Multiliteracies in Motion

"The contributors to this inspiring book (they include some of the most well-known and innovative thinkers in the field) provide a range of reflections, speculations, investigations, and practical applications all centering on the uneasy relation between schools, in many ways still bastions of mono-literacy, and the new multiliteracies."

(Theo van Leeuwen and Gunther Kress, From the Foreword)

The realities of new technological and social conditions since the 1990s demand a new approach to literacy teaching. Looking onward from the original statement of aims of the multiliteracies movement in 1996, this volume brings together top-quality scholarship and research that has embraced the notion and features new contributions by many of the originators of this approach to literacy.

Drawing on large research projects and empirical evidence, the authors explore practical and educational issues that relate to multiliteracies, such as assessment, pedagogy and curriculum. The viewpoint taken is that multiliteracies is a complementary socio-cultural approach to the new literacies that includes pedagogy and learning. The differences are addressed from a multiliteracies perspective—one that does not discount or undermine the new literacies, but shows new ways in which they are complementary.

Computers and the Internet are transforming the way we work and communicate and the very notion of literacy itself. This volume offers frontline information and a vital update for those wishing to understand the evolution and the current state of literacy theory in relation to multiliteracies.

David R. Cole is Senior Lecturer in English and Pedagogy at the University of Technology, Sydney, Australia.

Darren L. Pullen is Lecturer in ICT, Health Science and Professional Studies in the Faculty of Education at the University of Tasmania, Australia.

Multiliteracies in Motion

Current Theory and Practice

Edited by
David R. Cole
University of Technology, Sydney
Darren L. Pullen
University of Tasmania

Routledge
Taylor & Francis Group
NEW YORK AND LONDON

First published 2010
by Routledge

605 Third Avenue, New York, NY 10017
4 Park Square, Milton Park, Abingdon, Oxon OX14 4RN

Routledge is an imprint of the Taylor & Francis Group, an informa business

Typeset in Minion by Wearset Ltd, Boldon, Tyne and Wear

Library of Congress Cataloging-in-Publication Data
Multiliteracies in motion: current theory and practice/edited by David R. Cole, Darren L. Pullen.
p. cm.
1. Literacy–Study and teaching. 2. Literacy–Research. 3. Computer literacy. 4. Educational technology. 5. Education–Effect of technological innovations on. I. Cole, David R. II. Pullen, Darren L.
LC149.M8495 2010
302.2'244–dc22

2009023203

ISBN13: 978-0-415-80156-0 (hbk)
ISBN13: 978-0-415-80157-7 (pbk)
ISBN13: 978-0-203-86403-6 (ebk)

Contents

Foreword

Theo van Leeuwen, University of Technology, Sydney, and Gunther Kress, Institute of Education, London

Perhaps some 10 years ago, a Swedish PhD student showed us an "educational CD-ROM" she was working on—a Swedish localization of a Microsoft product, in fact. It had an "environmental" interface of the kind that was popular then—rooms or landscapes in which users could click on various objects. In this case it was a classroom with various teaching aids on tables and on the walls—books, pictures, tape recorders (it *was* 10 years ago), and of course computers. And then, in a corner at the back, there was a teacher, sitting behind a table with a vase containing a single flower. All those teaching aids could be clicked on, leading the user to a range of learning activities, often in game-like formats—all, that is, except one. You guessed it, the teacher.

This book, *Multiliteracies in Motion: Current Theory and Practice*, deals with all the issues called up by that interface: the need for schools to engage with multiple literacies and multiple technologies; to know more about the informal ways children learn outside school; to bring aspects of the child's lifeworld into the school; to replace instructional pedagogies with open-ended learning processes aimed not at transmitting knowledge, but at creating new kinds of subjects for new social futures that can incorporate all the diversities and divergences of today's globalized world.

Taking their cue from the influential 1996 article, "A pedagogy of multiliteracies: designing social futures," by the New London Group, the writers who have contributed to this inspiring book (they include some of the most well-known and innovative thinkers in the field) agree that the premises of that intervention are still valid, however much may have changed since then—there were no multi-level Internet games in 1996, for instance—and they provide a range of reflections, speculations, investigations, and practical applications all centering on the uneasy relation between schools, in many ways still bastions of mono-literacy, and the new multiliteracies.

In the midst of it all, there is the teacher, surrounded by technologies which may be new to them, but are already second nature to their pupils and by injunctions to bring the outside world into the school—as though school itself no longer has anything to offer. Teachers are caught between the tides of government interventions, which at one time seek to steer them back to "basics," and then at others open doors to new directions, and called upon to "change" and to have their "beliefs disrupted" by experts, while working in an institution which has not changed its basic premises for more than a century, despite opening its doors to new technology.

We hope this book will inspire them, and help them understand how to continue their important work in this ever-changing, multi-everything world.

Preface

This collection is, in our view, a selection of the highest quality work that is currently being undertaken around the globe in the field of multiliteracies and technology-enhanced education. The contributors include some of the most important figures presently involved with moving this area of inquiry forwards.

We truly hope that this volume will inspire, inform and intrigue teachers, educational researchers, trainee teachers and university lecturers. It is designed to be an inclusive publication that points to the benefits of multidisciplinary work in education while retaining strong knowledge fields.

The book is organized into four parts. Part I discusses multiliteracies and classrooms, and includes chapters on science education, Chinese early-years education and multimodal ESL teaching. Part II contains work on multiliteracy theory that covers the new media and new learning, agency in computer-mediated education, and the politics of desire that surrounds the contemporary teacher's body. Part III looks at the pedagogy of multiliteracies, with chapters that examine a professional change program for teachers, the disruption of teachers' beliefs through digital technology, and how to use culturally relevant curriculum through multiliteracies. Part IV focuses on multiliteracies and practice, with chapters that cover assessment, reading habits, English teaching with multimedia and the construction of a virtual school for teacher training.

This volume is distinctive in that it provides coverage of the ways in which multiliteracies permeate educational practice around the world. This is a continuing and important story that looks to align pedagogy, knowledge fields and the social/cultural factors involved with learning.

Darren and I would like to acknowledge Naomi Silverman for her help in bringing this volume to publication. We would also like to mention Geoff Riordan, Andrew Jakubowicz (UTS) and Ian Hay (University of Tasmania) for giving us dedicated time to work on this significant volume.

1 Introduction to Multiliteracies in Motion

Current Theory and Practice

David R. Cole, University of Technology, Sydney and Darren L. Pullen, University of Tasmania

Introduction

Western civilization stands at a turning point. On one side of this point are the structures and forms that have upheld its institutions and systems in the past. On the other stands possible ways forward that address the complicated situation of the present, where global economic fluctuations dominate social life in ever more powerful ways, and the purposes and through-lines for educational practice are increasingly more obscure given these tremendous fluctuations. One might legitimately ask the question: Why turn back the clock and re-examine the notion of "multiliteracies," that was positioned by the New London Group in 1996 as a useful term to give sense to the ways in which literacy practice is colliding with new technological modes of representation and shifting heterogeneous demographics? To answer this question one must consider the changes that are taking place in the educational world, and the ways in which literacy practice has dealt with these changes through classroom innovation, research into best practice, and theorizations of the critical factors that are animating change and making change more than a rhetorical call to arms for politicians or system managers intent on improving efficiency or introducing new technology due to commercial concerns. Change has become closely aligned with all aspects of literacy through the ways in which education has necessarily evolved under pressure from oscillating financial circumstances, and the adaptive and flexible elements inherent within multiliteracies make it a well-designated fit to keep on explaining continual literacy morphology. In this first section, we will explain the elastic connection between multiliteracies and changing literacies.

Multiliteracies in Motion

The first element that has determined that the notion of multiliteracies has survived beyond its initial conception is the multiple part of the idea. Multiple doesn't mean infinite, nor does it mean a vague number more than one. Multiple means a definite number of factors that converge on one point of literate behavior. For example, literacy instruction has been dominated by the reading and writing of printed text for a number of years. Students are asked to read a printed text and write out answers that explain their understanding of the text. This type of activity—called reading comprehension—has also come to dominate literacy examinations of basic skills. In terms of multiliteracies, the questions inherent within reading comprehension exercises are expanded beyond a dualistic notion of reading and writing, and include aspects such as visual literacy if images are involved in the source material, and critical literacy, that is the purposeful questioning of text for prejudice or silences and that might determine the political or social usage of the text in question. Multiliteracies is therefore a platform for the multiple elements that converge in educational practice as it is performed in formal and informal situations.

The second element of design that has allowed multiliteracies to remain in motion beyond its conception concerns the potential division between formal and informal learning situations. Research in this field has established that learning can happen in groups, and can be associated with informal, social and any loosely connected activity between participants (Hager & Smith, 2004). For example, many youths all over the world now learn a plethora of skills through multi-level gaming activity played on the Internet. They learn by competing together in virtual worlds practically unimaginable in 1996, which are rapidly being transformed by participant demand for new challenges and different ways to meet online via sophisticated role-play and imaginative scenarios. The technology that accompanies these games is being developed at a rapid speed, and is an area of learning driven by demand and the new ways in which digital technology offers rapid virtual interconnection on multiple simultaneous levels (Cole, 2007, 2005a). Multiliteracies incorporates this dramatic development in learning potential through the notion that social futures are being decided in the playing out of multiple literate behaviors. This idea of the New London Group accompanies the more recent development of the "new literacies" (Coiro, Knobel, Lankshear & Leu, 2008), which aim to map this new terrain of technologically mediated social connections, yet remains beyond the new literacies in that the map that may be produced by the accumulation of many new literacies still counts for something according to multiliteracies: i.e., a social future.

The notion of multiliteracies therefore contains a subtle yet important idea of power that has also allowed it to remain in motion. At the time of the conception of multiliteracies, the Internet was the new power broker, and theorists gave it dramatic and unqualified affordances—summed up through terms such as "global village" or "online communities" (Cole, 2005b). As the technology of the Internet moved out of purely academic and high-level commercial use, and became a familiar node of access for all offices, schools and homes, social scientists tried to track this movement and give it names that reflected the new societal groupings that were emerging. This process became embroiled within what became known as the "rhetoric of the technological sublime" (Jones-Kavalier & Flannigan, 2006), where new social terminology and modes of explanation were interwoven with new types of interactivity and communication sparked by digitized technological development. At base, the naming and understanding of all new Internet communities and modes of socialization are offshoots of this "entanglement." In contrast, established forms of power have been strikingly untouched by whatever new digitally augmented forms of socializing have emerged. For example, the power structures and hierarchical formations that are apparent through schooling have not changed due to the emergence of the global Internet. Universities have diversified and expanded to a certain extent via modes of distance learning, where students can complete degrees by using virtual portals, online material, and taking part in academic chat forums. However, even this activity is strangely reminiscent of the types of learning that were already apparent in universities before the Internet came into being. Assignments are still marked in the same ways, and academic careers are guided by highly structured and enforced types of criteria for advancement. So how does this relate to multiliteracies and the type of power that it entails?

Multiliteracies does not use the metaphors and analogies of online connectivity to hypothesize new societal tendencies. If one takes the virtual world that is represented by the Internet as a starting point, it could be said that it is complete in itself, as everything about it works through the way in which the connection has been established. Online dating works through the age-old processes of attraction and repulsion. Finding work on the Internet still requires a follow-up interview, a well-designed CV, and positive body language and appearance once contact between employers and potential employees has been established. Complete power relationships are therefore outside of the sphere of influence of the new literacies. Yet the new literacies are immanent to the power relationships that occur due to connectivity that one might discover online and by degrees in the ways in which society as a whole is changing. So there is a latent form of power inherent in the literacies that occur due to the net, and this has had an impact on social life. Multiliteracies sums this type of latency up by positing positive steps towards a better social life, rather than by establishing idealistic revolution due to digital innovation. For example, multiliteracies are concerned with the establishment of civil and pluralistic society, and this will happen through strengthening educational mores. The method for doing this is exemplified by the way in which the initial argument was constructed, and this is another element that has made multiliteracies endure and has put it into motion.

This element is the fact that the New London Group (1996) were comprised of an aggregate of 10 multidisciplinary individuals. Academics came together from the fields of linguistics, education, literary analysis, the sociology of education, and cultural studies. This richness has colored the argument from the start, and given depth and a broad perspective that could be added to in the future. Multiliteracies is in motion because it may be applied to other fields of interest such as diversity studies or organizational theory. This makes multiliteracies by its very nature expansionary and emergent.

The coming together of diverse intellectual concerns has not become stuck in a dead end of redundant thought. This is also a function of the fact that there is much detail to add to the construction of the multiliteracies argument. This has happened over time, and in particular by the series of essays contained in *Multiliteracies: Literacy Learning and the Design of Social Futures* (Cope & Kalantzis, 2000). This current volume fills in more of the gaps in the argument, as the authors of this collection are also interdisciplinary and concerned with similar aspects of emergent literacy practice. This parallel focus brings to the fore the last element of change that has cast multiliteracies into motion, and has to a certain extent defined one of its central concerns. That is the way in which meaning can be made through literate behavior.

There is a particular tension in Western literacy teaching that the New London Group successfully characterized. It could be argued that children are sheltered from the realities of the learning that takes place in literacy through fairy stories, phonics and set-piece skills exercises that are designed to enhance their use of language. Progressive educationalists have updated this picture, and pointed out that the use of language corresponds to context and social correspondences in terms of being meaningful (Kress, 2006). The notion of multiliteracies builds upon the progressivist perspective of education by deciding upon the design of social futures as giving literate behavior the most cogent meaning. Students should, according to this perspective, be engaged in actively designing their social futures when "doing literacy." The multiliteracies movement therefore has consequences in terms of text choice, text analysis, and textual synthesis and representation. All of this work has to be integrated into the design of social futures, which are continually rushing into the fields of knowledge of students and teachers as society progresses, and new social conditions become apparent. Literacy is, according to multiliteracies, deeply dependent on social–cultural factors that are always in motion, and often have unknown trajectories, especially given the current dramatic economic fluctuations that are presently starting to determine new models of work and communication.

Current Theory and Practice

The notion of multiliteracies has endured and it is in motion due to the elements listed and explained above, but what makes it particularly pertinent to be included in a collection of chapters about current literacy theory and practice such as this volume? The attribute that perhaps best suits multiliteracies to the contemporary educational scene is its ability to absorb and integrate with other theories of education that are crowding in on practice in terms of having commonly understood explicatory power. One such theory is "affect theory." Affect theory has a long history in Western thought, dating back at least to the work of Baruch Spinoza (1677/1993). It looks to explain the ways in which emotions work in human cognition by making connections between the mind, desire, rationality, language, and the unconscious. Affects have been theorized as possessing a charge or relative power above their position as connective devices between operative points in human communicative functioning (Fiumara, 2001). This potential has allowed affects to be positioned as points of intensity in various fields of inquiry such as literary analysis (Holland, 1968), social cognition (Forgas, 2001), psychoanalysis (Freud, 1953) and human geography (Thrift, 2004). The multidisciplinary nature of affect theory also makes it suitable for education in terms of lending explicative power to a teacher's work.

This is where one might discern a connection between multiliteracies and affect theory. Multiliteracies is also about the work of teachers, but addresses it through the ways in which pedagogical mores may be understood as being in motion from "overt instruction" to "transformed practice." Transformed practice is when a teacher is able to switch between available curricula designs and assimilate their teaching style with the social–cultural factors that are determining the behavior of the cohort in any particular context (including the use of digital technology). Affect theory is also about change, but acts as a vital connection between the internal state of the teacher (how they are feeling) and the social–cultural consequences of their actions (Hargreaves, 1994). For example, a teacher that is feeling overwhelmed and drowning in the behavioral issues of a particular class will have less impact in terms of making knowledge work to the benefit of that cohort. Both affect theory and multiliteracies are therefore critically determined by issues of power and shifting social–cultural factors. This important relationship in current literacy theory and practice is represented below:

Figure 1.1 shows how multiliteracies and affect theory may be conjoined through a concern for power in education, and this conjunction is played out in literacy classrooms. This perspective on current literacy theory and practice is further updated by adding the development of Multiple Literacies Theory (MLT) (Masny & Cole, 2009) to the fold. The forward motion of

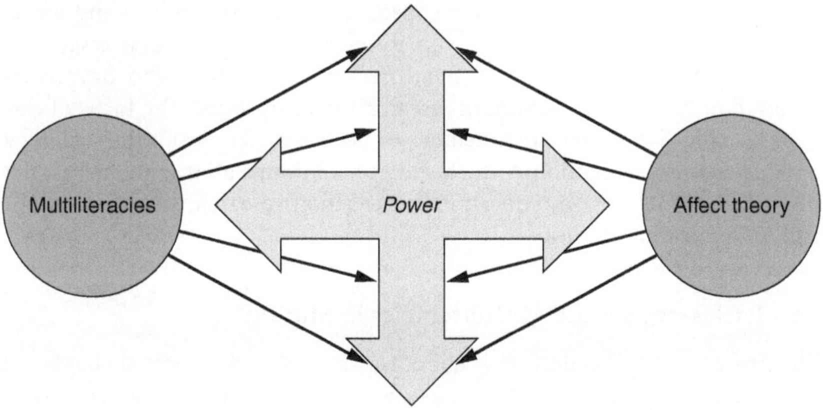

Figure 1.1 The Relationship between Multiliteracies and Affect Theory.

multiliteracies is hindered somewhat by the possible homogenizing effects of stipulating that the multiple aspects of literacy are tied to literacy in terms of multimodality (Kress & van Leeuwen, 2001). Multimodality is the switching potential inherent in different modes of literate progression, and owes its heritage to genre theory and systemic functional linguistics. This part of multiliteracies is potentially homogenizing as there is something posited behind the switching mechanism, such as experience, agency, or identity. In contrast, MLT has multiplicities at the center of its construction of literacy and the different modes of literate behavior that may pass through any teaching and learning situation defined as "life." MLT also employs affect theory to help with the construction and representation of literacy as a fully multiple development. Investigations into writing systems for young literacy learners have shown that the emotional impact of environmental circumstances is a major component of becoming literate (Masny, 2006). Multiliteracies benefits from such insights taken from MLT as current theory and practice in the field of literacy continues to uncover how the multiplicity of literacies that are presently being named and explicated may be deployed in education, and what the consequences are in terms of becoming truly "multiply literate" today.

The Chapters of the Book

This book is a collective collaboration of authors taken from the United States, Australia, China, and the United Kingdom. It is certainly dominated by academics working in English-speaking universities, though this domination should not be seen to be an empire-building enterprise. The focus and point of updating the multiliteracies project is to chart the relationship between changing conditions in the world of literacy representation and what we understand as educational practice. Far from excluding other theories and explanatory mechanisms for understanding changes in literacy, this collection of chapters, with a focus on multiliteracies, is designed to open up the field. This is because the scope of such a collection is ambitious, global and inclusive. The authors include some who were involved in the first essay that appeared in the *Harvard Educational Review*, and others who have been involved in literacy and education research for many years. The focus of this book is multidisciplinary, and includes work that is taken from the sociology of education, social semiotics, the history of communications, linguistics, the philosophy of education, educational and action research, literary analysis, and ICT education studies.

Part I: Classrooms and Multiliteracies in Motion

The first part of this collection is about classrooms, and the initial chapter of this part, by Beryl Exley and Allan Luke, is called, "Uncritical Framing: Lesson and Knowledge Structure in School Science." The authors take us into the world of science education, and the issues that surround this practice in contemporary education. They compare a traditional science curriculum with one based on the multiliteracies framework. This comparison is not to place one type of science training over another, but to see how both construct central notions of science through practice. This chapter employs Bernstein's knowledge classification and pedagogical framing in order to open up relevant sociological questions for the comparison. The authors look at primary science education and a popular Australian program that links science with literacy. The results of this study show how multiliteracies pedagogy could be applied to science classrooms, and the benefits for teachers and learners that would ensue. The authors do not, however, dismiss the traditional modes of science education, but analyze in detail the connections and points of contact of each model of education through sociological investigation and description of classroom practice.

The next chapter, "Image, Voice, and the Making of the School-Literate Child: Lessons from Multiliterate Teaching in China," shifts the focus of inquiry to China. The authors, Bette Zhang Bin and Peter Freebody, investigate the ways in which young children are acculturated in Chinese classrooms through multiliterate practice. This detailed and culturally specific study analyzes the mixture of text, image, genre and voice that permeate the early-years experiences of school children in China. Children in China are introduced to the notion of schooling and being schooled through textbooks that contain cultural and social messages. This chapter picks apart these messages, and shows how multiliteracies can be used to understand the ways in which the socialization of schooling in effected in different parts of the world. In particular, the authors highlight the use of the term *yuwen* in Chinese educational practice. It refers to the teaching of reading literature, though is a difficult term to precisely translate as it simultaneously makes reference to social, political, cultural and disciplinary ideas that are hard to understand outside of the Chinese context. The authors show how all the different elements of *yuwen* come together in the chapter, as well as examining several typical textbooks. In so doing, they build a picture of multiliterate practice in Chinese early-years education. This is a moving and close reading of Chinese textual practice that belies specific cultural and social directives that have a long history in Chinese society and that are realized in particular ways through the construction of school-age texts.

Chapter 4 of this volume, "Introducing Multimodal Literacy to Young Children Learning English as a Second Language (ESL)" is by Len Unsworth and Robyn Bush. The authors have taken the teaching experiences of the second author as the starting point for this chapter. Robyn teaches in an area of Sydney where 92% of the children have a language background other than English. This could be a hindrance to the usual running of the classroom, but the authors show how deploying multimodal text within a systemic functional linguistic framework can turn this situation around. They argue that multiliteracies is a development from functional systemic linguistics in the way in which multimodality underpins meaning-making with text, and the consequent switching between different modes or genre approach to speaking, reading, and writing. This chapter includes detailed textual suggestions for teachers to use in the classroom, as well as information and mechanisms for the use of these texts. The authors cover the oceans and sea creatures, environmental issues, and caring for pets through this highly structured and detailed approach to ESL literacy teaching and learning. The chapter concludes with a suggestion that teachers may use these ideas as a blueprint for action research about their own practice involving ESL teaching and multimodal text.

Part II: Multiliteracies Theory in Motion

The next part of the book examines the theoretical aspects of multiliteracies. Chapter 5, "New Media: New Learning," has been written by Bill Cope and Mary Kalantzis. The authors argue that the global spread of the new media has fundamentally changed the ways in which people learn. New media are defined by the digital applications of a range of information and communications devices. The problem that the authors point out in this theoretical approach to multiliteracies is that these devices are usually not used in schools to the benefit of the new learning. The authors take evidence from the history of communications that suggests how the "newness" of the new media is constructed. For example, they argue that hypertext is an extension of what books have always done (i.e., cross-reference and point the reader to different parts of the text). Virtual reality is another example of how different media have brought to the fore questions of verisimilitude. In contrast, the authors offer four dimensions of the new media that are new: (1) agency; (2) divergence; (3) multimodality; and (4) conceptualization. The chapter juxtaposes these four dimensions with four dimensions of the new learning: (1) designers; (2) learners differences; (3) synaesthesia and; (4) metacognition. This important chapter is an updated account of multiliteracies theory; the authors argue that contemporary education practice will advance once the four dimensions of the new media are reconciled with the four dimensions of the new learning.

In Chapter 6, "Multiliteracies and the Agency Involved with Computer Operations in Education," David R. Cole and Darren L. Pullen have constructed their theoretical approach to multiliteracies by examining the ways in which students learn in contemporary society. They take the fictional idea of cyberpunk and the socio-cultural notion of techno-tribalism as a basis for understanding the agency of computer operations in education. Cyberpunk is a useful way to figure computer-mediated agency, as it gives the user a landscape to live in where movement is global and power concerns are immanent to everything that happens. The authors take the example of global capital movements to demonstrate the argument on cyberpunk and agency. Global capital and the ways that it is moved provide a connection between our lives and the ways that they are being changed due to the use of computers. Students may change their identities on the net in their pursuit of different social, political, and cultural options, and this chapter deals with these radical possibilities in terms of multiliteracies and viable ways in which these unstable aspects of contemporary social life may be incorporated into education. The authors include an individual story from qualitative research to illustrate the consequences of seriously considering cyberpunk and computer operations in education. Techno-tribalism acts as a collective and sociological platform for computer-mediated agency, and broadens the argument of this multiliteracies chapter from the more individualized concerns of cyberpunk. The authors include the example of free-party organization in the UK to show how techno-tribal agency may be actualized in practice.

The last chapter of the theoretical section focuses on multiliteracies and the politics of desire, and was written by David R. Cole. The author argues that the contemporary educational scene has been affected by a new moral perception of a teacher's work by the intrusion of media systems into the classroom. Multiliteracies theory is added to in this chapter by the construction of a new "teacher's body" that is able to deal with the morphology of the new media by being absolutely open to change. David R. Cole uses ideas taken from Elizabeth Grosz and Gilles Deleuze and Félix Guattari to make a new body that is synthetic and flexible, communicable through the digital medium and able to connect internal desire with the external surveillance of desire. This chapter takes multiliteracies theory in a new direction, and gives teachers different options when considering their lives and the ways in which they are described, especially through media reports. The "teacher's body" of this chapter projects sexuality as a partial object, and shows how this could help to alleviate some of the suffocating moral discourse on sexuality and pedagogy that potentially demonizes teacher's desires.

Part III: The Pedagogy of Multiliteracies in Motion

Part III of this collection looks at the pedagogy of multiliteracies, which has always been central to the framework. Chapter 8, "Using the Principles of Multiliteracies to Inform Pedagogical Change," was written by Geoff Bull and Michèle Anstey. The authors have developed a professional development program for teachers in schools that engages them in action-learning to change their literacy pedagogy. This program has been successfully implemented in the state of Queensland, Australia, where multiliteracies has perhaps been most extensively used for teaching and learning in schools. The authors of the chapter are also facilitators of this process of change, and point to the multiliteracies framework as being pertinent to today's educational situation, in that it ties pedagogy with literacy practice. They therefore give the participants in their program an understanding of multiliteracies and the ways in which its usage may change their literacy teaching. Teachers are, importantly, constructed as learners in this chapter. The authors include in this work their construction of what it means to become multiliterate, as well as a multiliterate matrix that gives the teachers engaged with the action-learning program the opportunity to monitor their progress and to reflect on what in their practice might still need attention. Examples of this reflective attitude are interspersed throughout the chapter. The authors reflect upon what happened during the teacher sessions, and give the reader a practical means for changing teaching practice based on the principles of multiliteracies.

The next chapter of this book is called, "Disrupting Traditions: Teachers Negotiating Multiliteracies and Digital Technologies," and is written by Elizabeth Petroelje Stolle and Gustavo E. Fischman. The authors of this chapter have taken Prensky's notions of digital natives and digital immigrants as a starting point to investigate current changes in pedagogy. The issues at stake in this chapter are the power relationships that are established through pedagogy, and how teachers might be dealing with a potential loss of control due to the introduction of digital technology. The writers have used educational research methods to look at how teachers conceptualize literacy and pedagogy, with particular attention to the realities of working with digital technology in education. The researchers found that digital technology was disruptive to the usual running of the classroom, and they have developed an entertaining analysis of this disruption to draw out the consequences for pedagogical purposes. They conclude that teachers now have to navigate and negotiate their way around any power relationships that might be established in the classroom due to digital technology, and the application of the multiliteracies framework (i.e., transformed practice) is one such method to achieve this.

Chapter 10 completes the pedagogy section of the book. "Using Multiliteracies to Facilitate Culturally Relevant Pedagogy in the Classroom," by Louanne Ione Smolin and Kimberly Lawless, examines the multiple parts of multiliteracies with respect to making connections between cultural diversity and pedagogical choice. This can be a challenging aspect of a teacher's job, and the authors show how it may be achieved through and alongside the use of technology. The authors argue that much of the lives of contemporary students are spent online and in digital environments, and this now represents a significant part of their cultural makeup. Teachers should be aware of these digitally cultural forms and acculturations, and may use the multiliteracies framework as an effective means of incorporating them into their social practice of teaching. This means constructing educationally enriching situations that show the students how to use the knowledge and skills that they have learnt on their electronic adventures. The authors give two examples to illustrate their argument: the first involves bilingualism, the second a community learning center. Students from different contexts are asked to research and represent their findings on these topics, which help them to make connections with their local communities. This chapter shows teachers how to be culturally inclusive and how to use technology in their curriculum planning to break down pedagogical barriers such as the transmission model of knowledge.

Part IV: Multiliteracies in Practice

The ultimate part of the book concerns multiliteracies in practice. Chapter 11, "Multiliteracies and Assessment Practice" was written by Ian Brown, Lori Lockyer and Peter Caputi. Assessment is a vital part of educational practice, and this chapter looks at the different assessment options that one might apply to the multiliteracies framework. The team looked at new developments in curriculum construction in New South Wales (NSW) and Queensland, Australia that have included multiliterate ways of working, and ask the question as to whether the concomitant assessment practices that are currently being used have kept up with the pace of change encapsulated by new digital curriculum content. The answer is inevitably "no," especially as standardized literacy testing does not assess the broad range of skills that are involved with the multiliteracies framework. This testing has become the norm set against a political background of conservative ideology that positions literacy as a skill-based grouping of cognitive qualities such as spelling, reading, and writing of printed text. The team gives a different way to assess multiliterate practice that has been taken from ICT education studies. This alternative is an evidence-centered assessment design that has three parts: the student model, the task model, and the evidence model. The authors show how this model works in practice by applying it to a case study of using news media in NSW. However, the results of the project point to the ambiguous nature of assessment practice in the light of complex multimodality.

Chapter 12 is about young Australians reading in a digital world, and was written by Jennifer Rennie and Annette Patterson. The authors have surveyed over 600 14-year-old children in an Australian city. The focus of the survey was children's out-of-school reading habits, and the definition of "reading" that the researchers used included the social practices involved with any type of electronic or mobile media. The study also looked to ascertain the level of pleasure that the readers were achieving with respect to the different reading options that are now available in a multiliterate digital world. The analysis of the data includes a focus on the gender divide in teenage reading habits, as well as defining the shifts and tendencies in the ways in which young people are reading today. This is a lively and informative chapter that leaves the reader with a vivid and detailed picture of the ways that children are reading out of school when they have access to emerging digital technology. It will also help educators construct new reading curricula, given new electronic trends and multiliterate options.

The next chapter is called "Multiliteracies: Resources for Meaning-making in the Secondary English Classroom." Douglas McClenaghan and Brenton Doecke have written about the teaching experiences of Douglas as a secondary English teacher, and have drawn out the implications for the purposes of multiliteracies practice. This chapter pays close attention the ways in which educators ask their students to write. This gesture in educational practice is now potentially transformed, given the fact that there are many new multimedia representational options. This chapter charts several of these options through examples of student work where they are using multimedia to express themselves. The examples that the authors have chosen show how intense and complicated multimedia student representation can be when handled by a sensitive educationalist. This chapter points out the subtle ways that text represents life and vice versa, and how pedagogy may interpret and reinvent text in the classroom. This writing shows how students may be inspired by the use of multimedia to tell their stories, and how a teacher may balance creativity with direction to achieve substantial multiliterate outcomes.

The last chapter of this collection is called, "A Virtual School for Rethinking Learning," and was composed by Julie Faulkner and Gloria Latham. The authors have focused on a pedagogic experiment that looks to disrupt some of the norms of teaching. They have used a virtual construct of a school to encourage pre-service student teachers to think about what it means to become a teacher, and what potential challenges they might face in the profession. This fascinating approach to learning opens up many questions about technology and teacher training, as the researchers are using virtual reality to explore preconceptions about teaching. To get to this level of serious thought about the social stereotypes and normative functions of teaching in our society is not an easy task, as anyone involved with teacher training would know. This important virtual experiment therefore has broad implications outside of the training course in which it is embedded, and it is a fitting finale to finish off this collection of chapters on the future of education and multiliteracies.

Conclusion

This collection goes from current classroom literacy practice to the future of education. It includes evidence and theory taken from a range of sources, spread between four continents. The basic message of the book is that literacy teaching and learning—even though in a potential state of digitally inspired flux and economic variation, can still be a singular and joyous activity. Even if the outside, interconnected, and globally mediated world seems to be irrevocably oscillating and potentially dangerous to established norms, literacy seems to hold some sort of shelter. Perhaps this is because deep inside literacy practice there are ways of doing things that have changed little. This is why the ultimate point of this collection is to touch the inner lives of literacy educators, not to distract them from their purpose, but to add to them in order to strengthen the ways in which education functions, and to potentially make their lives better:

> This intensive way of reading, in contact with what's outside the book, as a flow meeting other flows, one machine, among others, as a series of experiments for each reader *in the midst of events that have nothing to do with books.*
>
> (Deleuze, 1990/1995, pp. 8–9 (emphasis added))

References

Coiro, J., Knobel, M., Lankshear, C., & Leu, D. J. (Eds.). (2008). *Handbook of research on new literacies.* New York: Routledge.

Cole, D. R. (2007). Virtual terrorism and the Internet E-Learning options. *E-Learning,* 4(2), 116–127.

Cole, D. R. (2005a). Learning through the virtual. *CTheory.* www.ctheory.net/articles.aspx?id=445.

Cole, D. R. (2005b). Reading in the future: literacy and the time of the internet. *Reconstruction,* 5(2). Retrieved 3 February 2008 from http://reconstruction.eserver.org/052/cole.shtml.

Cope, B., & Kalantzis, M. (Eds.). (2000). *Multiliteracies: Literacy learning and the design of social futures.* London: Routledge.

Deleuze, G. ([1990] 1995). *Negotiations, 1972–1990* (M. Joughin, Trans.). New York: Columbia University Press. (Original work published 1990.)

Fiumara, G. C. (2001). *The mind's affective life: A psychoanalytic and philosophical inquiry.* Hove: Brunner-Routledge.

Forgas, J. P. (Ed.). (2001). *The handbook of affect and social cognition.* Mahwah, NJ: Lawrence Erlbaum.

Freud, S. (1953). The interpretation of dreams (J. Strachey, Trans.). In J. Strachey (Ed.), *The Pelican Freud library—Volume 4.* Harmondsworth: Penguin Books.

Hager, P., & Smith, E. (2004). The inescapability of significant contextual learning in work performance. *London Review of Education,* 2(1), 33–46.

Hargreaves, A. (1994). *Changing teachers, changing times: Teachers' work and culture in the postmodern age.* New York: Teachers College Press.

Holland, N. N. (1968). *The dynamics of literary response.* New York: Columbia University Press.

Jones-Kavalier, B. R., & Flannigan, S.L. (2006). Connecting the digital dots: Literacy of the 21st century. *EDUCAUSE Quarterly,* 29(2), 8–10.

Kress, G. R. (2006). Reimagining English: Curriculum, identity and productive futures. In B. Doecke, M. Howie, & W. Sawyer (Eds.), *Only Connect: English teaching, schooling and community* (pp. 31–42). Kent Town, SA: Wakefield Press (AATE).

Kress, G. R., & van Leeuwen, T. (2001). *Multimodal discourse: The modes and media of contemporary communication.* New York: Oxford University Press.

Masny, D. (2006). Learning and creative processes: A poststructural perspective on language and multiple literacies. *International Journal of Learning,* 12(5), 147–155.

Masny, D., & Cole, D. R. (2009). *Multiple Literacies Theory (MLT): A Deleuzian perspective.* Rotterdam: Sense publishers.

New London Group. (1996). A pedagogy of multiliteracies: Designing social futures, *Harvard Educational Review,* 66, 60–92.

Spinoza, B. ([1677] 1993). *Ethics and treatise on the correction of the intellect.* (A. Boyle, Trans.). London: J. M. Dent.

Thrift, N. (2004). Intensities of feeling: Towards a spatial politics of affect. *Geografiska Annaler: Series B, Human Geography,* 86(1), 57–78.

Part I

Classrooms and Multiliteracies in Motion

2 Uncritical Framing

Lesson and Knowledge Structure in School Science

Beryl Exley and Allan Luke, Faculty of Education, Queensland University of Technology

Introduction

There is contention over the shape and formation of science curriculum and, ultimately, over what will count as scientific knowledge, skill, capacity and world view. The Cold War set the policy context for an ongoing focus on science education across Western nations. Sputnik-era US and UK educational policy offered a broad premise for the purpose of school science: in a risky geopolitical environment, high levels of advanced scientific expertise were central to the national interest and necessary for the maintenance of military/industrial and technological power. Half a century on, in the context of global economic and environmental crisis, as a justification for digital, industrial and biomedical innovation, the rationale for the production of *scientific capital* is central to curriculum settlements and educational policy in Europe, Asia and the Americas.

The Australian federal government's 2008 commitment to a National Science Curriculum has revived debate over what will count as scientific knowledge and literacy in schools. In early 2009 the national newspaper, *The Australian*, an influential player in educational policy, criticized the National Curriculum Board's (2008) argument for a "thematic" approach to science education. "In all disciplines, there is no substitute for teaching the basics" (Curriculum Values, *The Australian*, March 17, 2009, p. 11) , its editorial column read, restating its consistent argument for basic skills, facts and knowledge and a universal focus on canonical disciplinary and literary content (Luke, 2009).

The framing paper commissioned by the National Curriculum Board (2008) attempts to strike a balance between the production of high levels of scientific expertise and the production of a broad scientific literacy for everyday life and civic participation:

> The main objective of school science education is to develop young people's science capabilities. It is imperative that Australia's future citizens have scientific knowledge and understanding that enable them to make personal and societal decisions on the basis of evidence and

> reason.... [P]eople who are scientifically capable can make informed decisions about the products they buy, the food they eat, the environment in which they live or the lifestyle they adopt.
>
> (p. 1)

It acknowledges "a core body of science knowledge and understanding that is fundamental to the learning of science." Yet it cautions that current science curricula "tend to be knowledge-heavy and ... alienating for a number of students" (p. 3). The argument is that a school science curriculum should focus less on content transmission and more on "big ideas," exploring their disciplinary basis and affiliated ethical applications and social implications. Specifically:

> The school science curriculum should ... explore complex issues to enable students to understand that the application of science and technology to the real world is often concerned with risk and debate.... The inclusion of complex issues should not be avoided.... The idea is to use them to promote a more sophisticated understanding of the nature of science and science knowledge. Young people need to understand that decisions concerning science applications involve constraints, consequences and risks. Such decision-making is not value-free. In developing science capabilities, students learn about the influence of particular values in attempting to balance the issues of constraints, consequences and risk.
>
> (p. 4)

An Australian research report commissioned for the federal government by Goodrum, Hackling and Rennie (2001) described the current situation in classrooms:

> The actual picture of science teaching and learning is one of great variability but, on average, the picture is disappointing.... In some primary schools, often science is not taught at all.... When students move to high school, many experience disappointment, because the science ... is neither relevant nor engaging and does not connect with their interests and experiences. Traditional chalk-and-talk teaching, copying notes, and "cookbook" practical lessons offer little challenge or excitement to students.
>
> (p. viii)

An international decline in adolescent interest in school science is well documented (e.g., Millar, 2006; Reiss, 2007; Lavonen, Gedrovics, Byman, Meisalo, Juuti & Uitto, 2008; Relevance of Science Education, 2008). PISA (Programme for International Student Assessment) describes declining learner motivation and involvement in school sciences for a significant number of 15 year olds in the 58 participant countries (OECD, 2006). The PISA study also reports that globally 5.2% of participants were unable to complete Level 1 tasks at the lowest achievement level. In addition, just under 20% of participants, on average, were not proficient at Level 2 tasks. This means that approximately 25% of secondary school learners would be unable to participate effectively and productively in life situations related to science (OECD, 2006).

Lee and Erdogan (2007) explain the declining engagement by reference to current science teaching practices that discourage students' natural curiosity. In a major address to the World Conference on Science and Technology Education, Fensham (2007) argued that comparative employment prospects and negative media images of science may be responsible. But Fensham also refers to the problem of primary school teachers' lack of pedagogical strategies and content knowledge. The Australian Deans of Science are also skeptical about the disciplinary content knowledge of teachers. Many secondary school science teachers have completed less than one year of university science study, and many primary school teachers have no university-level science study.[1]

Science curriculum and pedagogy debates turn on several key issues:

1. How to increase the scientific content knowledge of teachers while altering traditional content transmission curricula and pedagogy;
2. How to balance the developmental acquisition of scientific facts, concepts, procedures and field knowledge—"the core body of scientific knowledge" (e.g., technical knowledge)—with the need for informed "personal and societal" decision-making (National Curriculum Board, 2008) about current scientific and technological issues (e.g., a broad general scientific literacy).

These are not abstract paradigm debates, but practical everyday curriculum and pedagogic dilemmas.

To reframe the current curriculum debates, this chapter examines two different versions of "science" that are generated by different curriculum and instructional orientations. Here we contrast a more traditionally scaffolded content-based science program with a multiliteracies approach to teaching science. The latter approach draws on the "pedagogy of multiliteracies" model (New London Group, 1996), featuring shifting pedagogic orientations and text designs. We use Bernstein's (2000) sociology of knowledge to compare the knowledge "classification" and pedagogical "framing" of the two approaches. Our claim is that the traditional content-based program, while direct and accessible, reduces the focus on "critical framing" and "transformed practice." These, we argue, are essential to prepare students for the critical analysis of scientific practices and issues called for by the National Curriculum framing paper and other current policy documents. Yet it is not our contention that one approach is superior to the other—simply that they construct scientific knowledge differently, through different modalities, towards different ends.

Multiliteracies, Knowledge Classification and Pedagogic Framing

Long before the current economic crisis, the core argument of "the pedagogy of multiliteracies" (New London Group, 1996) was that the advent of new technologies and global structures of cultural and economic exchange required an ambitious, futures-oriented educational agenda. The New London meetings were held in the midst of an educational and curriculum policy debate over the efficacy claims and equity effects of: direct instruction versus "holistic" teaching; "critical" versus "genre" approaches to early literacy instruction; and "skills" versus "constructivist" instruction. The assumption was that many of these longstanding binary arguments over pedagogy misconstrued teaching/learning relations in classrooms, advocating a single-lensed approach to teaching/learning. Hence, the "pedagogy of multiliteracies" argued that there was a central place for direct instruction in a critical educational project (cf. Luke, 2008). Further, it described an oscillating approach to print and digital media, texts and pedagogies, where teachers would use diverse repertoires in response to learners' diverse cultural and linguistic knowledge, and the particular fields, modalities and designs under study. The proposed model was not a repetitive linear sequence for lessons and units. Instead, it offered a description of pedagogic repertoires to be revisited at different levels across a lesson, unit or project, and across the teaching of different designs for meaning.

The four non-hierarchical and non-linear components of that pedagogy are: situated practice, overt instruction, critical framing and transformed practice (New London Group, 1996). Accordingly, learning would entail: (1) experiential immersion in a range of designs and texts; (2) direct access to a technical metalanguage that has utility across the range of designs and requisite field/content knowledge to make sense of these; (3) an analysis of the cultural and material consequences for a range of producers, audiences and users; and (4) the opportunity to critically "remake" texts across a range of sites for varied social and intellectual purposes. The designs might include linguistic, visual, auditory, spatial and gestural design and their multimodal intersections.

The New London work has informed school-based projects in Australia (Cazden, 2000; Kalantzis & Cope, 2005; Exley, 2007b; Henderson, 2008; Mills, 2007; Exley, 2008a), Malaysia (Samuel, 2002; Pandian & Balraj, 2005), Italy (Exley, 2008b), Singapore (Tan, 2008), South Africa (Bond, 2000; Newfield & Stein, 2000; Wits University Multiliteracies Group, 2001) and elsewhere. Much of this classroom-based developmental work has been concentrated in literacy education and new media/technology studies, with a strong focus on multimodal text analysis and production.

In observational coding work on Singapore classrooms, teachers' shifts in pedagogic repertoire were described using the metaphor of "weaving" (Luke, Cazden, Lin & Freebody, 2005; Kwek, 2005; Cazden, 2006): the processes whereby teachers systematically shift between kinds and levels of knowledge and kinds and modes of interactional discourse structures, systematically building upon knowledge so students can make connections. Weaving entails the restaging of interactional zones and face-to-face patterns of interaction around text to generate and foreground specific elements of tool use and knowledge. Singapore researchers observed lessons for shifts in interactional "phases" (Mehan, 1996) that marked movement in kinds and levels of knowledge: for instance, from the known to the new, local to global, everyday to technical, commonsense to scientific, concrete to abstract, and so forth.

In sociological terms, these shifts in the structure and sequence of classroom phases mark out observable relations of knowledge (curriculum) and control (pedagogy), or, in Bernstein's (2000) terms, classification and framing. Classification refers to the relative strength and weakness of categories and taxonomies of knowledge. With strong classification (++), "each category has its unique identity, its unique voice, its own specialized rules of internal relations" (Bernstein, 2000, p. 7). Affiliated with traditional, canonical curriculum, strong classification of a topic, field, discipline or "school subject" (Deng & Luke, 2008) marks out boundaries of inclusion and exclusion for what will count as knowledge that are clear and transparent to teachers and learners. In strong classification the rule is: "Things must be kept apart" (Bernstein, 2000, p. 11). Conversely, in instances where the classification of school knowledge is weak, there are less specialized discourses, less specialized identities and less specialized voices. With weak classification (– –), affiliated with multidisciplinary and integrated study, the rule is: "Things must be brought together" (Bernstein, 2000, p. 11) around a unified theme, topic or project.[2]

Bernstein's concept of framing refers to the social and discourse relations of pedagogy: the intersubjective relations of teachers and learners that "frame" and mediate knowledge. "[F]raming is concerned with *how* meanings are to be put together, the forms by which they are to be made public, and the nature of the social relationships that go with it" (Bernstein, 2000, p. 12). Framing therefore is the realization of the "form of control which regulates and legitimizes communication in pedagogical relations: the nature of the talk and the kinds of [pedagogic] spaces constructed" (Bernstein, 2000, p. 12). Strong framing (++) occurs when the teacher has more control over the selection, sequencing, pacing, criteria and social relations of classrooms. Here a teacher is asserting authoritative control of social relations, modes and forms of representation; pedagogic practice is "visible"; the rules for acquiring knowledge are explicit. Weaker framing (– –) is generally affiliated with more student-centered pedagogy, where students may assert what appears to be more overtly agentive speaking positions, epistemic authority and interactional strategies.

Because it accommodates and encourages shifting relations of classification and framing, a multiliteracies pedagogy has the potential to address the competing aims of science education outlined at the onset of this chapter. As a template it can accommodate: direct instruction in traditional content, formulae and concepts of science education (e.g., explicit technical metalanguages, categories, taxonomies); hands-on activities and experiences with a range of tools and technologies for "doing science" (e.g., procedure, process, data collection and analysis); and critical engagement with the variable social and cultural applications, uses and consequences of scientific knowledge (e.g., human and environmental implications, ethics, consequences, risk). Further, it stresses the recontextualization of student learning and knowledge in the production of multimodal texts.

In what follows, we describe two approaches to the teaching of science in the middle primary years: (1) a scripted biology unit in a widely adopted recent Australian science program (Australian Academy of Science, 2005); and (2) a science-inspired inquiry-based project developed by a primary teacher working with one of the authors (Exley) in a mid/low socio-economic multi-age classroom. Our analysis identifies and compares the pedagogic repertoires used, the different technological modalities in play, and the patterns of knowledge classification and pedagogic framing.

The Scripted Program Approach

Primary Connections: Linking Science with Literacy is a popular model of school science adopted in over 40% of Australian primary schools. The program was produced by the Australian Academy of Science and received $10.7 million in federal funding for development and implementation. *Primary Connections* sets out to lay "the foundation for a scientifically literate society where people can make informed decisions about a multitude of things that affect them" (Australian Academy of Science, 2005, p. iv). The program is organized through conceptual strands, which aim to "harness students' natural curiosity, nurture their sense of wonder, and develop their passion for exploring how the world works" (p. iv). The *Primary Connections* Stage 3 Interim research and evaluation report revealed that learners from the intervention sample "achieved significantly higher mean literacies of science processes and some aspects of attitude to school science than students in comparison classes" (Australian Academy of Science, 2008, p. 16).

We examine one part of the *Primary Connections* suite, a Stage 3 "Life and Living" unit, *Marvelous Micro-organisms* (Australian Academy of Science, 2005), selected because its content interested one case-study class. This unit is recommended for learners in their sixth or seventh year of schooling. Each unit comes with direct instructions for teachers on lesson planning, preferred interactional structures, appropriate responses and follow-up activities, in typical teacher guidebook format (cf. Apple, 1990). Box 2.1 provides an overview of the suggested sequence and foci of the eight lessons.

The unit introduces procedural knowledge for hands-on activities and engagement with basic scientific facts. These activities and the knowledge derived from them are treated as neutral scientific operations and facts, "beyond criticism" (Luke, DeCastell & Luke, 1989) of teachers and students.

Box 2.1 Lesson Sequences in Marvelous Micro-organisms Unit

Lesson 1—The Y Factor
Session 1—Exploring Bread
Session 2—The Bread-Making Process
Session 3—Anton van Leeuwenhoek: Microscope Maker
Lesson 2—Yeast Feast
Lesson 3—Putting the Heat on Yeast
Lesson 4—Knead the Loaf
Lesson 5—Food Observations
Lesson 6—Mystery Molds
Session 1—A Nightmare in my Lunchbox
Session 2—Investigating Molds
Lesson 7—Medical Micro-organisms
Lesson 8—Micro-organisms Experts

A key lesson outcome for Lesson 3 (p. 22), *Putting the Heat on Yeast*, is for learners to "plan an investigation, with teacher support, of the effect of temperature on the activity of yeast." In the teacher's manual, the first two lesson steps (p. 22) are written as:

1. Review Lesson 2. Focus students' attention on the use of warm water, and the fact that the bottles were put in a warm place. Ask students to reflect on what they know about yeast and temperature. Record what they know in the class science journal.
2. Discuss students' suggestions for an investigation to determine the temperature that best promotes yeast activity. Encourage students to think about testing the yeast in cold, warm and boiling water. Discuss how they will make this a fair test (by changing one variable, measuring another variable, and keeping all other variables the same). Read through an enlarged copy of "What's the best temperature for yeast to be active?" (Resource Sheet 4), and review the purpose and features of procedural texts. Focus students' attention on the safety issues surrounding this activity. Explain the class safety plan for using hot water. Suggest that one team member holds the bottle of warm water while another puts on the balloon.…

Resource Sheet 4 (Australian Academy of Science, 2005, p. 23) details the aim, equipment list and activity steps. The first five activity steps are listed as:

1. Make labels for the three bottles, showing your team members' names and the following information:
   - Bottle 1: Hot water
   - Bottle 2: Warm water
   - Bottle 3: Cold water

2. Place the funnel in the mouth of each bottle and add the ½ teaspoon yeast and ¼ cup sugar. Mix the yeast and sugar together.
3. The manager takes Bottle 1 to the "safety zone" where your teacher will carefully add ½ cup hot water to the bottle. Mix it gently.
4. Put the opening of the balloon over the mouth of the bottle. Pull the stem part of the balloon down so that it will not come off easily. If it is loose, stick it down with a piece of masking tape to make it airtight.
5. Repeat this process for the warm water and cold water…

Here the textbook scripts teacher and student interaction—with a strong focus on exact reproduction of the experimental procedure. While Step 2 of the lesson draws out learners' suggestions for an investigation to determine the temperature that best promotes yeast activity (p. 22), the students are not encouraged to put their ideas into practice. Irrespective of what ideas students generate, Resource Sheet 4 offers only *one* sequence of actions and one pathway for thinking through the issues. Learners who do not offer up the "right" answers are "encouraged" to "think about testing the yeast in cold, warm and boiling water" (p. 22).

The sequencing of the lesson is scripted and pacing for hands-on activities is strongly framed. For example, in the hands-on activity, "What is the best temperature for yeast to be active?" Step 7 leads an imperative: "Place the bottles in a warm place and leave for one hour. After an hour, come back to your bottles" (p. 23). There is little decision-making on the learners' part about pacing and sequencing of science activities. The focus is on precision and procedure. Possible problems, such as "pull[ing] the stem part of the balloon down so that it will not come off easily," are anticipated, with preferred solutions: "If it is loose, stick it down with a piece of masking tape to make it airtight." Here, what counts as scientific knowledge is the replication of a given procedure to produce an expected and accepted finding.

As indicated in Box 2.1 above, the *Marvelous Micro-organisms* unit lays out a plan for eight lessons that build towards a concluding assessment task in Lesson 8. Item 1, below, is the assessment task as it is explained to the teacher, and items (2) and (3) are listed as optional tasks (pp. 49–50).

1. Explain that students are going to work in teams to develop a presentation about the role of micro-organisms in their lives. Review the micro-organisms that students have learned about in the unit—yeast and molds. Discuss what type of information students could include in their presentations, for example:

   - What are micro-organisms?
   - What conditions do micro-organisms like yeast and mould need to grow?
   - What role does yeast play in bread-making?
   - How do micro-organisms affect our lives?

Explain the information that you will be looking for to assess students' presentations:

- well-organized information
- evidence of research into the topic (optional)
- evidence of knowledge of topic
- clear oral communication
- evidence of cooperative team work
- creative presentation.

2. **Optional:** Students use their understanding and experience of micro-organisms to participate in whole-class, small-group or individual construction of a narrative text about micro-organisms, for example, "The mystery of the multiplying mould."
3. **Optional:** Students write questions and answers from their information reports for a game show. Collate the questions and play a quiz game, for example, a quiz called "The Micro-organism Factor."

Assessment Task 1 requires learners to communicate how micro-organisms affect their lives. There is the possibility of multimodal text production. Yet it is not clear how the strongly classified content knowledge and strongly framed pedagogies of Lessons 1–7 (i.e., a learner's fundamental sense of scientific knowing beyond recitation of science facts about yeast, mould and medicines) will enable or set the ground for a reframing and transformation of textual designs. Specifically, the task is focused on micro-organisms "in their lives," with little resourcing or specification of everyday applications (other than bread-making) of the experimental procedure and finding. While general criteria are specified, there is little discussion of the different audiences and effects of modes and genres of representation. Finally, while the assessment criteria for the more traditional Assignment 1 are detailed—no criteria to guide student performance are introduced for Assignments 2 and 3.

Assessment Item 2, construction of a narrative text about micro-organisms, also has the potential for a demonstration of science content knowledge. However, there is nothing in the lesson that establishes the shifting of textual designs or, in this case, acknowledges the complex differences and functional purposes of scientific exposition vis-à-vis narrative. Simply, narratives have distinguishing textual and linguistic features that differ from those expressed in texts in Lessons 1–7. Students are being asked to move to and across specialized representational designs and modalities, with no discussion of their features, characteristics or audiences, or specific uses and consequences.

Assessment Item 3 draws on derived senses of science knowledge and fundamental senses of reading science texts and writing science content in a quiz format. The innovation in mode and medium for these two optional assessment items are attempts to translate scientific knowledge into popular cultural forms. The approach has some merit "in that ... [popular cultural texts] have the potential to motivate learners, stimulate their engagement, and scaffold their learning of science" (Fang, 2006, p. 515). However, there is no critical analysis here of the particular textual designs in question (narrative, television quiz shows), their contexts or features. It is noteworthy that these two assessment items—designed to connect the more traditional knowledge of scientific facts and procedures into students' everyday lives and media experience—are the least scripted activities.

Classroom discourse and social interaction is also strongly framed, with explicit prescription of the teacher's role and actions. For example, in Lesson 8, where the assessment task and further options are outlined, the role of the teacher as an "explainer," "reviewer" and "discussant" are clear:

> *Explain* that students are going to work in teams to develop a presentation about the role of micro-organisms in their lives. *Review* the micro-organisms that students have learned about in the unit—yeast and molds. *Discuss* what type of information students could include in their presentations.
>
> (pp. 49–50, emphasis added)

The actions of the learner are set out in sequences of imperatives: "Explain the information that you will be looking for to assess students' presentations" (p. 50).

Table 2.1 summarizes the lessons, describes the pedagogy and engaging modes, and analyzes curriculum knowledge and pedagogic practice according to Bernstein's notion of classification and framing.

Primary Connections Marvelous Micro-organisms unit is, then, a strongly classified curriculum delivered through strongly framed, highly directive pedagogies. What counts as scientific knowledge is set out through a prescriptive set of content and procedures for teachers and students. The result is an explicit instructional focus on the acquisition of basic scientific facts and concepts, with the aim of the replication of a set of experimental procedures. This is reinforced in the pedagogical modes, which include background reading, teacher-based discussion, and hands-on replication of an experimental procedure. Throughout the unit, there is a strong emphasis on teacher-directed activities and explicit teaching. The major assessment is a group report/presentation. The optional assessment activities, designed to engage and motivate students, are weakly framed and without the clearly articulated criteria or specifications affiliated with a higher-stakes assessment. The activities designed to engage and motivate students (e.g., personal narratives, media game show performance) are clearly adjunct to the unit and less explicitly connected with salient scientific issues or contents.

There are several relevant issues here. First, the lesson covers a range of modalities (e.g., visual, spoken, written) and textual designs (e.g., expository, procedural, narrative) with almost no explicit attention paid to specific linguistic features, varied audiences, social uses and purposes. The result is a largely decontextualized production of facts, procedures and findings, with little direct application or connection with student background knowledge—other than the content around bread, lunchboxes and food. Second, there is no critical framing—the discussion of "risk," "values" and possible related "issues" that feature in the broad scientific literacy we described at the onset of this chapter.

A Multiliteracies Project Approach

So how might "complex social and critical issues associated with scientific evidence and knowledge" (National Curriculum Board, 2008) guide a comparable unit of study? This case study was based on a single multi-age class (ages: 7–10 years) in a small primary school in an inner-city suburb of Brisbane, the capital city of Queensland, Australia. Bushland State School (pseudonym) is set in a mid-to-low socio-economic community—as its name implies, surrounded by bushland. Learner and parent surveys indicate that the school's curriculum and pedagogy reform of the past four years has gained significant parent and community support. Teachers have developed and implemented "student negotiated" long-term curriculum projects with the aim of increasing learner engagement and improving overall literacy achievement.

In their planning, these projects adopted a general multiliteracies approach that: (1) foregrounds inquiry and situates content and its modes of representation in the "lifeworlds" of learners; (2) provides overt instruction that names and theorizes content and modes of representation and extends these into new knowledge; (3) integrates critical framing at every stage; and (4) culminates in the application of content and modes of representation for real audiences.

The impetus for the eight-week multiliteracies project was the Australian Academy of Science's *Primary Connections Marvelous Micro-organisms* (2005) unit. The teacher, Mrs. Sarah Bellum (pseudonym), with over two decades of primary teaching experience, implemented the unit as intended from Lessons 1–7. She did not undertake Lesson 8, the culminating assessment task or either of its two options. In an interview where she was asked to evaluate the unit discussed above, she described the careful scaffolding of science content for teachers and students as "helpful and valuable." However, in relation to the overall aims and educational value of the unit, she stated: "You get to the end and you close the book.... I was left thinking, what's next? It didn't feel as though we had actually accomplished anything substantive, anything we could relate to or get our teeth into." From Mrs. Bellum's perspective, *Marvelous Micro-organisms* provided background reading and a range of hands-on activities that extended content knowledge. But in itself, it failed to deal with the crucial questions of critical engagement and relevant application issues.

She began the next phase by negotiating an inquiry question with her 19 middle-primary learners. The focus was on the role of micro-organisms in food and medicine: "Micro-organisms: Good or Bad?" The learners were fascinated with the notion that some micro-organisms were helpful to their

Table 2.1 Analysis of Marvelous Micro-organisms Unit

Summary of Lessons		*Description of Pedagogy*	*Modes*	*Classification*	*Framing*
Lesson 1—The Y Factor	Session 1—Exploring Bread	Situated practice that elicits what students know about bread, the bread-making process and the yeast micro-organism. Overt instruction to record differences between breads, including reading bread labels	• Talk (sharing and discussion) • Print (recording)	++	++
	Session 2—The Bread-Making Process	Overt instruction for constructing flow chart of how bread is made	• Print (flow chart) • Visual (flow chart)	++	++
	Session 3—Anton van Leeuwenhoek: Microscope Maker	Overt instruction for reading information sheet on Anton van Leeuwenhoek	• Print (reading) • Talk (initiate, respond, evaluate and exchange)	++	++
Lesson 2—Yeast Feast		Overt instruction—read, discuss and enact a procedural text "What happens when yeast is mixed with sugar and water?"	• Print (reading) • Talk (discussion) • Doing (procedural text)	++	++
Lesson 3—Putting the Heat on Yeast		Overt instruction—read, discuss and enact a procedural text "What is the best temperature for yeast to be active?"	• Print (read) • Talk (discuss) • Doing (procedural text)	++	++
Lesson 4—Knead the Loaf		Overt instruction—observe bread-making process and draw conclusions about role of yeast in bread-making process	• Observation • Print (record)	++	++
Lesson 5—Food Observations		Overt instruction on summarizing, representing and explaining observations about yeast micro-organisms	• Talk (explaining) • Print (summary) • Visual (flow chart)	++	++

Lesson 6—Mystery Molds	Session 1—A Nightmare in my Lunchbox	Overt instruction for planning, conducting and recording investigation of the conditions that affect mold growth on food	• Doing (manipulative observation with microscope) • Visual (labeled diagram) • Print (recording) • Print (reading)	++	++
	Session 2—Investigating Molds	Overt instruction for reading resource sheet on molds			
Lesson 7—Medical Micro-organisms		Overt instruction for reading about the role of micro-organisms in the discovery and development of the antibiotic penicillin.	• Print (reading) • Print (writing reflection)	++	++
Lesson 8—Micro-organisms Experts		Transformed practice where students prepare a presentation that represents what they know about micro-organisms	• Talking (group report) • Gestural (live presentation) • Possibility of digital presentation (written and visual) • Print (written and visual for narrative) • Talk (closed interrogates and declaratives for quiz/game show)	++	+

everyday lives while others were harmful. Learners' motivation was enhanced by the introduction of a situated role-play drama where two bumbling "scientists" (acting principal and Exley in role) made regular visits to the classroom. One of the bumbling scientists, Professor Von Spacey (Exley in role), presented the learners with a pseudo-fictional observation, that good micro-organisms used in foods and medicines were starting to disappear from the world. She had reason to believe that her arch-enemy, the dastardly Dr Stickeminabottle (acting principal in role), was developing a plot to rid the world of good micro-organisms so to encourage the growth of the bad micro-organisms. He explained to the students his belief that the world population would recognize that he held the balance of power for he would be the only one able to control the existence of harmful micro-organisms. This would then allow Dr Stickeminabottle to realize his lifelong goal—to take control of the world and all of its riches.

The situated role-play drama created a moral tension for the learners. They had to decide if they would support an attempt to re-establish the status quo of micro-organisms, or if they would side with a plan to rid the world of helpful micro-organisms and promote the growth of harmful micro-organisms. Each "scientist" visited the classroom briefly on half a dozen occasions in role to engage in non-scripted conversation about what new knowledge the learners had found and the progress of their moral discussions. So that the role-play had a sense of purpose, learners set about researching both standpoints. It was not practical that both scientists continued their whimsical behavior. The scientists and learners reached an agreement: the learners would continue to examine the inquiry question. They would then have to collaborate as a community and decide which of the two scientists could have access to their new-found knowledge. In short, they were entering into debate about the ethics of scientific knowledge and the disparate possibilities science created for reality.

The two scientists never visited together; rather learners were only exposed to one viewpoint at a time in order to highlight the contending issues and justifications. Working in small teams, and guided by their teacher and additional adult advisors, the learners decided to:

- undertake learner-led inquiry and activities so as to learn content information and engage with science processes;
- decide which scientist's actions they could morally support;
- design and present a multimodal hortatory (call to action) text using the newly acquired computer animation software, Kahootz 3.0 (Australian Children's Television Foundation, 2007), at a community vote which would determine which scientist would be given the learners' research findings and which scientist would be banished from practicing science.

Alongside this six-week-long cycle of critically framed situated practice and overt instruction focused on science content (micro-organisms) and multimedia (using a digital microscope and the Kahootz 3.0 software), Mrs. Bellum set up a department-approved asynchronous online forum so that learners could post questions, findings and/or continue their real-time conversations with each other and the two bumbling scientists virtually. The 19 learner participants were all given a separate password to access the site on one of two networked computers in the classroom or from an external service provider (e.g., home). This online forum was not core to teaching and learning; rather learners were invited to participate if and when they felt like it over the life of the project.

The choice made by Mrs. Bellum to avoid summative assessment in the forum ensured the space was casual and optional (see Exley, 2007a). An analysis of the student contributions made to the online forum revealed the potential for online forums to contribute to the experience of scientific enquiry in and through wider learning spaces, in particular non-school sites and (parts of) the World Wide Web community.

The findings also suggest that ICTs are a mechanism for allowing some learners the chance to regain control over the learning experience; that is, weaken the interactional framing of school science. The online forum demonstrated potential for supporting the diverse needs of learners operating on asynchronous schedules while also creating connectivity amongst learners, experience sharing and information flow.

Learners also had access to three other significant adults during the project:

- An industry-based scientist (the father of a learner at the school) who visited the classroom on a few occasions to calibrate the newly purchased digital microscope and the aging manual microscopes bequeathed from a nearby secondary school; attend to the learners' request to prepare slides to examine micro-organisms in food and creek water; and add half a dozen posts on the forum that answered learners' questions about micro-organisms.
- A parent of a learner in the class with an interest in the computer animation software (Kahootz 3.0) who supported the learners' explorations of the program and who also made a dozen posts to the forum site regarding the mechanics of Kahootz 3.0.
- A final-year pre-service teacher from a local university who worked in collaboration with Mrs. Bellum for a month, and made half a dozen posts to the forum site that suggested learners visit some useful websites about micro-organisms. It was up to the learners at what level they engaged with these alternative media.

The focus here is on content relevance, a citizenship/society/socio-scientific foci, and a pedagogy that focused on scaffolded and structured inquiry that was also sufficiently weakly framed to offer students choice in knowledge content and pedagogical practice. Mrs. Bellum's approach weakened the classification of what counted as science knowledge, encouraging crossover in online and face-to-face discussion from scientific field knowledge to the students' everyday lives and larger societal issues. Learners, then, were able to exercise, by degrees, power over the curriculum and control over the selection, sequencing, pacing and interaction patterns. This was most evident when the learners were working on Kahootz.

Despite her interest in ICT and desire to learn, Mrs. Bellum observed that the students had more ICT content knowledge and were building upon their bases more rapidly. They were recontextualizing knowledge and understandings from their outside-of-school ICT use and were even finding answers to ICT problems in outside-of-school time by entering into discussion with their peers on the online forum. That is, the shifting of pedagogic modalities from face-to-face and print-based to online was generating dialogue and engagement. Observing these gains, Mrs. Bellum deliberately did not strengthen the classification of curriculum and framing of pedagogy to the point she was forcing all learners through scripted pedagogy.

While the instructional classification remained weak, the roles and interventions of the five adult experts were carefully structured. Here scientific knowledge was formed not solely from strongly bounded content knowledge and content assessment, rather also within the realm of expert/novice pedagogy and student work groups. This participatory approach encouraged students to generate diverse viewpoints on "expert knowledge," and bring these together for deliberations. The situated role-play drama was indeed central in creating the moral problem and need for detailed scientific exploration. Yet the students' solutions were not pre-determined, emerging from unpredictable and indeterminate conversations. The underlying tenets of Mrs. Bellum's weakly classified curriculum and weakly framed pedagogy resonates with Lemke's (2007, p. 2) statements on science and scientific learning:

> Science cannot be equated with its products: what science says about the world is not science itself. Science itself is the human activity that produces these statements and theories, and to learn science is not to learn what the last generation of scientists thought the world was like; it is to learn how each new generation of scientists re-makes our view of the world.

Applying an analytical lens to the multiliteracies project reveals the shifting classifications of scientific knowledge and framing of pedagogy for science (Table 2.2).

At the onset of this chapter, we noted that one of the key dilemmas for science education was to bridge traditional knowledge of facts, concepts and procedures with substantive and authentic applications, issues and debates. The New London Group (1996, p. 67) argued for a focus on learners developing "the capacity to speak up, to negotiate, and to be able to engage critically with the conditions" of their lives and their futures in complex new times. This multiliteracies project was a deliberate attempt to draw on the strengths

Table 2.2 Micro-organisms: Good or Bad? Multiliteracies Unit

Unfolding of the Project	*Description of Pedagogy*	*Engaging Mode*	*Classification*	*Framing*
Negotiation of an inquiry question—Micro-organisms: good or bad?	Critical framing—to interpret the social and cultural context of science	• Talk (negotiating and considering alternative viewpoints) • Written (recording)		
Introduction of situated role-play drama with two bumbling "scientists," each seeking knowledge about micro-organisms for very different purposes: one to take control of the world, the other to maintain the status quo. Multiple visits over the course of the project	Critical framing—by standing back from what the students are studying and viewing it critically in relation to its context	• Talk (negotiating persuasive speech from and with bumbling "scientists")	–	–
Students' questions inspiring science content focus (e.g., students wanted to look at live micro-organisms in pond water under a microscope, in food products, in medicine)	Overt instruction—of student inspired science content, scaffolded by teacher and industry-based scientist	• Talk (focus on "what"—science content) • Manipulation of science equipment	–	+

continued

Table 2.2 Continued

Unfolding of the Project	*Description of Pedagogy*	*Engaging Mode*	*Classification*	*Framing*
Students continue discussions, albeit virtually, on system-sanctioned forum site	Situated practice—conducted online asynchronically, in school and out of school	• Digital (acquiring and developing competencies for text production) • Print (reading and writing screen text)	– (students had maximum control over what was brought in as science content)	– (students have maximum control over the pedagogic relationship between acquirers, whether that be adult and learner; learner and learner)
Conscious awareness and control over computer animation program, Kahootz 3.0.	Overt instruction—at times weakly framed overt instruction, at other times, more strongly framed overt instruction. Learners could gain skills at the point of need. Overt instruction does not imply direct transmission, drills and rote learning; rather students were self-learners and impromptu peer tutors for each other Critical framing—visual, spatial and gestural design	• Digital (acquiring and developing competencies for text production)	Ranges from – to + (rather than offer pre-sequenced activity, student need dictated what content was brought in and how it was structured)	Ranges from – to + (student had options for structuring the pedagogic relations)

Teacher and students compare and contrast target text samples (hortatory exposition), that is, the structure of language	Overt instruction—use of metalanguage, language of reflective generalization that describes the form, content and function of hortatory exposition (call to action) Critical framing—linguistic design	• Print (comparing hortatory expositions) • Multimedia (comparing non-print-based hortatory expositions)	++ (teachers' expertise in this area and need to focus learners on significant textual features of genre returned strong classification of knowledge)	Ranged from + to ++ (students deconstructed some sample texts in groups but also participated in strongly framed lessons)
Systematic, analytic and conscious understanding of meaning and processes of linguistic, audio, spatial, visual and gestural *design* for production of multimedia text (public presentation)	Overt instruction in form of active intervention on the part of the teacher and other experts (including peers) that scaffold learning experiences and activities within the community of learners	• Talk (discussion) • Print (reading and writing the words) • Digital (production of Kahootz computer animation presentation) • Visual (design) • Spatial (design)	++	++
Culminating task—presentation of hortatory expositions for public audience (parents, carers, siblings), community ballot to decide which scientist would have access to the learners' knowledge and which would be banished from practicing science forever	Transformed practice—demonstration of design and carrying out, in a reflective manner, new practices embedded in their own goals and values	• Talk (present to audience) • Manipulative (present digital file of Kahootz 3.0) • Gestural (design) • Auditory (design)	–	–

of the traditional and progressivist curricula, while also ameliorating some of their more notable weaknesses.

Mrs. Bellum took the role of an expert facilitator, with other adults introducing existing facts, concepts and procedures where relevant. The overall aim was for the learning community to undertake a long-term research project and construct an original text for public consumption. In this project, Mrs. Bellum's curriculum philosophy was progressivist in orientation, with a strong emphasis on students' background knowledge and "absences" in experience and knowledge (Kalantzis & Cope, 2005). However, there are several practical problems with the approach: (1) teacher preparation workload increases; (2) there is a risk that transparency and predictability of curriculum is reduced, with learners' unfamiliarity with constructivist pedagogies reducing the benefit of applications (Bernstein, 2000); and (3) learners' beliefs become the reference point for knowledge making, with excessive time pursuing the "wrong leads" (New London Group, 1996).

While students were involved in negotiating the inquiry topic, and advancing the critical framing, Mrs. Bellum systematically introduced relevant content "just in time." She further strengthened the classification and framing when introducing specific designs; both the computer animation program and the culminating presentation required direct instruction on technical, linguistic and semiotic design. While the textbook lesson maintained strong classification and framing throughout, this teacher developed a unit built upon content knowledge, weakening the classification and framing to enable students to explore the issues and make judgments—then, strengthening the classification when students moved towards the production of new designs.

Towards Critical Scientific Literacies

As in many contemporary issues in curriculum, there is a tendency in academic and public debate towards binary arguments: the basics *or* higher order work, direct instruction *or* immersion, rote *or* critical knowledge, teacher *or* learner-centered instruction, and so forth. While these categories may make conceptual sense, provide structurally tidy analyses and conveniently lend themselves to media reporting and editorial comment, current debates over science education risk an oversimplification of the actual work and challenges facing teachers and learners.

The element of the multiliteracies pedagogy that we have highlighted here is the possibility and the practicality of oscillating or "weaving" pedagogical modes, framings and classifications across a unit of work (Cazden, 2006; Luke, 2008). It is only through these shifting frames that teachers and learners can both engage with key facts, concepts and procedures with some degree of accuracy and precision; *and* connect with background knowledge, increase motivation and interest to engage in new scientific knowledge thinking; and explore opportunities to engage with the complex ethical and moral, social and cultural issues around the applications of science in everyday community and civic life.

It is perhaps too easy to juxtapose these two approaches to instruction and make normative pedagogical and, indeed, policy claims of the efficacy of Mrs. Bellum's integrated unit; that this form of the "curriculum-in-use" (Luke et al., 1989) is intrinsically superior in efficacy to an official, textbook-based, scripted curriculum. Indeed, the textbook lessons are more of a "closed text" (Luke, 1989), using imperatives, setting clear behavioral limits and thresholds in discourse exploration of issues and alternatives. But the risk here is a simple binary, with a strong moral sanction for progressivist and learner-centered instruction. Despite the direct involvement of one of the authors in the second part of the unit, we want to move away from such a stance, given the nature of the debates over science education. Our concluding case here is simple: differing classifications and framings have potentially different cognitive and social effects that constitute different kinds of scientific knowledge and capacity.

There is a place for both. As Mrs. Bellum reported to us, the coverage of scientific content knowledge and procedure of the textbook was "valuable." This is a particularly salient point given the recognition of the problem of primary teachers' threshold of core scientific knowledge, concepts and procedures. Yet the problem, she went on to comment, was that something was missing: it didn't seem to lead to "substantial" work. Our analysis suggests that while the strong classification and framing applied to the content and procedures in the textbook lessons, there was little attention paid to the technical features of the text designs required of the students. Further, the critical framing work around audiences, applications and relevant ethical issues was altogether absent, possibly implied but not systematically introduced in the adjunct assignments in Lesson 8.

At the same time, Mrs. Bellum recognized and addressed the potential problems with learner-centered, weakly classified classification and framing: specifically, that learner background knowledge could not form the sole platform for substantive engagement with issues, and that the shifts in modalities (from spoken dialogue and dramatic role-play, to digital animation and online dialogue, to hortatory multimodal text) required explicit instruction on design characteristics and technical features. To address the former, she used "experts" who provided technical information and scientific knowledge via student requests. To address the latter, she strengthened the classification and framing as each design was introduced. Finally, the culminating task required that the students synthesize new knowledge and understandings into a publicly presented standpoint on the possibilities of micro-organisms in everyday life.

The challenges facing science education are to move students from the known to the new, and in so doing both introduce them to a corpus of scientific knowledge, strategies for thinking and working like scientists, and using scientific knowledge to engage with salient issues in their current and future lives. We concur with Goodrum et al.'s (2001, p. 15) broad goal for school science, to teach students of the need to be "skeptical and questioning of claims made by others about scientific matters ... able to identify questions and draw evidence-based conclusions, and ... make informed decisions about the environment and their own health and well being." Our position—particularly enhanced by current debates over war, weapons of mass destruction, new economic and political formations built around sciences of energy, DNA, nano and digital technology—is that the tie-up and linkage between the analysis of society and a critique of science has become crucial. The state has, in effect, militarized science for geopolitical and economic purposes (Graham & Luke, 2003, 2005).

In conclusion, the "pedagogy of multiliteracies" model entailed a principled movement between different forms of curriculum and pedagogy that expanded one science-inspired project. We have described here a science-based multiliteracies project undertaken in a Year 4/3 mainstream multi-age Australian classroom, where one teacher worked with a community of learners to orchestrate shifting knowledge classifications and pedagogic framings. This version of science enables a renewed focus on critical framing and mastery of new modalities and designs. Curriculum materials like the *Primary Connections* unit can set the grounds for learners to enter into discussion about the ethics of the distribution of scientific knowledge through multiple perspectives, learn to explore the power of public debate and speaking positions, and—importantly—come to understand the different text practices that are required to engage with scientific knowledge. But in and of themselves, such traditional lessons cannot deal with the demands for increased learner engagement, motivation and a critical analysis of scientific applications and issues. What is needed is a pedagogy of multiliteracies that systematically shifts levels of classification and framing, that integrates new knowledge with critical framing, and that weaves across a diverse repertoire of instructional and curriculum strategies, including overt instruction.

Acknowledgments

The authors, listed in alphabetical order, thank the teachers, professional colleagues and students who participated in the study. We also wish to thank Steve Ritchie and Courtney Cazden for editorial comments and advice.

Notes

1. In a 2007 appraisal of the teacher expertise situation in Australia, Goodrum noted that: early childhood teachers' expertise is in the child development; primary teachers' expertise is usually literacy, then maths, then the other curriculum areas find a space; and secondary teachers traditionally had a major in science, yet the field is now populated by teachers teaching out of their field, for example, health and physical education teachers with expertise in human body physiology but limited content knowledge in physics, chemistry and early sciences.
2. As Bernstein (2000) recognizes, classification of knowledge is not the artefact of curricula, schools and classroom pedagogy alone: "because communication from the outside is less controlled ... identities are not [solely] established by the organi-

sational structure. . . ." (p. 11); that is, different framings and classifications are part of dominant, normative relations of selective knowledge production and reproduction.

References

Apple, M. (1990). Restoring the voice of curriculum specialists. *Education Digest*, 56(2), 48–52.

Australian Academy of Science. (2005). *Primary connections: Linking science with literacy. Marvelous micro-organisms, stage 3, life and living.* Canberra, Australia: Australian Academy of Science.

Australian Academy of Science. (2008). *Primary connections: Linking science with literacy. Small study—Big success story.* Canberra, Australia: Australian Academy of Science.

Australian Children's Television Foundation. (2007). *Kahootz 3.* Australian Children's Television Foundation. Retrieved July 2, 2007, www.kahootz.com/kz.

Bernstein, B. (2000). *Pedagogy, symbolic control and identity: Theory, research, critique* (Rev. ed.). Maryland, USA: Rowman & Littlefield Publishers.

Bond, D. (2000). Negotiating a pedagogy of multiliteracies: The communication curriculum in a South African management development programme. In B. Cope & M. Kalantzis, (Eds.), *Multiliteracies: Literacy learning and the design of social futures* (pp. 311–320). South Yarra: Macmillan Publishers.

Cazden, C. (2000). Four innovative programmes: A postscript from Alice Springs. In B. Cope & M. Kalantzis, (Eds.), *Multiliteracies: Literacy learning and the design of social futures* (pp. 321–322). South Yarra: Macmillan Publishers.

Cazden, C. (2006, January). Connected learning: Weaving in classroom lessons. Keynote address, *Pedagogy in Practice 2006 Conference.* University of Newcastle, Australia, January 18, 2006.

Curriculum Values. (2009, March 17). *The Australian*, p. 11.

Deng, Z., & Luke, A. (2008). Subject matter: Defining and theorizing school subjects. In F. M. Connelly, M. F. He & J. Phillion (Eds.), *The Sage handbook of curriculum and instruction* (pp. 66–87). Thousand Oaks, CA: Sage Publications.

Exley, B. (2007a). MUDS in the classroom: teachers' learning, epistemic potential and pedagogical dilemmas. *Australian Journal of Middle Schooling*, 7(1), 17–19.

Exley, B. (2007b). Meanings emerging in practice for linguistically and culturally diverse students: An early years Multiliteracies project. *International Journal of Pedagogies and Learning*, 3(3), 101–113.

Exley, B. (2008a). The senses of scientific literacy in a middle years multiliteracies project. *Australian Journal of Middle Schooling*, 8(1), 12–16.

Exley, B. (2008b). Communities of learners: Early years students, new learning pedagogy, and transformations. In A. Healy (Ed.), *Multiliteracies and diversity in education: New pedagogies for expanding landscapes* (pp. 126–143). South Melbourne: Oxford University Press.

Fang, Z. (2006). The language demands of science reading in middle school. *International Journal of Science Education*, 28(5), 491–520.

Fensham, P. (2007, July). *Policy issues for science education.* Discussion Paper presented at the World Conference on Science and Technology Education, Perth, Australia.

Goodrum, D., Hackling, M., & Rennie, L. (2001). *The status and quality of teaching and learning of science in Australian schools.* Canberra, Australia: Department of Education, Training and Youth Affairs.

Graham, P., & Luke, A. (2003). Militarising the body politic: Weapons of mass instruction. *Body and Society*, 9(4), 149–168.

Graham, P., & Luke, A. (2005). The language of neofeudal corporatism and the war on Iraq. *Journal of Language and Politics*, 4(1), 11–39.

Henderson, R. (2008). Mobilising multiliteracies: Pedagogy for mobile students. In A. Healy (Ed.), *Multiliteracies and diversity in education: New pedagogies for expanding landscapes* (pp. 168–200). Oxford University Press: South Melbourne.

Kalantzis, M., & Cope, B. (2005). *Learning by design*. Altona, Victoria: Common Ground Publishing.

Kwek, D. (2005, May). Classroom interaction as aesthetics experience: The praxis of aesthetics and flow in weaving. Paper presented at the *International Conference on Redesigning Pedagogy: Research, Policy, Practice*, Singapore.

Lavonen, J., Gedrovics, J., Byman, R., Meisalo, V., Juuti, K., & Uitto, A. (2008). Students' motivational orientations and career choice in science and technology: A survey in Finland and Latvia. *Journal of Baltic Science Education*, 7(2), 86–103.

Lee, M.-K., & Erdogan, I. (2007). The effect of science-technology-society teaching on students' attitudes toward science and certain aspects of creativity. *International Journal of Science Education*, 29(11), 1315–1327.

Lemke, J. L. (2007). *Teaching all the languages of science: words, symbols, images and actions*. Retrieved July 2, 2007, from University of Michigan Website: www.personal.umich.edu/~jaylemke/papers/barcelon.htm.

Luke, A. (1989). Open and closed texts: The ideological/semantic analysis of textbook narratives. *Journal of Pragmatics*, 13, 53–80.

Luke, A. (2008). Pedagogy as gift. In J. Albright & A. Luke (Eds.), *Pierre Bourdieu and literacy education* (pp. 68–91). New York: Routledge.

Luke, A. (2009). Curriculum in context: Introductory Essay. In M. Connelly, J. Pillion & M. F. He (Eds.), *Sage handbook of curriculum* (pp. 145–152). London: Sage.

Luke, A., Cazden, C., Lin, A., & Freebody, P. A. (2005). *A coding scheme for the analysis of classroom discourse in Singapore*. CRPP technical paper. Singapore: National Institute of Education, Centre for Research in Pedagogy and Practice, Unpublished report.

Luke, C., deCastell, S. C. & Luke, A. (1989). Beyond criticism: The authority of the school textbook. In S. DeCastell, A. Luke & C. Luke (Eds.), *Language, authority, criticism: Readings on the school textbook* (pp. 245–260). London: Falmer Press.

Mehan, H. (1996). A new reproduction of inequality under the New capitalism? *Organization*, 3(3), 419–429.

Millar, R. (2006). Twenty-first century science: Insights from the design and implementation of scientific literacy approaches in school science. *International Journal of Science Education*, 28(13), 1499–1521.

Mills, K. A. (2007). Have you seen Lord of the Rings? Power, pedagogy and discourses in a multiliteracies classroom. *Journal of Language and Identity in Education*, 6(3), 221–241.

National Curriculum Board. (2008). *National Science Curriculum: Framing Paper*. Retrieved February 1, 2009, from www.ncb.org.au/verve/_resources/FramingScienceFINAL_090109.pdf#xml=http://search.curriculum.edu.au/texis/search/pdfhi.txt?query=framing+paper+science&pr=www.ncb.org.au&prox=page&rorder=500&rprox=500&rdfreq=500&rwfreq=500&rlead=500&rdepth=0&sufs=0&order=r&cq=&id=49c322dea6.

New London Group. (1996). A pedagogy of multiliteracies: Designing social futures. *Harvard Educational Review*, 66(1), 60–93.

Newfield, D., & Stein, P. (2000). The multiliteracies project: South African teachers respond. In B. Cope & M. Kalantzis (Eds.), *Multiliteracies: Literacy learning and the design of social futures* (pp. 292–310). South Yarra: Macmillan Publishers.

OCED. (2006). *Assessing scientific, reading and mathematical literacy: A framework for PISA 2006.* Paris: OECD Publishing.

Pandian, A., & Balraj, S. (2005). Approaching learning by design as an agenda for Malaysian schools. In M. Kalantzis & B. Cope, (Eds.), *Learning by design* (pp. 285–314). Altona, Victoria: Common Ground Publishing.

Reiss, M. (2007). Comment: Bottom of the class. *The New Scientist*, 196(2623), 23.

Relevance of Science Education. (2008). *Relevance of Science Education.* Retrieved October 18, 2008, from www.ils.uio.no/english/rose.

Samuel, M. (2002). Sustainability revisited: Lessons from a Malaysian multiliteracies project. In J. Lo Bianco (Ed.), *Development and Language: global influences and local effects* (pp. 287–294). Melbourne: Language Australia Limited.

Tan, J. P.-L. (2008). Closing the gap: A multiliteracies approach to English language teaching for "at-risk" students in Singapore. In A. Healy (Ed.), *Multiliteracies and diversity in education: New pedagogies for expanding landscapes* (pp. 144–167). South Melbourne: Oxford University Press.

Wits University Multiliteracies Group. (2001). Exploding the monolith: Multiliteracies in South Africa. In M. Kalantzis and B. Cope (Eds.), *Transformations in language and learning: Perspectives on multiliteracies* (pp. 121–155). Retrieved from www.the-Learner.com.

3 Image, Genre, Voice, and the Making of the School-literate Child

Lessons from Multiliteracy Teaching in China

Bette Zhang Bin, University of Queensland, and Peter Freebody, University of Sydney

Introduction

Our aims in this chapter are to document the ways in which young school students are acculturated into the uses of texts that combine verbal and imaginal information, and to explore the possible consequences of that acculturation process. We pursue these aims from a historical perspective and through detailed examinations of school texts given to students beginning education in the People's Republic of China (PRC). In the PRC, *yuwen* is the term used to describe reading, literacy, language, literature teaching, and learning in school. In this chapter, we first examine constructs from the history of early reading education and how they compare to the assumptions and practices of early language education embodied in *yuwen*. We then turn to an examination of a small sample of the first *yuwen* texts currently used in schools in the PRC. Specifically, we use a multiliteracies framework to analyze three aspects of *yuwen* texts, focusing on mixtures of modalities, genres, and voices. Through these analyses we argue that *yuwen*, literacy and reading, and the acculturation of the literate student-subject more generally, together entail an inscription of particular attributes of the "school-literate" child, and, further, that it is only through detailed analyses of the materials of literacy and language education that the nature and consequences of such inscription processes can be made visible.

Mixing Modalities, Genres and Voices in Early School Literacy

The multiple functions performed by the official textual materials used in schools to help youngsters learn to read and write constitute the theme of this chapter. We consider these textual materials as instances of multiliterate practice, as both visual and linguistic objects. This chapter builds on work that we have presented elsewhere (Freebody & Baker, 1985; Freebody & Zhang, 2008; Zhang & Freebody, 2009; Zhang, 2006). Words and images are often mixed in early school reading materials (Unsworth, 2001), including in the Chinese examples we discuss here, and our focus is on how image, syntax, and genre structure these early educational materials and constitute important authorial practices for young people. Key concerns for us are how these young children's school reading materials structure everyday life, project particular futures, and deeply conjoin private and public interests.

There is no straightforward translation of "reading" and "literacy" in Chinese. Specific contextual information is usually needed to give a listener some general idea: a colloquial translation of "reading" in Chinese, for instance, is *yuedu* (阅读), a term usually associated with the act of reading. To make sense, the object(s) of this action—as types of books or documents—need to be signaled in the word itself. The materials and the process are conjoined in the naming of the activity. "Literacy" is translated via several concepts in Chinese, such as "*qimeng jiaoyu*" (启蒙 教育), "*wenmang*" (文盲), "*saomang*" (扫盲), or "*shizi*" (识字). To translate these Chinese terms back into English literally, they become, respectively, "enlightenment/cultivation education" (*qimeng jiaoyu*), "literate/word blindness" (*wenmang*), "eradicating blindness" (*saomang*), and "word-recognition" (*shizi*) (see Zhang, 2006). As we see, Chinese school education in "reading" is conceptualized, conducted, and even named in ways that do not assume the independence of this idea from a range of particular practices, problems, goals, and materials.

As discussed in Freebody and Zhang (2008), *yuwen* is a term used in the PRC to refer to the teaching of reading literature in school.[1] It is difficult to provide an English version of *yuwen* that adequately reflects the social, political, cultural, and disciplinary ideas that this notion carries (Cheng, 1998). Historically, the teaching of early reading was called "interpreting and reading the classics" (*jianjin dujin*), but the 1920s brought the establishment of a formal set of school curriculum subjects, and the teaching of contemporary Chinese language was placed under two headings: National Literature (*guowen*) and National Language (*guoyu*). In 1950, *yuwen* was introduced into the school curriculum, but until 2001 it was used to indicate two distinct aspects of teaching Chinese—language (*yu*) and literature (*wen*). Until recently these denoted separate programs of instruction and learning.

A Mixing of Modalities: Naming the Gateway

For Chinese school children, first encounters with reading in school (*yuwen*) do not focus on word recognition. In the first 3–5 weeks of school the major learning tasks are "entrance education" and *pinyin*. These are undertaken largely with look-and-say pictures (see Hu, 2004; Hudson-Ross & Dong, 1990; Ingulstrud & Allen, 1999; Sheridan, 1990). Among the groups of entrance education pictures, the one shown here (Figure 3.1) is the first in the sequence. At this age, children are prompted to recognize some basics of school behavior, such as, as suggested in this picture, greetings and acceptable ways of speaking, including in *putonghua* (see Zhang & Freebody, 2008).

Figure 3.1 Entrance Education (*Yuwen I*, pp. 2–3).

This picture is exceptional in that no captions appear. Earlier editions of *yuwen* books use speech bubbles with words such as *laoshi hao* ("teacher good"). The absence of verbal expressions in words in this picture is significant. Ways of greeting have changed considerably in China since the 1980s. During the national campaign of "Constructing Material and Spiritual Civilization" in the 1980s, expressions such as "How are you?" "Excuse me" and "Thank you" were explicitly propagated as the basics of a civilized language. Also around that time, people's professions and positions started to emerge as the favored style of address instead of the earlier "comrade." By the 1990s it was common to address people in terms of gender (Mr., Mrs., and Miss), even though they carried a slight satirical hint of corporate lifestyle.

In Figure 3.1, no cues are given to the characters' possible utterances. According to the teacher's manual accompanying this book, "simple polite language" is encouraged rather than specified, and the emphasis is on letting students sense the warmth of the teacher, a respect for the country when saluting to the red flag, and so on. As such, the picture is designed to "say without words," a design that seems to imply a guessing game, the answer to which children are expected either to know or to discover.

This is a narrative picture representing "entering" school. It is narrative in the sense that the represented participants are connected by vectors and represented as doing something to, with, or for each other that we infer to entail a succession of events (Kress & van Leeuwen, 2006). The human figures presented on the left side of the picture are paired, with hands gesturing greeting (teacher–pupil), departing (mother–daughter and father–son) or talking (two students). Cutting across the picture is a school fence, a strong vector signifying a border-crossing point. The large-letter poster on the fence, "Welcome New Students," presents an interpretive frame for engaging the picture. On the left of the fence there are eight human figures; on the right, the represented participants include a building, a flag, trees and a flower-bed, and four human figures. The strong diagonal line formed by the gated fence creates the setting and the narrative.

A sign saying "New China Road Primary School" on the right side of the fence, and a small shelter-like building on the left support the narrative. The sign indicates that this is a school, and a school in China ("new" differentiating it from "traditional"). The human figures on the left of the fence are the most salient participants in the image. The fence line links the actors walking toward the school. In this picture, except for the female figure, we see the actors standing beside the gate in positions that project their attention toward the school. The three adult–child pairs are linked by raised arms, signifying departure and entering. The children are entering.

This is an ordered scene that can be read using Kress and van Leeuwen's "four-block positioning device" (1996). The top-side information is taken to convey meaning of "ideals" and the bottom side of "realities." The ideal is idealized or generalized information; the real presents more specific, concrete information. The left-side information is presented as "given," and the right side as "new." The given is presented as commonsense, self-evident, or already in semiotic play in the text, and the new is novel, problematic, and/or challenging. In this picture, the top section is a school environment, perhaps an ideal one; the bottom section presents a "familiar" scene for young viewers—people accompanying and "talking" to one another. The left side of the picture, as a given, tells the young readers a fact—that child-characters are now leaving people they know and going, by themselves, independently, into a school. The three children are shown in three distinct phases of movement from their adult parent-guardians toward the welcoming teacher: one is already with the teacher with no accompanying parent evident; one is waving to his father from a distance; and one is still with her mother, who is pointing to the gate. School-related elements are presented on the right side as new to new students. Depicted in the bottom-right section are, apparently, two school mates (their school bags are on their backs and they are walking toward the gate) walking and talking, signifying a new student-to-student relationship.

The representation of school is accompanied here by a raised national flag, a surrounding leafy environment, the fence, and the words on the fence. In this picture, we see a bar fence, which came to replace the traditional solid brick "compound" walls of the 1980s. At the time, there were national debates about walls, so even this fence is a static narrative. School and university walls were taken to symbolize a closed educational system in China, in contrast to open educational systems imagined to be in the West. The bar fence appears to be more transparent than the traditional brick walls. In this picture, the shelter-like building on the right border side of the fence is marked with a sign "Message Office" (*Chuanda Shi*), which is a distinctive marker of an institution in China, and the gate officer has the power to check and potentially block the entrance of incomers. The female figure beside the gate is the only person in the picture facing readers, holding books in her hands. We can also tell this is a recently constructed scene because of the attire (all the females in the picture wear skirts), and the backpacks that the youngsters carry.

The picture "entrance education" is one that virtually every Chinese student beginning school will see within the first few days of school. Before any explicit word recognition has been introduced to students, this picture affords messages about school culture at the first moment of students' school careers—their gateway to school. Through the look-and-say reading lessons, children are implicitly positioned to recognize school, and schooled forms of demeanor and interaction. They are also "put into the picture," projected into a new and unfamiliar environment. Given and new are not just grammatical categories in this instance; they represent a social and cultural rite of passage.

The display and formatting of *yuwen* materials show the main themes underlying contemporary Chinese reading education. In that sense they are material expressions of a theory of beginning readers as learners, and as new to institutional public life. Traditionally, the layout of Chinese writing is right–left, vertical reading order, without punctuation. The use of left–right horizontal format started in 1915 as a convenience in scientific texts and formulas. Together, the top-to-bottom and left-to-right horizontal order, and the use of punctuation, set the textual formatting apart from tradition; the simplified characters with *pinyin* on top of each distinguish these as PRC early-school reading materials. The sequence of events in a typical *yuwen* lesson is structured by the ordering of written text in the upper section and the picture in the lower section of each page. Consistently, text lessons (*kewen*) are structured with numbered titles, bodies of texts, key vocabulary, and following exercises. These visual semiotics suggest information about the structural order of meanings, as indicated by Kress and van Leeuwen (2006), and signify the pedagogical procedures that are to deliver the knowledge.

When students move on to word recognition and text comprehension lessons, there emerges a fine-tuning of the integration of written texts and images, each giving cues that help construe and contextualize the meanings made available in these ensembles. The integration is neither random nor accidental. Kress and van Leeuwen (2006) have pointed out that visual layout, the maneuvering of spatial arrangements of blocks of texts and pictures, and the handling of various graphic devices and ensembles are, together, intended to afford and reinforce particular social practices. Visual and verbal devices are employed to give meaning to certain discourses prevalent in contemporary China.

Mixing Genres: Toward an Imagined Landscape

Like verbal texts, images carry particular orders that help construe meaning (Emmison & Smith, 2000). In their analyses of early-school reading materials, Baker and Freebody (1989) identified textual features and interpretive frames through which children are acculturated to become school-literate. Baker and Freebody describe these as "specialized school genres." These textual genres relate to phoneme–grapheme relations, as well as genre-based transitions from oral to literary written patterns, such as expository, narrative and experiential (see Martin, 1997). A point that Baker and Freebody reiterate is that textual formalities represent neither natural nor neutral bodies of knowledge, but are rather products of cultural technologies, providing versions of the world that can in turn be interrogated. In the first-year *yuwen* books, for instance, a salient textual feature is the mixing of narration and exposition (for detailed discussion, see Zhang, 2006). *Drawing Hometown* (translation and Figure 3.2) shows some of these features.

> **Drawing Hometown**
> Children love their hometown, and also love to draw their beautiful hometown.
>
> Tao Tao's hometown is by the sea. In his drawing, the sea is so blue, and so broad. The ships are full of fish and shrimps. The boy who is collecting shells in bare feet is Tao Tao.
>
> Shan Shan's hometown is in the mountain. In his drawing, the mountain is so high, and the water is so clear. The houses have tall and big trees in front and back. In the picture, Shan Shan is carrying a little bamboo basket for picking up mushrooms in the forest.
>
> Ping Ping's hometown is on a plain. In her drawing, the plain is so smooth and so stretched-out. There are golden crops, snow-white cotton flowers, and vast patches of jade green vegetable fields. In front of the houses, there are chickens and ducks; behind the houses, there are emerald green bamboo trees. The little girl running around the fields is Ping Ping.
>
> Qing Qing's hometown is on the prairie. In her drawing, the prairie is endless. The grass grows green and is dense. The sheep are strolling around. A handsome horse is running from a far distance. Qing Qing is riding on the horse's back looking after the sheep.
>
> Jing Jing's hometown is in the city. In his drawing, the city is so beautiful. The streets are wide, the buildings are tall, and the city is dotted with central street parks. The little boy running towards the science and technology palace is Jing Jing.
>
> Little friends, your hometowns must be very beautiful as well. Let's draw them together.
>
> (*Yuwen II*, pp. 102–105)

This text has a mixture of narrative structures, such as third-person narration, and expository structures. The latter are a striking feature of the first year

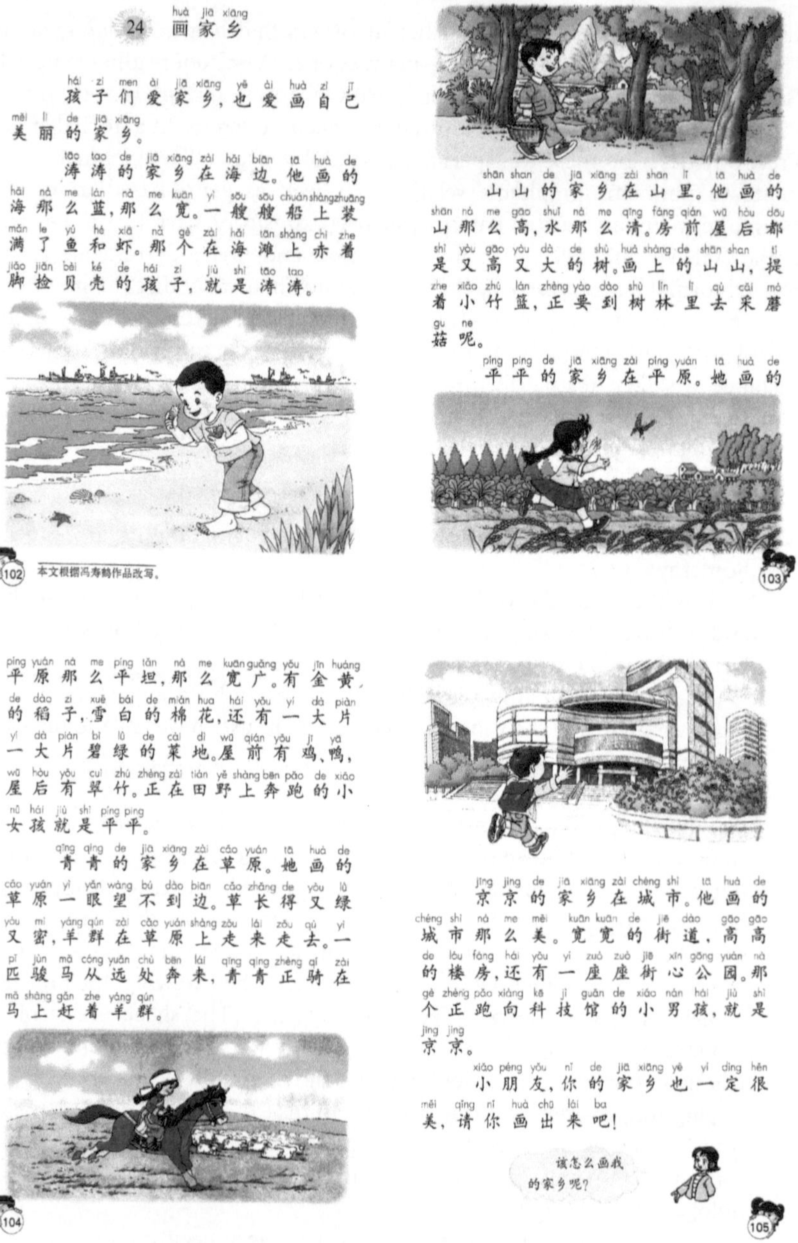
24 画家乡

孩子们爱家乡，也爱画自己美丽的家乡。

涛涛的家乡在海边。他画的海那么蓝，那么宽。一艘艘船上装满了鱼和虾。那个在海滩上赤着脚捡贝壳的孩子，就是涛涛。

本文根据冯寿鹤作品改写。

102

山山的家乡在山里。他画的山那么高，水那么清。房前屋后都是又高又大的树。画上的山山，提着小竹篮，正要到树林里去采蘑菇呢。

平平的家乡在平原。她画的

103

平原那么平坦，那么宽广。有金黄的稻子，雪白的棉花，还有一大片一大片碧绿的菜地。屋前有鸡、鸭，屋后有翠竹。正在田野上奔跑的小女孩就是平平。

青青的家乡在草原。她画的草原一眼望不到边。草长得又绿又密，羊群在草原上走来走去。一匹骏马从远处奔来，青青正骑在马上赶着羊群。

104

京京的家乡在城市。他画的城市那么美。宽宽的街道，高高的楼房，还有一座座街心公园。那个正跑向科技馆的小男孩，就是京京。

小朋友，你的家乡也一定很美，请你画出来吧！

105

Figure 3.2 Drawing Hometown (*Yuwen II*, pp. 102–105), pp. 102–103.

yuwen books: there is a starting point introducing a general topic, a sequence of elaborations, and finally a moral implication. *Drawing Hometown* follows this expository pattern, starting by asserting a proposition (paragraph 1), followed by five paragraphs of elaborations, and concluding with imperatives that reinforce the initial proposition statement. This kind of beginning–middle–end construction is different from the story grammar that is often associated with children's narratives, which generally shows a pattern of setting (character, location); episodes (initiating event, response, and attempts); and consequences/reactions/resolutions. The typical episodic structures relating to story grammar, with a string of internal responses, conflicts, reflections, and so on, do not characterize *yuwen* texts. In *Drawing Hometown*, the "middle" is another unique instance, providing elaborations that can be multiplied with no narrative-structural implications, apparently endlessly.

As demonstrated in *Drawing Hometown*, expository features are also observable in the five elaboration paragraphs (paragraphs 2–6), the employment of relational processes in the five elaboration sequences, and the repeatable pattern of elaborations. The rhythmic pattern is repeated through syntactic structures, such as "X is by a" (e.g., "Tao Tao's hometown is by the sea"), or "X is a" (e.g., "the sea is so blue"). Each of the elaborations uses an identical syntactic relational process to start identifying a geographic feature, mapped out spatially (sea, mountain, plain, the prairie, city). Further, each of the geographic features is construed through two modes of relational processes: attributive and identifying. By supplying the related attributive (e.g., the sea is blue and broad), or by use of an identifier (e.g., the ships are full of fish and shrimp), an abstraction effect is achieved (drawing on Halliday, 1994, 2002). This abstraction is realized through either abstraction in the same order, such as sea and blue, or through a categorical nominal group, such as fish and shrimp. Human agency is absent from these clauses. Of course, as indicated in the text, this is a construction of an imagined hometown. In other words, it is a constructed inter-subjectivity, but it is rich in unspecified authorial intention.

In school, beginning readers are often positioned to appreciate such a deliberately imagined hometown picture. As demonstrated in the text, the sequences of articulation of each hometown are construed to be repeatable, and each is illustrated with a picture. The repeatable and imitable patterns can serve as a substitute-form of drill exercise as necessary, for the students to imagine what they can call out as "the hometown" as required at the end of the texts. But the employment of relational processes functions to reconfigure human activities as static, agentless, and abstract—as ideas. Table 3.1 is a summary of agents and processes from paragraphs 2–6, in which the agentless clauses (18/20) are prevalent. In other words, geographic features and objects are endowed with pre-supposed attributes as given by nature. Child readers are positioned to appreciate and accept these categorized conceptions composed and imposed through the text.

Abstraction and agency can also be approached from a different angle. In each of the landscapes, a young inhabitant is presented to associate with the

Table 3.1

Agents/categorization	*Processes*
Hometown	is
Sea	is
Ship	are
Boy	is
Mountain	is
House	have
Shan Shan	is carrying
Plain	is
There	are
Girl	is
Prairie	is
Grass	grows
Sheep	are strolling
House	is running
Qing Qing	is riding
City	is
Streets	are
Buildings	are
City	is dotted
Boy	is

geo-features, identified in sequence from their abbreviated names: Tao Tao (literary meaning is "wave"), Shan Shan ("mountain"), Qing Qing ("green"), Jing Jing ("city"). The presence of a human figure in each of the pictures enables the reader to make a connection between people and the land; people's identities are bound into the land. The landscape of the country is mapped across east and south-east coastal lines, mountainous areas in the west and north-west, the middle inland agricultural area, and the prairie in the north and north-west. In alignment with the four natural geographic features is the city. Hence, the country is presented both with some vast natural nostalgic features, and with some modern, more hard-headed signs of construction. This geo-centric representation makes it possible to render China as landscapes rather than as a political entity. Although a human figure is represented in each of the landscapes, he or she is not presented as an agent; linguistically, no material process is established, and visually no action line/vector is involved; instead, the human "appears," functioning as one of the static elements of each scene.

So in the five elaboration paragraphs, a major concern in each of the landscapes is shown to be the attributes of the land. These are created through modes of relational processes: attributive and identifying. There are two types of attribution, one describing color and the other describing size; the nominals are concerned with resources (Table 3.2).

A rich vocabulary is employed to convey a sense of magnitude for the intended first-year readers: broad, high, tall, big, stretched-out, vast, endless,

Table 3.2

Geo-identified	*Attributive*		*Resources*
	Color	*Size*	
Tao Tao (sea)	Blue	Broad	Fish, shrimp, shells
Shan Shan (mountain)	Clear	High, tall, big	Mushrooms, trees
Ping Ping (plain)	Golden, snow-white, jade green, emerald green	Smooth, stretched-out, vast	Crops, cotton, vegetables, chicken, duck, bamboo trees
Qing Qing (prairie)	Green	Endless, dense	Horse, sheep
Jing Jing (city)		Wide, tall, center	Street, building, park, science and technology palace

and wide. These adjectives present a category of attributes associated with what can be called "hometown" and country. Each of the sites is represented with concrete material resources: sea—fish, shrimp, shells; mountain—mushrooms and trees; plain—crops, cottons, vegetables, chickens, ducks, bamboo and trees; prairie—sheep and horse; city—streets, buildings, parks, and science and technology palace. Many of these are transferable into food. The sense of magnitude is also reflected in the following exercise text, *How Big is Our Mother Land* (p. 112).

> When the snowflakes are dancing in the Great Xing Anling Mountain Range, the willow trees are sprouting along the Chang Jiang River, and the flowers are blossoming in the Hailan Island. How big is our motherland.

In this case, magnitude is brought about by the signs of the four seasons made visible at one time. The country and its landscapes are represented through a temporal order; by depicting climatic features in the geographic locations. Great Xing Anling Mountain Range represents the northern frontier, Chang Jiang River represents the middle area, and Hailan Island represents the far southern frontier. Snowflakes dancing, willow trees sprouting, and flowers blossoming represent different seasons, and by assembling all the seasons in one text, the extensiveness of the country is thus achieved. This exercise text was used as a main text in previous *yuwen* editions. In a contrast to the temporal mapping of the national landscape conducted in exclamatory language, *Drawing Hometown* engages in textual exposition, didactically presenting a more familiar countryside to its young readers.

The identifiable human figures in each hometown landscape are dressed in contemporary or ethnic costume. The resources are oriented to consumption and cosmopolitanism, no longer to the production resources such as minerals, oil, or agricultural crops, as portrayed in some of the traditional texts. In *Drawing Hometown*, the landscape is created through two dominant colors, natural blues and greens; but the text is designed to command love for the country rather than appreciation of the daily lives going on in the towns and on the land.

The text, *Drawing Hometown*, begins with an assertion: "Children love their hometown, and also love to draw their beautiful hometown." In omitting any hedges such as "some children love," or "children may love," an emotional obligation of children to the country is established. Following the descriptions of the features of the country, the text concludes: "Little friends, your hometown must be very beautiful as well." The strong modality writes out other possibilities that may not be counted as "beautiful." The imperative created through "Let's draw them together" demands action, conjoining the pedagogical and the patriotic. Although there are no adult figures presented in the text, an adult authority is established through the address of "little friend," and the following persuasion from the same authorial source—"let's." What is called for from the young readers is a collective imagination, a shared moral, aesthetic, and affective value, brought about through the maneuvering of verbal and visual devices.

A Mixing of Voices: The Moon's Wish

A systematic mixture of modalities and genres is a persistent feature of the *yuwen* texts for beginning students. There is a high density of textual structuring conveying explicit themes, techniques and skills for reading words and texts, and literary effects in these texts. This multiplicity, along with the ambiguity of the Chinese scripts and texts (Ku & Anderson, 2003; Li, Gaffney & Packard, 2002; Shu, 2003; Wu, Li & Anderson, 1999), conveys some shared features with school language-reading materials: an intention to balance information to be acquired with stories to be enjoyed, a transition from oral stories to written expositions, and the apparently collaborative nature of authorship ("let's..."). What is purveyed in particular is the need to move beyond the narrator's apparently simple conveying of characters' utterances. As in oral conversational events, topic and content are produced by speakers. In books, "the narrator takes over some of the work of signaling the sense of what is going on; this sense, which the narrator's interjections assist, becomes the context for the interpretation of characters' speeches" (Baker & Freebody, 1989, p. 87). Early-school materials represent beginning steps toward the fuller interpretive authority of the narrator. The interleaving of talk and narration hence is significant in examining the silent adult presence, the narrator's textual practices by which stories and expositions are assembled.

When examining the author's interweaving of narration and talk, a key practice is the reporting of speech (Vincent & Perrin, 1999). Generally, in contrast to the function of indirect speech of the "she said that..." variety, which cues the reader into the fictional nature of the narration, the choice of directly reporting the speech is seen to give "factuality" to the fiction. Direct speech functions to convey "the sense of an actual record rather than the sense of a likely or possible rendition of what might have been said or thought" (Baker & Freebody, 1989, p. 83); this is a way of constraining the varieties of interpretation that operate in normal human interaction. We can see this at work in a *yuwen* text, *A Wish of the Moon*, shown below (also see Zhang & Freebody, 2008). The quoted speeches, particularly presented through the mother and daughter discussion in paragraphs 4–7, show this interpretive effect.

A Wish of the Moon

Late at night, the moon penetrated inside through the curtain. It saw a little girl sleeping on her bed, with a backpack beside, and in it there were fruit and snacks.

The moon talked to itself, "Tomorrow the children are going to have a picnic in the suburb. I should go to discuss with Grandpa Sun, and let's have a good day tomorrow."

The moon went inside the window of another family. It saw a little girl taking care of her sick mother.

Mother said, "Zhengzheng, go to bed early. Don't be too tired. Tomorrow you're going to have a picnic in the suburb."

"Mum, I don't want to go."

"You should go tomorrow and have a good time with your friends!"

"But the doctor said that you haven't recovered yet!"

The moon left quietly from the window. It thought, "Let me go to have a talk to Grandpa Thunder, and let's have rain tomorrow!"

Two days later, it was a bright sunny day. All the children, without one less, walked in rows happily towards the suburb.

(*Yuwen II*, pp. 30–32)

In this text, scenes of two families are presented, accompanied by two illustrations (Figure 3.3). The families are shown as the targets of the moon's gaze. Fantasy and commonsensical resources are needed to interpret the objects displayed. In the two families portrayed, one is presented with some iconic symbols: "a little girl sleeping on her bed, with a backpack beside, and in it there were fruit and snacks." The related picture is presented at the top of the text frame, with a girl lying on her bed, her eyes closed, and holding a teddy bear. This family scene is set as a background for the story; young readers are expected to recognize both the situation, as a room like their own, and the symbolic meanings attached to the backpack, fruit, and snacks. Specifically, these signal preparation for an outing rather than for school. Chinese school students generally do not stay in school during the lunch break in the way that Western students do. These symbols also indicate the contemporariness of the events, scenes, and objects, all identifiable as household items, establishing the currency of the implied readership. In this apparently "familiar" family story,

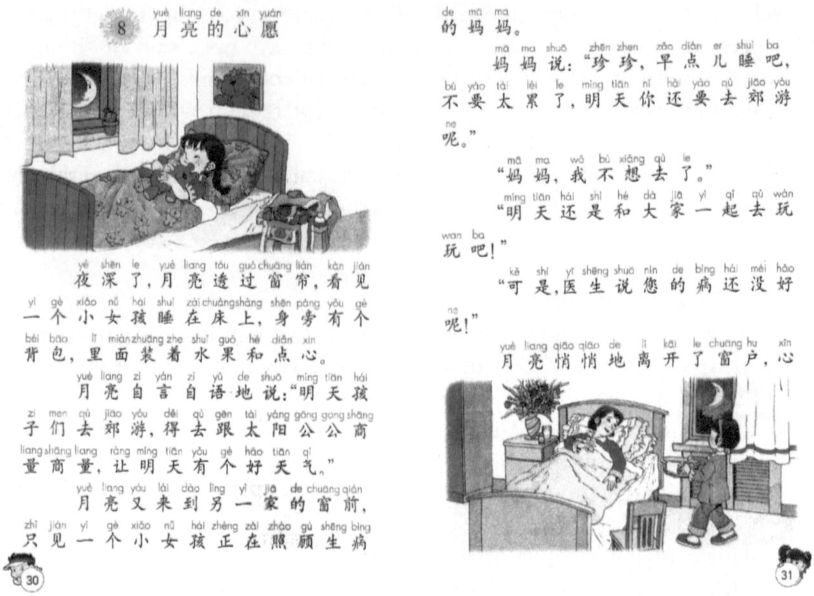
8 月亮的心愿

夜深了，月亮透过窗帘，看见一个小女孩睡在床上，身旁有个背包，里面装着水果和点心。

月亮自言自语地说：“明天孩子们去郊游，得去跟太阳公公商量商量，让明天有个好天气。”

月亮又来到另一家的窗前，只见一个小女孩正在照顾生病的妈妈。

妈妈说：“珍珍，早点儿睡吧，不要太累了，明天你还要去郊游呢。”

“妈妈，我不想去了。”

“明天还是和大家一起去玩玩吧！”

“可是，医生说您的病还没好呢！”

月亮悄悄地离开了窗户，心

30

31

Figure 3.3 *A Wish of The Moon* (*Yuwen II*, T8, pp. 30–31), pp. 30–32.

the mother–daughter conversation is presented. In the illustrated picture (bottom-right side), readers see the mother lying on the bed, the girl approaching her with a washing-basin.

These portrayed events are evidently in a post-Mao Deng China, a period in which social disparity is an indisputable fact. In this text a daughter from a clearly disadvantaged background is seen exercising a determination to attend to her sick mother regardless of the prospects for her own enjoyment, and this is portrayed as a valued attribute. In China's situation, insofar as people are, and have to live, under the mercy of the moon, to be consoled and supported by family members seems to be a realistic, unremarked feature of daily life. But when child readers are positioned to accept misfortune as fact or fate, the social inequity becomes de facto a built social reality.

Conclusions about Multiplicity: Medium-level Symbolic Violence

We began this chapter with a description of the historical context of early Chinese education. We argued that constructions of the school subject of "reading" in China can be seen as a discursive tradition that has moved on from centuries-long Confucian texts and teaching practices (Yuan, 2001; Zhang & Zhong, 2003), to standard Chinese *putonghua* and literary texts and their particular nationalist purposes, and on toward a distinctive form of modernization and "scientific thinking," retaining some linguistic, visual, and cultural features along the way, often reconfiguring them into new cultural formations (Zhu, 1992; You, 2005). We briefly explored the formation of the school subject *yuwen* in this process, and then examined three texts currently in use in the PRC. Among other things, the three texts show the heavy duty performed by images in conveying interpretation. The positioning of textual elements, including ensembles of words and images, relates directly to what Kress and van Leeuwen (2006) considered to be the meaningfulness worked up in the order of the layout. The meaning and value of the reading path and the positioning practices that we delineated together imply that readers should and will follow certain reading routines (Ingulsrud & Allen, 1999), and it is learning both the contents of these routines and the simple fact of their institutional existence that forms part of the multi-functionality of the design of these materials. These routines intensify a process whereby the public is made personal and vice-versa.

In their analyses of early reading in English language, Baker and Freebody (1989) discussed the abstraction of human experience entailed in the process of moving from oral to oral *and* written language experience. As part of this they showed how distinctive "specialized school genres" are inserted into the materials made for early literacy education in Western settings. Clearly the images and written texts we examined here constrain and complement each other in the formation of these specialized genres: the images enhance the factuality, recognizability, and familiarity of the texts. In particular the expository procedures of written texts are complemented by apparently "personalized," quasi-narrativized illustrations. Whether this generic hybridity is taught explicitly or implicitly, Chinese schooling requires that a hierarchy of genres be mastered: narrative description (*jixu wen*, for instance, a major task in primary school, the writing of descriptions of persons or events), expository (*shuoming wen*, for instance, the writing of practical notes, manuals or technical essays), and argumentation (*yilun wen*, for instance, making comments on certain social phenomenon, speeches, reports, and so on). We have aimed to illustrate that the affordances of verbal and visual materials built into hybrid genres in the introduction of young students to this hierarchy constitutes a combination that is well-suited to educational acculturation—a pedagogy for learning knowledge ideology (Freebody, 2008).

Both psychologically oriented reading research and observational studies of reading pedagogy have tended to overlook the social and historical context of the practices and materials of reading in school (see, for example, Sheridan, 1990; Shu, Chen, Anderson, Wu & Yue, 2003). Few research programs have examined literacy movements as data (Hayford, 1987; Woodside, 1992 are exceptions). For instance, the most widely cited research survey of Chinese educational systems and practices (Rawski, 1979), covers an extensive range of issues relating to literacy education in China's last dynasty, but, as with many others, does not deal in any depth with the construction of the school subject of "reading" in China, or with how it is a significant part of the broader political and cultural movements of revolution and modernization, and the acculturation of individuals who can embody those movements. Abstract accounts of literacy practices tend not to link these movements with mundane materials, practices, and policy formations in which they are visible in any accountable way.

Early-education Chinese *yuwen* texts display explicit thematic topics—thought, science, and humanity, in hybrid forms—themselves mixtures of residual and emergence, modernity, tradition, and revolution (see Brown, 1987; Ding, 2001; Pepper, 1996; You, 2005). It is only through detailed analyses that we can document the features that make the school children in different sites experience distinctive textually mediated literate worlds. Here we have used Chinese materials to help us see more clearly how an appreciation of the multiliteracies framework—drawing our attention to the multiplicities of materials, modalities, and cultural settings—might also help us see the acculturational work done around us every day by more familiar educational materials, materials that we see but generally do not notice.

Note

1. See Ministry of Education, 1999, 2001a, 2001b; *Yuwen*, 2001; and Teachers' Manual, 2001.

References

Baker, C. D., & Freebody, P. (1989). *Children's first school books: Introductions to the culture of literacy*. Oxford: Basil Blackwell.

Brown, H. O. (1987). American progressivism in Chinese education: The case of Tao Xingzhi. In R. Hayhoe & M. Bastid (Eds.), *China's education and the industrialized world: Studies in cultural transfer* (pp. 120–138). New York: M. E. Sharpe.

Cheng, D. (1998). *On the subject of Chinese [Yuwen xueke lun]*. Changsha: Hunan Education Publishing House.

Ding, G. (2001). Nationalization and internationalization: Two turning points in China's education in the twentieth century. In G. Peterson, R. Hayhoe, & Y. Lu (Eds.), *Education, culture, and identity in twentieth-century China* (pp. 161–186). Ann Arbor: University of Michigan Press.

Emmison, M., & Smith, P. (2000). *Researching the visual: Images, objects, contexts and interactions in social and cultural inquiry*. London: Sage.

Freebody, P. (2008). Critical literacy education: On living with "innocent language." In B. V. Street & N. H. Hornberger (Eds.), *Encyclopedia of language and education, Volume 2: Literacy* (pp. 107–119). Heidelberg, Germany: Springer Scientific.

Freebody, P., & Baker, C. D. (1985). Children's first reading books: Introductions to the culture of literacy. *Harvard Educational Review*, 55, 381–398.

Freebody, P., & Zhang, B. (2008). The designs of culture, knowledge, and interaction on the reading of language and image. In L. Unsworth (Ed.), *New literacies and the English curriculum: Multimodal perspectives* (pp. 23–46). London: Continuum.

Halliday, M. A. K. (1994). *An introduction to functional grammar* (2nd ed.). London: Edward Arnold.

Halliday, M. A. K. (2002). *On grammar*. London and New York: Continuum.

Hayford, C. W. (1987). Literacy movements in modern China. In R. F. Arnove & H. J. Graff (Eds.), *National literacy campaigns: Historical and comparative perspectives* (pp. 147–172). New York and London: Plenum Press.

Hu, Y. (2004). The cultural significance of reading instruction in China. *The Reading Teacher*, 57, 632–639.

Hudson-Ross, S., & Dong, Y. R. (1990). Literacy learning as a reflection of language and culture: Chinese elementary school education. *The Reading Teacher*, 44, 110–123.

Ingulsrud, J. E., & Allen, K. (1999). *Learning to read in China: Sociolinguistic perspectives on the acquisition of literacy*. Lewiston: The Edwin Mellen Press.

Kress, G., & van Leeuwen, T. (1996). *Reading images: The grammar of visual design*. London: Routledge.

Kress, G., & van Leeuwen, T. (2006). *Multimodal discourse: The modes and media of contemporary communication*. London: Arnold.

Ku, Y. M., & Anderson, R. C. (2003). Development of morphological awareness in Chinese and English. *Reading and Writing: An Interdisciplinary Journal*, 16, 399–422.

Li, W., Gaffney, J. S., & Packard, J. L. (Eds.). (2002). *Chinese children's reading acquisition: Theoretical and pedagogical issues*. Boston, Dordrecht and London: Kluwer Academic Publishers.

Martin, J. R. (1997). Analysing genre: Functional parameters. In F. Christie & J. M. Martin (Eds.), *Genre and institutions: Social processes in the workplace and school* (pp. 1–39). London: Cassell.

Ministry of Education, PRC. (1999). The Chinese Communist Party Central Committee State Council's decision on further deepening educational reform and an overall promotion of quality education, 1999, No. 9 (*Zhonggong Zhongyan Guowuyan Guanyu Shenghua Jiaoyu Gaige Quanmian Tuijing Suzhi Jiaoyu de Jueding*). Retrieved July 6, 2003, from www.moe.edu.cn/wenxian/07.htm.

Ministry of Education, PRC. (2001a). The State Council's decision on the reform and development of basic education 2001, No. 21 (*Guowuyuan Guanyu Jichu Jiaoyu Gaigey yu Fazhang de Jueding*). Retrieved July 6, 2003, from www.moe.edu.cn/base/zonghe/01.htm.

Ministry of Education, PRC. (2001b). An outline of basic education reform—interim (*Jichu Jiaoyu Kecheng Gaige Gangya—shixing*). Retrieved July 6, 2003, from www.moe.edu.cn/jcheng/ziliao/02.htm.

Pepper, S. (1996). *Radicalism and education reform in 20th-century China*. Cambridge: Cambridge University Press.

Rawski, E. S. (1979). *Education and popular literacy in Ch'ing China*. Ann Arbor: University of Michigan Press.

Sheridan, E. M. (1990). Primary Chinese language instruction in the P.R.C. *Reading Psychology: An International Quarterly*, 11, 141–150.

Shu, H. (2003). Chinese writing system and learning to read. *International Journal of Psychology*, 38, 274–285.

Shu, H., Chen, X., Anderson, R. C., Wu, N., & Yue, X. (2003). Properties of school Chinese: Implication for learning to read. *Child Development*, 74, 27–47.

Teacher's Manual. (2001). *Teacher's Manual Books, I and II*. Beijing: People's Education Press.

Unsworth, L. (2001). *Teaching multiliteracies across the curriculum: Changing contexts of text and image in classroom practice*. Buckingham: Open University Press.

Vincent, D., & Perrin, L. (1999). On the narrative vs non-narrative functions of reported speech: A socio-pragmatic study. *Journal of Sociolinguistics*, 3, 291–313.

Woodside, A. (1992). Real and imagined continuities in the Chinese struggle for literacy. In R. Hayhoe (Ed.), *Education and modernization: The Chinese experience* (pp. 23–46). Oxford: Pergamon.

Wu, X., Li, W., & Anderson, R. C. (1999). Reading instruction in China. *Journal of Curriculum Studies*, 31(5), 571–586.

You, X. (2005). Conflation of rhetorical traditions: The formation of modern Chinese writing instruction. *Rhetoric Review*, 24(2), 150–169.

Yuan, Z. (2001). The status of Confucianism in modern Chinese education, 1901–49: A curricular study. In G. Peterson, R. Hayhoe, & Y. Lu (Eds.), *Education, culture, and identity in twentieth-century China* (pp. 193–216). Ann Arbor: University of Michigan Press.

Yuwen. (2001). *Yuwen Books I and II.* Beijing: People's Education Press.

Zhang, B. (2006). *Becoming school-literate in China: Historical, semiotic and interactional analyses of yuwen texts.* Unpublished PhD thesis. Brisbane: University of Queensland.

Zhang, B., & Freebody, P. (2008). Power, language, and literacy education: The case of early reading and writing in China. In T. Lê & M. Short (Eds.), *Critical discourse analysis: An interdisciplinary perspective.* New York: Nova Science Publishers.

Zhang, H., & Zhong, Q. (2003). Curriculum studies in China: Retrospect and prospect. In W. Pinar (Ed.), *International handbook of curriculum research* (pp. 253–270). Mahwah: Lawrence Erlbaum.

Zhu, W. (1992). Confucius and traditional Chinese education: An assessment. In R. Hayhoe (Ed.), *Education and modernization: The Chinese experience* (pp. 3–22). Oxford: Pergamon.

4 Introducing Multimodal Literacy to Young Children Learning English as a Second Language (ESL)

Len Unsworth and Robyn Bush, University of New England

Introduction

Increasingly, young children are developing their experience in English as a second language (ESL) in the context of their regular classroom learning in a range of curriculum areas. This is consistent with recent developments in communicative language teaching (CLT) focusing on content-based instruction (CBI) and is typical of the school language-learning context for many young children in Australia whose first language is not English. This chapter is based on the experience of one of the authors, Robyn Bush, working in one such context in a primary (elementary) school in the south-western suburbs of Sydney.

In this school 92% of the children have a language background other than English. The major cultural groups are Arabic, Vietnamese, Macedonian and Chinese. Many of the first languages of the students have different scripts, writing orientations and/or sounds from English. These factors are routinely incorporated in the kinds of learning experiences described in this chapter. However, since the focus here is on explicit teaching about the meaning-making role of images in multimodal texts, due to the constraints of space, the usual work dealing with orthographic and phonological issues will not be included. Cultural differences such as those related to the direction of writing, along with cultural "norms" about how texts are constructed affect the way a person reads an image/text. Such variations also need to be emphasized and investigated as part of the incorporation of visual literacy in ESL literacy teaching.

The classroom pedagogy outlined here derives from the Curriculum Area Multiliteracies and Learning (CAMAL) framework (Unsworth, 2001). This framework draws on and extends previous work applying systemic functional accounts of language and image to the articulation of pedagogic models of literacy and learning in school curriculum areas (Derewianka, 1990; Macken-Horarik, 1996, 1998; New London Group, 1996[1]). More specifically, the classroom work described in this chapter utilizes from the CAMAL framework parts of the Literacy Development Cycle (LDC). In its most generalized form the LDC (Figure 4.1) incorporates modeled, guided and independent practice in the comprehension/composition of multimodal texts in conventional and electronic formats.

The cycle can be entered at any point in planning learning experiences within a unit of work. If students are very familiar with a particular genre, modeled and guided practice may not be necessary. On the other hand, in introducing new genres, it may be advisable to extend modeled practice, curtail guided practice and postpone independent practice until a subsequent unit of work. It may also be the case that the LDC is applied differentially to a range of comprehension/composition activities within a unit of work. Some activities might involve modeled, guided and independent practice, while some require extended modeling, and others are undertaken as independent practice. The ways in which the parameters of the LDC are adapted will depend on the prior learning of the group and the range of experiences among students within the group. The broken lines indicate this kind of flexibility, as well as the lack of rigid boundaries around the categories of practice.

The development of students' reading of curriculum area materials is integrally related to the development of their capacity to compose the texts. The organization of teaching needs to take this into account. The LDC maintains the strategies of modeled, guided and independent practice for both reading and writing development, but the implementation steps differ for reading and writing. However, within reading and writing, the same implementation steps are used for modeled, guided and independent practice, as shown in Figure 4.2.

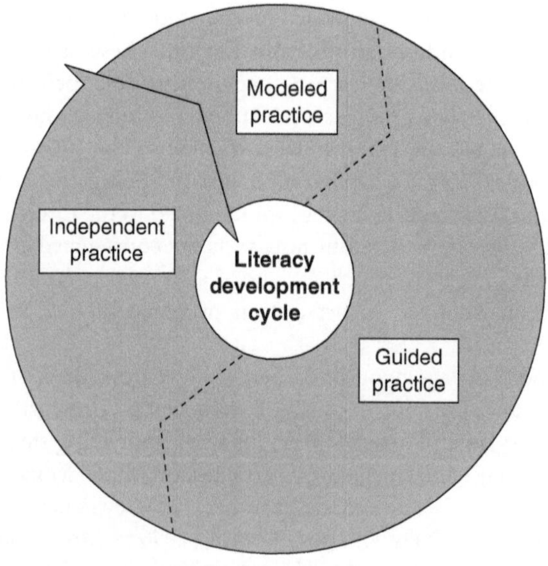

Figure 4.1 The Literacy Development Cycle.

Strategies	**Implementation steps**	
	Reading	Writing
Modeled practice Guided practice Independent practice	• Orientation to the text • Reading the text • Working with the text • Reviewing reading	• Orientation to text • Writing the text • Reviewing writing • Publishing writing

Figure 4.2 Strategies and Implementation Steps in the Literacy Development Cycle.

This chapter is based on the articulated teaching of multimodal literacy and curriculum content in integrated programs of classroom learning activities. Three such classroom programs are:

- sea creatures and life in the oceans (lower primary);
- environmental issues in picture books (middle primary);
- caring for pets and the role of learning about disease and parasites (upper primary).

Teaching points related to visual literacy are included to provide discussion topics during modeled reading/viewing activities. Instructions on possible learning sequences are intended as examples only. The suggested activities suited the students and the context in the south-western Sydney school in question. However, they may need to be altered for other schools to ensure local knowledge and students' learning backgrounds are incorporated into the planning.

There are five literacy-related goals for the learning experiences described:

1. To read inter-modally. That is, they would learn that in order to optimize their understanding of the information provided in the texts they would need to read both images and verbiage and relate the understandings they derived from both.
2. To read critically. In this case the critical dimension entails learning to detect inconsistencies within and across segments of different information books dealing with the same topic.
3. To develop a metalanguage dealing with the visual and verbal meaning-making resources deployed in the text segments they studied.
4. To recognize the layout and structural elements of information reports in factual texts.
5. To compose their own information report using language and images to record additional knowledge they gained on one aspect of the topic.

The Oceans and Sea Creatures: Learning Experiences in Science and Literacy

Building the Field

If possible, organize a preparatory school excursion to an aquarium as an effective basis for enhancing the children's background knowledge and experience prior to intensive science and literacy lessons. Students from the example school attended an excursion to Sydney Aquarium prior to the unit's commencement.

Modeled Reading: Orientation to the Text

Following the visit to the aquarium, devote time to recapitulating the children's experiences at the site and rehearsing orally what they had observed and learned. Link to images of sea creatures and oceans, and the children's own written recounts of the aquarium experience. On the basis of this shared understanding, introduce systematic technical knowledge about the ocean environment and distribute images of ocean habitats of various sea animals.

Following this exploration, and consistent with the LDC, select a suitable information book outlining the levels of the sea habitat (in this case, Gray, 2001, pp. 3–4) to be used in modeling the reading behaviors the teacher intended the children to eventually engage in independently.

Reading the Text: Teaching Points: Divergence

The verbiage and images are set out on the double-page spread in a portrait orientation to simulate the levels of the various zones at successive depths in the ocean. Pictorially, these levels are allocated equal proportions of the layout space and hence are not to scale. The text states:

- The sunlit level is 150 meters deep.
- The twilight zone starts at 150 meters below sea level and finishes around 1000 meters below the surface.
- The midnight zone starts at the end of the twilight zone and continues to the seabed, possibly being as deep as 4000 meters, and more than 6000 meters in some trenches.

This non-scale depiction of the sea levels used in the layout is also repeated in small diagrams showing the three main ocean depth zones at the beginning of each descriptive paragraph. Hence, what is stated in the verbiage about the relative depths of the different ocean zones contradicts the visual information as these are strongly represented as being equivalent. This is an example of "divergence" between images and verbiage.

Highlighting divergence can increase awareness of the need to read all modes of communication constructed within any multimodal text. Such highlighting makes conflicting information explicit to students, providing the opportunity for teachers to emphasize the importance of the critical dimension of multimodal reading.

Working with the Text

Make 1 meter equal to 1 millimeter and mark these depths out on the playground using a piece of chalk. Then compare the real scale to how the levels are visually represented in the book.

Reading the Text: Teaching Points

Hierarchy of Information: Layout

Direct the students' attention to the structure of the text through naming the main features:

- main heading
- introduction
- sub-headings
- descriptive paragraphs
- "extra facts."

Select students to affix pre-prepared labels next to the corresponding section on the information report. Emphasize how the font size and position of each section will help the reader distinguish between the different sections of the report. Highlight and encourage discussion about the reasons why:

- the introduction is positioned under the main heading;
- the largest font is the main heading;
- the medium-sized font is the introduction;
- the smaller font is used for the descriptive paragraphs;
- the smallest font is used for diagram labels and extra information.

These are elements of *visual literacy* that may be ignored by students and, in the experience of one of the authors, by some ESL learners who are too preoccupied with translating the written text to notice the layout. These visual clues can support students when:

- participating in text prediction exercises;
- decoding unfamiliar vocabulary;
- obtaining an overall picture of the subject being reported rather than just remembering snippets of information.

Hierarchy of Information: Labels

Small labels attached to the images of the sea creatures link the animals to the zones they live in. These labels are "buried" within the page layout due to their size and the obfuscation of the overpowering colors and images in the background. This implies that they are of lesser importance. However, they provide added information that stops students forming assumptions about the content in the images. An example would be the likely conclusion from the positioning of the naturalistic images of the octopus in the "twilight zone," that this is their habitat. However, the small italicized text states that "Octopuses and squid live in all the ocean zones including the twilight zones" (Gray, 2001, p. 3). If students scanned over this verbiage and did not pay attention to its significance due to its size and obscurity, they would be misinformed.

Guided Reading

For guided reading, use a text dealing with the same topic (in this case the teacher used Davies, 2004, pp. 6–7). This is especially important in working with ESL students. It not only assists in the consolidation of new vocabulary and grammatical structures, but also contributes to the familiarization of content and text form, facilitating the adoption of a critical stance in relation to the subject matter.

Orientation to the Text

Ask students (in the guided reading group) to discuss the images in this book in relation to their experience of the first book, and in relation to their prior knowledge, and ask them to predict what the text will be about. Record all contributions and display them. Have the Gray text nearby to provide opportunities for direct comparison. These activities can further consolidate new vocabulary and grammatical constructions, as well as intermodal and critical reading practices addressed during modeled reading.

In preparation for reading, the teacher should also review with the students their knowledge of the typical structural organization of information reports such as the modeled reading text and the one they are about to read. Ask students to assign labels to the different sections in the Information Report from the Davies text, as they did, as a class, during modeled reading of the Gray text (2001, pp. 3–4).

Reading the Text: Teaching Points

Pair Reading

Instruct all students to read the text silently. Nominate pairs of students to take responsibility for shared reading aloud of a text section allocated to them.

Direct pairs to prepare their text section for reading aloud. Invite each pair of students to read their allocated sections aloud. Monitor students' oral reading, noting quality of any student miscues and strategies for dealing with unfamiliar vocabulary. Ask the students to indicate the meanings conveyed by the images in the text. Establish a purpose(s) for reading the text, related to prior knowledge. Encourage discussion about the targeted audience—"Who might need this type of information?"

Layout: Topic Statement and Descriptive Paragraphs

The Davies text starts with the familiar on the left side, which is a large satellite photograph of the earth linked to information about its connection to oceans. The new information—the ocean zones—is stated on the right side of the double-page spread. This is different from the modeled reading text, which uses a vertically linear layout. Encourage students to explore the reasons for both layouts and provide suggestions as to why the author/editor (Davies text) chose this layout.

Background and Framing

The background color in the photographs in the Davies text mimics the colors of the levels of the ocean—blue for the surface level, navy blue for the middle ocean level and black for the deepest water. The background of the double-page spread is a different type of blue that contrasts with the photographs. This is a framing technique which makes a distinction between the photographs and the rest of the text. The modeled reading text (Gray, 2001) displays the animals as a part of the background, with no separation between the written paragraphs and the creatures. Integrating the animals strongly with the background stresses the link between an animal and its habitat. The Gray text uses minimal framing: the thick white, horizontal lines between each descriptive paragraph (defining each ocean zone) and a thin black line around the "Fishy facts" which signal additional information. During the guided reading session, discuss the purpose of framing and compare the usage of this feature in both texts.

Working with the Text

Adjectives

Since the text (Davies, 2004, pp. 6–7) does not include headings stating the ocean zones, ESL students may not clearly understand the distinctions indicated by the words "surface," "deeper," "middle" and "deepest." There are no measurements provided to show depth and no pictorial reference to support this vocabulary. Use this opportunity to explore comparative and superlative language with the students while using scale marks in the playground (as discussed earlier) to connect the grammatical concepts to the experiential learning at stake in the context of these books.

Difference in Information when Comparing Texts

Ask children to examine what each text says about the habitat of the octopus. The Gray text (2001, pp. 3–4) states that the octopus can live in all three levels of the ocean, while the Davies text asserts that it lives in the middle level. Contradictions like this can emphasize the need to research thoroughly. Ask students to create a table with two columns titled "similarities" and "differences." Instruct the group to record their observations during text comparison and share with the class at the conclusion of the lesson.

Reviewing Reading

In this phase students initially work in pairs or groups of three to read the text again in order to complete review tasks such as the following:

- Students to "mark up" a copy of the text with editorial changes. The student-editors' brief could be specified—delete peripheral information, suggest more examples, ensure all new technical terms are defined, change existing images or include additional images, etc.
- Generate a series of questions for the author(s) and/or editor(s) of the text.
- Annotate the images to show their relationship to the verbal text and the kinds of visual meanings they contribute.

Review tasks such as these can be distributed across the student groups. Once the tasks are completed, re-group the students so that each new group member has addressed a different question when working in the original groups. Provide time for students who completed different tasks to exchange and discuss their responses. Convene the whole group to discuss similarities and differences in thinking about the text, which emerge from their responses to these tasks.

Preparation for Student Research and Writing

The next part of the classroom work is to help the children to read a new text in order to obtain information as the basis for writing their own report on a particular sea creature and its habitat. In this case, the teacher decided that the class would investigate different types of crabs. She would eventually provide them with relevant websites from which they could obtain such information. However, in order to prepare them for this work she conducted a further modified guided reading lesson using a text about crabs (Gunzi, 1992, pp. 14–15). Rather than detailing the steps of the guided reading again, we will simply list some key features of this text that we would focus on in the "working with the text" phase.

Labels

One important feature of this text to take into account for ESL learners is the labeling of the two images of pie-crust crabs. Some labels are just large noun groups. For example, "Huge, blunt pincers with serrated (notched) edges for grasping food." Others are sentences that contain large noun groups "*Sharp claws at the tip of each leg* give the crab extra grip for scrambling over rocks." The density of information and unfamiliarity of such extended noun groups can make their comprehension difficult for ESL learners.

Working with the Text

Explore:

- what elements are needed to make a basic sentence (noun/pronoun, verb and rest of the sentence);
- how and why noun groups act only as part of a sentence;
- how noun groups differ from sentences.

The proforma, shown in Figure 4.3, can be used to explore these concepts. Initially the teacher can begin with subject matter well-known to the children and gradually build the complexity of the noun group before proceeding to do the same thing with the noun groups from the text.

Transitional Images

This text (Gunzi, 1992, pp. 14–15) uses naturalistic photographs of the crabs, albeit devoid of background and containing labels to focus on identifying the parts of the crab. This makes it more of a conceptual image than simply a photograph of a crab, and is hence what might be regarded as a type of

Number	Describer	THING / NOUN	Extra information
Two	large	hamburgers	
Two	large, mouth-watering	hamburgers	with extra cheese.
Two	large, mouth-watering MacDonalds	hamburgers	with extra cheese that ran over the edges.
Two	*huge*	*pincers*	
Two	*huge, blunt*	*pincers*	*with serrated (notched) edges.*
Two	*huge, blunt*	*pincers*	*with serrated (notched) edges for grasping food.*

Figure 4.3 Exploring Complex Noun Groups with Children.

"transitional image" (Unsworth, 2001, p. 103). The function of these images is to begin to move young readers from realistic images, which have a large representation in early childhood texts, toward becoming more familiar with abstract or schematic images typical of those used in science texts for older learners. The need to be able to interpret conceptual images will increase as children progress through school, studying more complex scientific concepts (Kress & van Leeuwen, 1996, p. 162).

Researching and Writing an Information Report on a Type of Crab

Computer access is required for this section. Demonstrate how to use the proforma provided in Figure 4.4 to record key information about a selected crab from the website of the *Australian Museum Online* (www.amonline.net.au/wild_kids).

Explain to students that they will be writing an information report about a crab to inform other students in their year. Their choices include: the ghost crab, the swift-footed crab, the sand crab and the soldier crab.

To demonstrate how to gather the information needed, choose "The Ghost Crab" on the Australian Museum Website. Show how to navigate through the website to find the list of crabs. Demonstrate how to:

- fill in the introduction by naming the type of crab and then classifying it;
- draw a picture of the crab in the box titled "Appearance" and label the crab according to its special features: "large eyes at the end of short eye stalks." Sentences should not be used. Encourage the use of noun groups. Explain that note-taking is preferable as it allows one to record more information in less time;
- locate "Diet" in the text and use bullet points to record the information quickly and concisely.

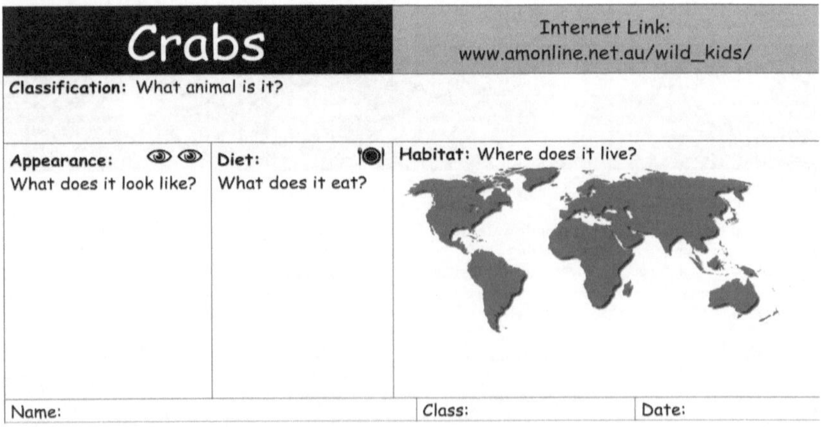

Figure 4.4 Scaffolding Children's Research: Note-taking Proforma.

- locate the habitat on the web page and mark it on the map on the worksheet under "Habitat."
- record any additional information under the map using bullet points. For example, "tropical and sub-tropical Australia."

Organize students into pairs and issue them a note-taking proforma. Assign each pair to a computer to research the crab of their choice.

Announce the next task: to write an Information Report from the notes. Model the writing using the notes made during the demonstration lesson. List a number of "sentence beginnings" on the board to which the students can refer during the writing activity. These sentence beginnings include singular and plural forms of "crabs" and pronouns, as indicated in Figure 4.5, to encourage students to use what they have learned about subject–verb agreement and reduce repetition in their writing.

Once the students' first drafts have been self-edited, edited by a peer and then the teacher, provide the resources to produce their final copy (a blank A4 page, a small blank map and their corrected first draft).

Conduct a modeled writing activity to assist students in thinking about possible designs for the layout of their Information Reports. This is an opportunity to review and consolidate earlier work on the relevance of different styles and font sizes. Provide font books that students can use to choose a style of writing to copy for their main heading. Demonstrate sketching a diagram of the crab. Explain the reason for the image position—for example, "I drew the crab in the middle of the page because it is the topic of the report. The central position emphasizes its importance." Attach labels to all the important parts of the crab. Next, indicate the possible positions for the introduction and descriptive paragraphs. Emphasize that the topic statement needs to be under the main heading and be written in medium-sized writing. Finally, show the students a small photocopied blank world map that can be stuck near the sub-heading "Habitat" to pictorially represent where the ghost crab lives, and include pictures of the crab's diet.

The students will then be prepared to start their own information report.

Singular	①	Plural	many
		Crabs	The crabs
A crab	The crab	They	These crabs
It	This crab	All crabs	Most of these crabs
The swift-footed crab	This crustacean	Swift-footed crabs	These crustaceans

Figure 4.5 Scaffolding Children's Writing of Sentence Beginnings.

An example of a student's written report on the "swift-footed crab" is provided in Figure 4.6. Computers can be used for the above demonstration and the students' text production.

Once the children have completed their "published" text, instruct them to scan their texts and use the PowerPoint program to create hyperlinked versions of their reports. The scanned reports are successively cropped to obtain separate images of the heading and introduction, the descriptive paragraphs, the main image and the habitat location map. Then the heading and main text are located on one PowerPoint page, with hyperlinks to the other components of the report on subsequent pages.

The PowerPoint document can simulate a website. Ask students why they would create a website about their crab and who their target audience might be. Emphasize that websites can be accessed by anyone around the world, so their reader demographic would be larger when published on the Internet

Investigating the Portrayal of Environmental Issues in Picture Books: Exploring Image/Text Relations in Narrating and Persuading

These learning activities are based on a picture book for middle primary school students. The book, *One Child*, was written by Christopher Cheng and

Figure 4.6 "An Information Report on the Swift-footed Crab" by Farouk Arnaout, Aged 6. Swift-footed crab.
Drawing by Farouk Araout. Used with permission.

illustrated by Steven Woolman (Cheng, 1997). The purpose of the book is to identify environmental problems and inspire students to take action and encourage other people to help. The book uses a primary-school-aged girl as the main character as a deliberate persuasive technique to allow the targeted audience to identify with her. This strategy encourages children to believe that they do not need to be an adult to make a difference. As the students uncover the layers of meaning incorporated in the images, they will be provided with ways they can help the environment and subsequently make the world a better place.

Modeled Reading: Orientation to the Text

Read the book without showing the illustrations. Instruct students to draw, act or present what they predict is happening in the images. Read the text while students are presenting their version. Once every group has presented, read the book again, this time displaying the images. Discuss how the images provide added information about the messages in the text. Arrange students into groups and instruct them to discuss their predictions in relation to the visual text. Following that, direct students to write about the similarities and differences between the stories portrayed by the images and the text.

Reading the Text: Teaching Points—Vertical Angle and Color Symbolism

The first double-page image shows a girl sitting on the floor watching television. The vertical angle is one where the reader is looking down at the child, reflecting her feeling of powerlessness. Explain the meaning constructed by vertical angles using reference to kings and queens on their thrones, where people "look up" to them. The high vertical angle in the Cheng text and the different tones of blue repeat and mirror the powerless and dissatisfied feeling that the participant is experiencing. The term "feeling blue," meaning "feeling sad," is embedded in Western culture, and it would be beneficial to explore this when looking at this image. This "feeling blue" is augmented by the text. The text describes environmental disasters, which the child responds to by saying "What can I do?"—she feels that the problem is too big and she is too small.

Working with the Text

Arrange students into small groups to analyze images from newspapers, magazines, children's magazines and comics. Make the sources known to the children so they can envisage a context and possible targeted audience. Ask students to work out the angle of depiction and agree on a possible explanation for the artist's choice. Invite students to present these findings to the class.

Provide students with the opportunity to compare the different images and how they highlight the child's varying degrees of power. These are:

- powerlessness in the image looking down on the child;
- equal power with the reader when the girl is on the reader's level. Since the targeted audience of the book is children, this angle communicates the idea that if she can do it, so can all children;
- increased power in the images where the reader is looking up at her while she is actively participating and thus making a difference.

Write the cultural meaning of all three angles (high, equal and low) on cardboard to be displayed in the classroom for future reference.

Reading the Text: Teaching Points—Framing and Color

The next double-page image uses framing to emphasize that big problems can be broken down into smaller pieces. An example of this framing can be seen in Figure 4.7. Triangular frames make up a large frame.

Color is also used to add to this meaning, where the illustrator has chosen two different color schemes to depict the problems and the solutions. All the triangular frames, except one, use grey, black and brown tones to create a dark, destructive feeling when displaying environmental devastation. One piece of this whole frame is a picture of the girl, planting a sapling. The colors used in this triangular frame are mainly tones of green, reflecting an environmental message.

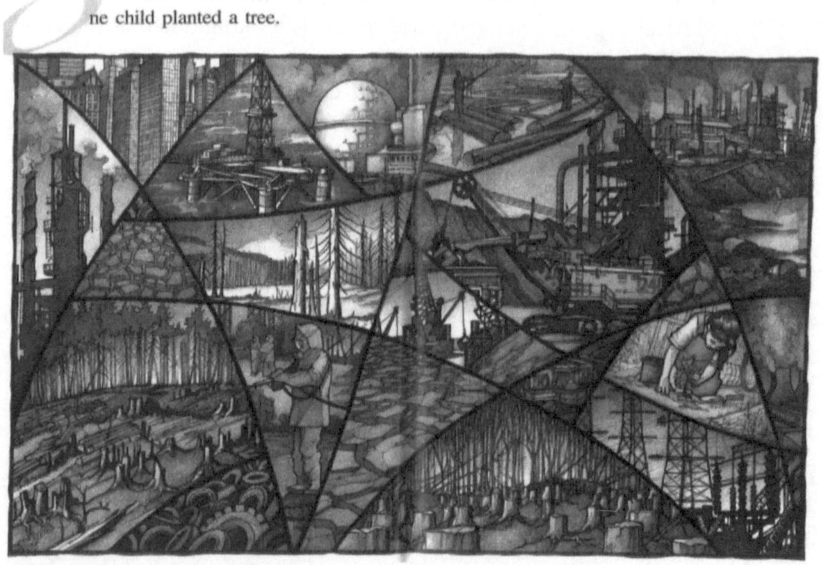

Figure 4.7 First Segmented Image.

Explain to the children that the color green, in Western culture, is a positive color. A green traffic light is used symbolically to instruct people to go. It can, however, be used to say someone is immature or to symbolize jealousy. In traditional Islamic cultures, green is a sacred color. In China, green jade represents perfection, immortality or longevity, strength and magical powers—a color associated particularly with the Ming dynasty. In the current climate, the color green is recognized by many cultures as representing plant life, and therefore has acquired a new symbolic quality, standing for environmental protection. It would benefit children to see the connections with the color green to the terms "being green," "Greenie" and to the international organization "Greenpeace."

These different interpretations of color need to be highlighted to students as they may not consider the author's or targeted audience's cultural background, but use their own to "read" images. In the case of some ESL learners' interpretations of color that are specific to their cultures, they may need to be compared with other interpretive possibilities. Exploration around the meaning of color in different cultures with students from different Australian community groups can enrich everyone's understanding, not just ESL learners.

In each consecutive page the girl's piece of the puzzle (her frame) is growing bigger. The color schemes chosen for her frame are green, blue, yellow and red. These colors become more significant later on in the book as they are used to accentuate the causal connections between the children's actions and the positive results on the environment. In Figure 4.8, the blue

Figure 4.8 Cause-and-Effect Image.

uniforms of the children depicted in the top frame relate to the image of the sky and its inhabitants on the following pages (Figure 4.9). The yellow uniforms and green vegetation in the image at the bottom in Figure 4.8 are color schemes that are replicated on the following page when showing the animals and environment prospering (Figure 4.9). This aims to implicitly connect the two pages, showing cause and effect—when the children helped the environment, the environment prospered. The frames are the same size and orientation on both double-page spreads. There are two frames on each spread that have a landscape direction, repeating and making the causal connection stronger.

Instruct students to examine this causal connection in groups. Ask them to compare the images and write down the differences and similarities into a table that they can then use to present their ideas to the class. Once the students have pointed out the similarities in the color scheme and framing on both pages, then a discussion can unfold as to the artist's reasons for this.

Exploring the other function of framing in this text is important as it impacts on the main message—tackling small problems one at a time to eventually solve the greater problem. The first segmented image encompasses the two pages, where the larger frame dominates the space. The next double page has two frames consuming each page, showing how the problem is getting smaller due to the action of the child. The next has four frames across the two pages, symbolizing a further break down.

Analyze the framing in the book where the large frame shows the overwhelmingly large problem. Encourage discussion around the symbolism,

Figure 4.9 Result Image.

showing how a problem can be broken up into little pieces and tackled more easily and effectively. Form groups and provide a photocopy of either the fifth, sixth or seventh double-page spread. Instruct students to record the processes by labeling each small piece of the puzzle.

Explain that frames are used to separate or join different ideas, participants or phenomena. The increasing inclusion of white space on each consecutive page highlights the separation between each small problem.

The environmental message first discussed by Rene Dubos, an advisor to the United Nations Conference on the Human Environment in 1972, was "Think globally, act locally." Refer to this message during modeled reading to explain how the framing in these images echo it.

Instruct students to analyze other texts related to framing—newspaper articles, posters, pamphlets and picture books. They can provide explanations on how thick frames separate elements and thin framing or an absence of framing joins elements together in varying degrees and for a range of purposes. Ask students to arrange images from the least amount of framing to most (a cline) and discuss reasons.

Objects Beyond the Frame

Figure 4.8 shows a large picture of the girl closing her eyes, looking towards the left side of the page, gazing into the past. This could symbolize her hopes that past achievements may influence other children to take action. Since she is superimposed over two frames containing children who are helping the environment, one can assume that she has indirectly influenced these students. The text consolidates this: "Just imagine if the children of the world did all that they could." Earlier in the book it states that she "wrote for the sea and sang for the sky and marched for the animals and spoke for the world," showing that she interacted with other people to persuade them to take action. The girl is out of the frame in the aforementioned page, occupying the space of the viewer. The absence of a frame joins people together—the participant is related to the viewer and the "real world." Whereas the fact that the girl is not present in the children's frame may suggest that they are strangers to her, they have been influenced by her actions (see Figure 4.8).

Three different animals, a toucan, an eagle and a butterfly, are overlapping the frame in Figure 4.9. This may symbolize animals escaping from repression due to the kindness of the children. They are free to leave the restraints of the segmented frames, and join the real "free" world. The images on earlier pages show animals behind bars and subjected to cruelty—these animals are contained within the frames much like they are in their cages.

Ask students to justify the different reasons why the illustrator would depict certain participants extending beyond the frame. Encourage discussion around the points mentioned above for the main character and the animals.

Working with the Text: Barrier Activity

CLT promotes the use of opportunities for students to use the targeted language when interacting with their peers. The following barrier activity requires students to be arranged into pairs. One of the pairs has the information, the other needs to get the information. The second player cannot look at his/her partner's page. They need to use language to find out the information. Once students feel comfortable identifying features of images using the visual metalanguage explored by the following activity, organize lessons that require students to justify why illustrators would use specific techniques to construct meaning.

Arrange students into pairs. Call one student Player A and the other Player B. Photocopy different images from the book. Give Player A an image. Provide Player B with the question table (Figure 4.10). Instruct Player B to ask Player A the questions about their image. Player B needs to record the answers Player A provides. Once Player B has filled in the columns, ask the student to look through the book and work out the image Player A has in front of them by using the information gained during the barrier activity. Discuss the number of guesses students needed to have to obtain the right image. For similar learning experiences, see Gibbons (1991, 1998).

Guided Reading

Select a variety of environmental texts suitable to the reading level of the students. Explore the visual elements discussed in the modeled reading session, relating these techniques to the author and illustrator's purpose. Organize language activities that explore the language related to persuasion to prepare students for their independent activities.

Independent Activities

To use the text for its intended purpose (to inspire students to act in favor of the environment locally), instruct students to identify an environmental problem within the school and devise a plan to break the problem into small manageable tasks to achieve the bigger goal. Environmental issues can include:

- litter
- erosion of soil (due to people walking on unpaved areas)
- lack of animal habitats.

Ask students to use digital photography to take some pictures to include in a poster, picture book, artwork, computer-generated text or another medium through which to educate and persuade other children. Remind students of the function of:

- colors
- framing

What colours are used in the image? 	What type of framing is used in the image? 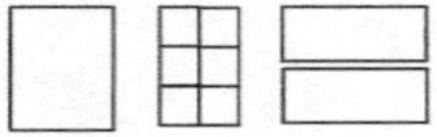	Is there anything extending beyond the frame? 	What is the vertical angle? ☑ Tick the right box.	Guess the image that your partner is holding.
			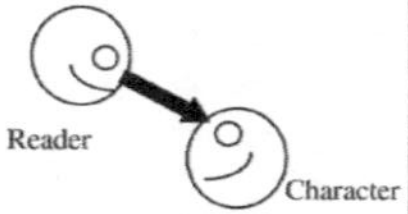 The reader is looking down at the character (High angle). ☐	
			 The reader is looking at the character on an equal level. ☐	
			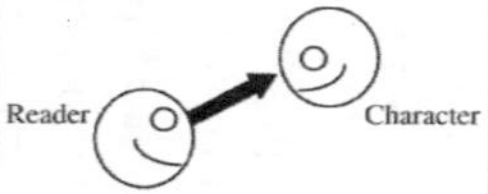 The reader is looking up at the character (low angle). ☐	

Figure 4.10 Barrier Game Question Table here.

- objects beyond the frame
- vertical angles.

Finally, ensure students use their text for its intended purpose, for example, ensure all posters are displayed, picture books are read to younger students and presentations are conducted in a forum—such as the student representative council meeting or a school assembly.

Caring for Pets and Learning about Science: Heartworm Disease

It is common in Australian schools for children in upper primary to study the effects of human activities on the environment within the Science KLA. The next sequence of activities introduces the life-cycle of a heartworm. The writing activity that follows focuses on how humans can affect this cycle, thus preventing pets suffering from heartworm infestation.

The resource used here is a website (Figure 4.11), which is linked to various websites related to pet health and disease control. It is an authentic text created for a real purpose rather than a text created purely for teaching primary students. It is not directly linked to selling a product, but it is created by Merial, a health company that produces pharmaceutical products and offers services for a range of animals. We have chosen this website because it

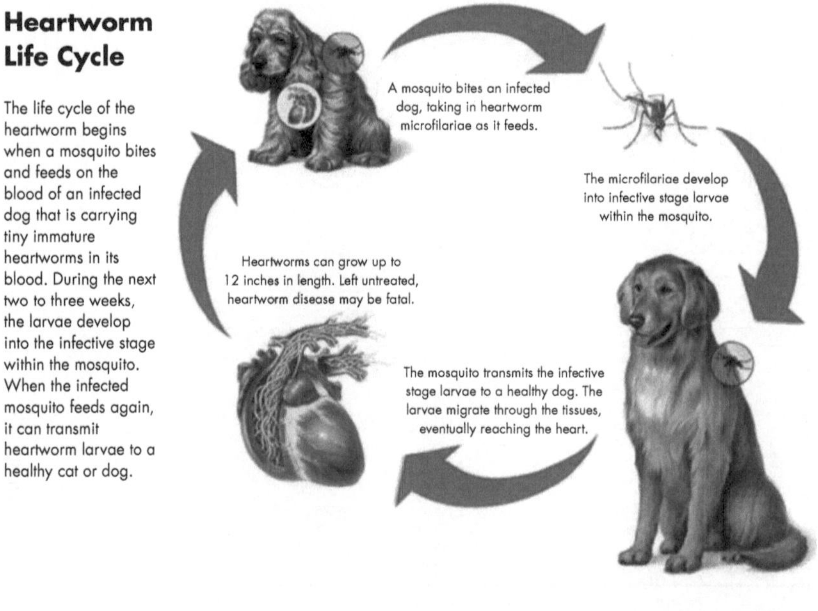

Figure 4.11 Merial Limited (2005) (source: Stopworms.com, 2006). "Heartworm Life Cycle" in Stopworms.com [online]. Monday May 22, 2008.

demonstrates the complexity of image/verbiage relations. We will suggest learning experiences that will alert children to this as we discuss the various features of the multimodal text.

Magnification

The representation of an "enlarged" image segment inside a circle is presumably meant to invoke the effect of a magnifying glass or microscope. While this may be familiar to adults, many of today's children are more familiar with "zoom" buttons in order to achieve magnified views. The magnification of the mosquito in the image is quite clear. However, the function of the circle around the image of the infected dog's heart is not clear. It may also be intended to signal magnification or simply to draw attention to the revealing of the dog's internal organs in an otherwise highly naturalistic image. Instruct students to find another technical image showing the size of a dog's heart in relation to the size of the animal to ascertain if the heart is magnified.

Cutaway Images

The dog's heart is a cutaway image. Children may not be familiar with this convention and with what a dog's heart looks like. Therefore, highlight this visual technique and discuss the depiction of the heartworms, which are not labeled.

Cycle

Although the image is represented as a cycle, it clearly has a starting point at the top left, with the image of the infected dog. This is consistent with the sequence of the main text. For children of Western cultures, it would also be the usual starting point. In the context of ESL teaching, the "left to right" conventions in negotiating textual layouts will need to be explicitly taught.

Image/Verbiage Relations

It might be assumed that the image is a "projection" of the main text, recapitulating its content in an alternative mode (Martin, 1994; Martinec & Salway, 2005). Such an interpretation might be sustained for part of the image—the images of the infected dog, the lone mosquito and the healthy dog, if we regard the captions as part of the image. However, only the first sentence in the caption accompanying the healthy dog is a recapitulation of the main text.

Here the page editor facility of the web browser (or colored highlighter pens with a hard copy of the text) is useful to color code corresponding segments of the caption texts and the main text. This will readily show that the second sentence in the caption accompanying the healthy dog ("The larvae migrate through the tissues eventually reaching the heart") is not represented in the main text, and nor is the information in the caption accompanying the heart ("Heartworms can grow up to 12 inches in length. Left untreated, heartworm disease may be fatal"). It will be realized that the caption accompanying the infected dog assumes knowledge of three concepts:

- the technical term, *microfilariae*;
- mosquito bites entail the extraction of blood from the victim;
- microfilariae are in the blood of the victim.

A non-technical equivalent of *microfilariae* is provided in the main text, and the second two concepts are also explicitly provided: "A mosquito bites and feeds on the blood of an infected dog that is carrying tiny immature heartworms in its blood."

Ask students to color code information that is in the main text but not in the captions. This will reveal that the phrase "During the next two to three weeks" is not represented in the caption dealing with the development of *microfilariae* into infective-stage larvae. It will also show that the main text indicates that heartworm can also affect cats, and that this is not indicated in the image captions.

If we look at the relationship between the caption texts and the images, we will note that the first clause and the image of the mosquito biting the infected dog are ideationally concurrent in that the meanings of the image and the language are re-presented in the alternative mode. We can refer to this image/verbiage relation as exposition. But the second two clauses ("taking in *microfilariae* as it feeds") are related consequentially to the information in the first clause and in the image.

In the case of the image of the mosquito and its caption text, the relation concurrence, exposition is between only one element of the verbiage, "the mosquito" and the whole image. There is no relation between the rest of the caption text and the image. The image of the mosquito biting the healthy dog does relate to the first clause of its juxtaposed caption text ("The mosquito transmits the infective stage larvae to a healthy dog"). But this is not a relation of exposition. It is rather a relation of complementarity or augmentation, where the text extends the meanings of the image. The text and image have in common the two participants, the healthy dog and the mosquito, but "transmits the infective stage larvae" is additional to the image.

There are a number of possible relations between the image of the dog's heart and its caption text. One of these is a spatial enhancement: the image makes explicit where the heartworms grow. It may also be possible to read an implicit enhancement: the image implies that heartworm multiplies to the extent that it occupies much of the heart, constricting blood flow, and that this is the manner in which "heartworm disease may be fatal."

When introducing learners to close reading of the image/verbiage relations as discussed here in terms of the relations between the images and their caption texts, it is recommended that teachers use the stages of the LDC

(Figure 4.1). That is, first modeling the reading of these relations and making explicit the metalanguage that describes them. Then in subsequent lessons, working with the children to guide their reading, understanding and naming of the image/verbiage relations. Finally, asking children to read such texts independently and then explicate the nature of the image/verbiage relations.

Writing Task

After the stages of LDC for reading, explain to students that their mission is to convince dog owners to be vigilant about the threat of heartworm by presenting a detailed outline of how to prevent heartworm infestation. They need to research different products that act as the "human intervention," preventing dogs and puppies from being infected. Resources they can use include:

- the local vet
- pamphlets from veterinarian clinics
- printed material: information books, encyclopedias
- websites.

They can use various methods to support their presentation:

- PowerPoint presentations
- photographs
- a poster
- concrete resources that are used to demonstrate the heartworm cycle and prevention measures
- DVD footage of an interview with an expert
- recording of an interview with an expert
- prompt cards.

Students will need lessons focusing on teaching the language of persuasion (selling the idea) and explanation (life-cycle and human intervention) before commencing the above task.

Conclusion

The kinds of learning activities outlined in this chapter indicate practical ways in which students learning English as a second language can be taught about image construction and images complementing the meaning-making resources of language in multimodal texts. What have been emphasized here are the details of practical implementation of simultaneous teaching of curriculum area content and meta-knowledge of how images contribute to the construction of meaning in those texts. This orientation has been adopted to show ESL teachers that such multiliteracies teaching can take place in the context of regular classroom work. What has not been attempted here is any indication of the range of image–text relations that are functionally significant across curriculum area teaching. Further work in this area in the context of regular classroom teaching in the primary school has been documented by Callow (Callow, 1999; Callow & Zammit, 2002), and the significance of image–text relations in learning school science has been shown in work by Lemke (2002), Thibault (2000) and Unsworth (1997, 1999, 2004), while van Leeuwen and Humphrey have done related work in school geography (van Leeuwen & Humphrey, 1996). Much is still to be done and it is hoped that this volume will encourage teachers to implement research in multiliteracies pedagogy in these and other curriculum areas in the context of their own teaching.

Note

1. What we are saying is that the New London Group (NLG) apply SFL (Systemic Functional Linguistics) accounts to "the articulation of models of literacy learning…." The NLG are quite explicit about SFL being fundamental to their work. There are many quotes that one could give here, for example, according to Halliday (1978): "A deep organizing principle in the grammars of human languages is the distinction among macrofunctions of language, which are the different functions of Available Designs: ideational, interpersonal and textual functions" (p. 20).

References

Callow, J. (Ed.). (1999). *Image matters: Visual texts in the classroom.* Sydney: Primary English Teaching Association.

Callow, J., & Zammit, K. (2002). Visual literacy: From picture books to electronic texts. In M. Monteith (Ed.), *Teaching primary literacy with ICT* (pp. 188–201). Buckingham: Open University Press.

Cheng, C. (1997). *One child.* Flinders Park, South Australia: Era Publications.

Davies, N. (2004). *Kingfisher young knowledge: Oceans and seas.* London: Kingfisher Publications.

Derewianka, B. (1990). Rocks in the head: Children writing geology reports. In R. Carter (Ed.), *Knowledge about language and the curriculum: The linc reader* (pp. 34–46). London: Hodder and Stoughton.

Flickr. (2008). *World map.* Retrieved December 1, 2008, from www.flickr.com/photos/29712230@N08/2861478881.

Gibbons, P. (1991). *Learning to learn in a second language.* Sydney: Primary English Teaching Association.

Gibbons, P. (1998) Classroom talk and the learning of new registers in a second language. *Language and Education,* 12(2), 99–118.

Gray, S. (2001). *Dk eyewonder: Ocean.* London: Dorling Kindersley.

Gunzi, C. (1992). *Look closer: Rockpool.* Pymble, New South Wales: Angus and Robertson.

Halliday, M. A. K. (1978) *Language as social semiotic.* London: Edward Arnold.

Kress, G., & van Leeuwen, T. (1996). *Reading images: A grammar of visual design.* London: Routledge.

Macken-Horarik, M. (1996). Literacy and learning across the curriculum: Towards a model of register for secondary school teachers. In R. Hasan & G. Williams (Eds.), *Literacy in society* (pp. 232–278). Harlow: Addison Wesley Longman.

Macken-Horarik, M. (1998). Exploring the requirements of critical literacy: A view from two classrooms. In F. Christie & R. Misson (Eds.), *Literacy and schooling* (pp. 74–103). London: Routledge.

Martin, J. R. (1994). Macro-genres: The ecology of the page. *Network*, 21, 29–52.

Martinec, R., & Salway, A. (2005). A system for image–text relations in new (and old) media. *Visual Communication*, 4(3), 337–371.

New London Group. (1996). A pedagogy of multiliteracies: Designing social futures. *Harvard Educational Review*, 66(1), 60–91.

Stopworms.com. (2006). Merial limited. Retrieved May 22, 2006, from www.stopworms.com/pets_lifecycle.html.

Thibault, P. (2000). *Multimodality and the school science textbook*. Paper presented at The multimodal discourse analysis conference, University of Sydney.

Unsworth, L. (1997). Scaffolding reading of science explanations: Accessing the grammatical and visual forms of specialised knowledge. *Reading*, 31(3), 30–42.

Unsworth, L. (1999). Explaining school science in book and CD rom formats: Using semiotic analyses to compare the textual construction of knowledge. *International Journal of Instructional Media*, 26(2), 159–179.

Unsworth, L. (2001). *Teaching multiliteracies across the curriculum: Changing contexts of text and image in classroom practice*. Buckingham: Open University Press.

Unsworth, L. (2004). Comparing school science explanations in books and computer-based formats: The role of images, image/text relations and hyperlinks. *International Journal of Instructional Media*, 31(3), 283–301.

van Leeuwen, T., & Humphrey, S. (1996). On learning to look through a geographer's eyes. In R. Hasan & G. Williams (Eds.), *Literacy in society* (pp. 29–49). London: Addison Wesley Longman.

Part II

Multiliteracies Theory in Motion

5 New Media, New Learning

Bill Cope and Mary Kalantzis, University of Illinois

Introduction

This chapter analyzes the distinctive features of what are often today called the "new media," a range of information and communications media using digital technologies, including technologies for the creation and storage of text, still and moving images and sound, and the distribution of this content through local computing systems and the Internet. The relationships of these new media to education vary from attempts at transliteration of the classroom and heritage learning relationships into the digital media, to educational projects as fundamental as changing the social relationships of learning.

Apparently New Media, Apparently New Learning

The new digital media will change the face of education. We've heard this said often, and more frequently since the invention of the Internet. One kind of response to this proposition is: "Impossible and besides inequitable, because not every student has a computer or internet access." On top of the other historic divides which mean that some kinds of learners perennially do better at school than others, we are adding another—a "digital divide" between those who can afford the technology, and those who can't (Cuban, 2001; Mitchell, 1995; Virilio, 1997). To this, contemporary technology innovators reply that digital creation and access media are becoming as ubiquitous as the telephone and the radio in an earlier era—cheaper desktop and laptop computers, mobile phones with comprehensive computing and Internet functionalities, portable reading devices, and devices for digital video and audio recording and playback, to name just a few areas of significant development.

Another kind of response to the new media is a rush to adopt. In that rush, we have seen teachers bring the new media into the classroom, as if the medium itself were the message. Instead of writing a story longhand on a piece of paper, students type it to a word processor, or a blog, or put together a video. There's something new here, to be sure, but just how new? Have the relationships of knowledge and pedagogy changed in any significant way? Is classroom discourse that much different? Often, the answer is "no," because we can use new technologies to learn old things in old ways. We can set up the new media devices in our contemporary world to do old-fashioned didactic teaching: the teacher or textbook publisher puts content into a learning management system; the learners work through the content step by step; the learners take a test at the end and get a grade that indicates whether they have passed or failed. We can use computers to re-create traditional, transmission pedagogies that embody a mimetic relationship to knowledge: absorb the theories, practice the formulae, learn the facts, appreciate the greats of the canon, internalize the socio-moral truths that others have deemed will be good for us (Kalantzis & Cope, 2008b). There are some differences, to be sure—the image of the solar system in the old science textbook stays still, but the planets move around the sun in the digital "learning object"—but the learners' relationships to knowledge and the processes of pedagogy have not necessarily changed in any significant way (Cope & Kalantzis, 2009).

Then there are the dedicated attempts to mechanize learning. Some of these are cheap enough for schools' meager budgets. Give every child a device that looks like a television remote control, ask a question, then instead of having just one student answer, all the students answer by pressing a button on their remote. In this way, the teacher gets a picture of what every learner knows, not just the child whose hand shoots up hand first. Or get the students to do online reading comprehension tests. The machine, rather than the teacher, scores the learner, which means students in the one class can be reading different books depending on their reading and interest levels (see, for instance, www.renlearn.com, used in some 75,000 schools). Put some of these pieces together into a "learning management system," and students can be assigned work, access that work, participate in class "discussions" and have their work scored. For its apparent novelty, this is called e-learning. Everything that could happen in a classroom can now happen though a computer network.

Many of these things are, in a technical sense, new to education. Schools have had to collect together new resources, teachers have had to master new technologies, and students have had to engage in new types of mediated activity as a part of their school work. But oftentimes the underlying learning relationships have barely changed. New media do not necessarily mean new learning. Old institutions have an enormous capacity to assimilate new forms without fully exploiting their affordances. From the scope of possibility in the new media, teachers and curriculum designers all-too-often selectively do things with them that are not much more than conventional.

New Media

What more could the new media do for education? How might they support a new learning? To answer these questions, we need first to explore what's new about the new media. We are going to focus on four dimensions of the new media which we would argue represent a significant break from the media of our habituated cultural and educational home—the media we have lived with for the duration of modernity thus far. To look at the new media and then to consider the possibilities for new learning in this way is not to imply that technologies are, on their own, agents of social change. Rather they are symptoms of social change, or fellow travelers on a journey of social transformation in which social conditions make the technologies imaginable then useable, and in which the technologies provide the affordances (the means of cultural production) for new social forms. The following four dimensions represent a schematic overview of key characteristics of the new media. In the last section of this chapter, we will explore the educational affordances of each of these dimensions. But before we start the four, a digression—what, textually speaking, is not new about the new media? We will take as cases-in-point, hypertext and virtual reality and ask the question: How different are the textual practices of the Internet from those of books and print literacy?

Hypertext, it is argued, is one of the most distinctive features of the digital communications environment, creating the possibility of non-linear readings and reader-chosen navigation paths. Even at first glance, hypermedia technologies are not so novel, tellingly using metaphorical devices drawn from the textual practices of the book, such as "browsing," "bookmarking," "pages" and "index." Moreover, when we examine the book as an information architecture, its characteristic devices are nothing if not hypertextual. Gutenberg's Bible had no title page, no contents page, no pagination, no index. In this sense, it was a truly linear text. However, within a century of Gutenberg's invention, the modern information architecture of the book had been developed, including regularly numbered pages, punctuation marks, section breaks, running heads, indexes and cross-referencing. Amongst all these, pagination was the critical functional tool (Eisenstein, 1979).

The idea that books are linear and the Internet is multilateral is based on the assumption that readers of books necessarily read in a linear way. In fact, the devices of contents, indexing and referencing were designed precisely for alternative lateral readings—hypertextual readings, if you like. And the idea that the book is a text with a neat beginning and a neat end—unlike the Internet, which is an endless, seamless web of cross-linkages—is to judge the book by its covers. A book does not begin and end at its covers, despite the deceptive appearances of its physical manifestation. It sits in a precise place in the world of other books, literally when shelved in a library, located in multiple ways by sophisticated subject cataloguing systems, and intertextually positioned by the apparatuses of attribution (referencing) and subject definition (contents and indexes).

As for hypertext links that point beyond a particular text, they do no more than what citation has always done, albeit much faster. The footnote developed as a means of linking a text back to its precise sources, and directing a reader forward to a more detailed elaboration (Grafton, 1997). The only difference between the footnote and hypertext is that in the past you had to go to the library to follow through on a reference. Books, in other words, have developed elaborate ways of bursting out of their covers, of always referring to the world outside their covers, including to other books. This relationship to other writing and other books comes to be regulated in the modern world of private property by the laws, conventions and ethics of copyright, plagiarism, quotation, citation, attribution and fair use (Cope, 2001a). So, for all the hype in hypertext, it only does what books have always done, which is to point to connections across and outside of a particular text.

Take also the hyperbole of the "virtual." There's not much about the virtual in the digital communications era which print and the book did not create as a genuine innovation 500 years earlier. The book as a communication technology brought modern people strangely close to distant and exotic places though the representation of those places in words and images on the printed page. So vivid at times was the representation, that the early moderns could be excused for thinking they were virtually there. So too, in their time, the photograph, the telegraph, the newspaper, the telephone, the radio and the television were all credited for their remarkable verisimilitude—remarkable for the "real" being so far away, yet here so easily, so quickly and so seemingly close and true to life. Each of these new virtual presences became a new kind of reality, a new "telepresence" in our lives. We virtually lived through wars via the medium of newspapers; and we virtually made ourselves party to the lives of other people in other places and at other times through the medium of the novel or the travelogue. In this respect, digitization is just another small step in the long and slow journey into the cultural logic of modernity. Digital reproduction and transmission of meaning simply reopens the fundamental questions of aura, authenticity and location raised by Walter Benjamin in the 1930s in his discussion of "the work of art in the age of mechanical reproduction" (Benjamin, 1970).

But here are four things which, we would argue, are new...

Dimension 1: Agency

One of the key differences between the old media and the new is in what we call the balance of agency. Whereas broadcast TV had us all watching a handful of channels, digital TV has us choosing one channel from amongst thousands, or interactive TV in which we select our own angles on a sports broadcast, or making our own video and posting it to YouTube or the Internet. Whereas novels and TV soaps had us engaging vicariously with characters in the narratives they presented to us, video games make us central characters in the story to the extent that we can even influence its outcomes. Whereas print encyclopedias provided us definitive knowledge constructed by experts, Wikipedia is constructed, reviewed and editable by readers and includes parallel argumentation by reader-editors about the "objectivity" of each entry. Whereas broadcast radio gave listeners a programmed playlist, iPod users create their own playlists. Whereas a book was resistant to annotation (the size of the margins and out of respect for its next reader), new reading devices and formats encourage annotation in which the reading text is also a (re)writing text. Whereas the diary was a space for time-sequenced private reflection, the blog is a place for personal voice which invites public dialogue on personal feelings. Whereas a handwritten or typed page of text could only practically be the work of a single creator, "changes tracking," version control and web document creation such as Google Docs make multi-author writing easy and collaborative authorship roles clear (Kalantzis, 2006a; Kalantzis & Cope, 2008a).

Each of these new media is reminiscent of the old. In fact, we have eased ourselves into the digital world by using old media metaphors—creating documents or files and putting them away in folders on our desktops. We want to feel as though the new media are like the old. In some respects they are, but in some harder-to-see respects they are quite different.

One important and underlying difference is what we call the changing balance of agency (Kalantzis, 2006b; Kalantzis & Cope, 2008b). The earlier modern regime of communications used metaphors of transmission—for television and radio literally, but also in a figurative sense for books, curricula, public information, workplace memos and all manner of information and culture. This was an era when bosses bossed, political leaders heroically led (to the extent even of creating fascisms, communisms and monolithic welfare states for the ostensible good of the people), and personal and family life (and "deviance") could be judged against the canons of normality. Not only have things changed in today's everyday life. The most advanced of contemporary workplaces devolve responsibility to teams and ask workers to buy into the corporate culture (Cope & Kalantzis, 1997). Neoliberal politics tells people to give up their reliance on the state and to take personal responsibility for their own welfare. Diversity rules in everyday life, and with it the injunction to feel free to be true to your own identity.

Things have also changed in the social relations of meaning-making. Audiences have become users. Readers, listeners and viewers are invited to talk back to the extent that they have become media co-designers themselves. The division of labor between culture and knowledge creators and consumers has been blurred. Consumers are also creators, and creators are consumers. Knowledge and authority are more contingent, provisional and conditional-based relationships of "could" rather than "should." This is what we mean by a "shift in the balance of agency," from a society of command and compliance to a society of reflexive co-construction. It might be that the workers creating bigger profits for the bosses, that neoliberalism "naturally" exacerbates disparities in social power, and that diversity is a way of putting a nice gloss on inequality. The social outcomes, indeed, may at times be disappointingly unchanged or the relativities even deteriorating.

What has changed is the way these outcomes are achieved. Control by others has become self-control; compliance has become self-imposed. New media are one part of this broader equation. The move may be primarily a social one, but the technology has helped us head in this general direction.

Whether it be in the domains of work, governance or cultural life, the command society is giving way to the society of reflexivity in which agency is more evenly balanced. Or so we might say in moments of strategic optimism. In moments of pessimism, we might experience these same phenomena as fragmentation, ego-centrism, randomness, ambiguity and anarchy. And when this pessimism turns to fear, we might want to return to earlier, simpler command structures—in nations, workplaces, households and schools.

Pessimists and optimists alike might agree that we are in the midst of a transformation that is creating new forms of subjectivity and new kinds of personality. These transformations can be viewed both from within a systems perspective and beyond it. From a systems point of view, these are the kinds of governance structures, the kinds of organization and the kinds of people required today, for the most conservative, small government and pro-enterprise points of view. We hear these points of view expressed in the public rhetoric of innovation and creativity, the knowledge economy, and individual autonomy and responsibility. Notwithstanding the high-sounding rhetoric, left to run their course, these transformations may only legitimate and even exacerbate systemic inequities.

History, however, is more open-ended than that. Inevitably, human systems are so complex that they allow possibilities outside the scope anticipated by their progenitors and apologists. For every moment when the ideologues of small government succeed in shrinking the state, there is another moment in which people learn the civilities of self-government in their various communities of practice; for every moment when command structures in workplaces are replaced by structures which ask workers to "fit" in with the workplace culture, there is another moment in which people acquire the collaborative competencies of socially directed work; for every moment when compliant personalities are replaced by the ego-centrism of individualism, there is another moment in which new relationships of co-dependence and mutual reliance are created and the bonds of sociability are extended and deepened. Whatever the domain, there is a shift in the balance of power and in the moral economy of agency which favors egalitarianism and liberty. And this is despite and beyond prevailing systems and structures of power. From this something genuinely new could emerge.

The trends, however, are always contradictory. Just as agency is passed over to users and consumers, power is also centralized in ways that become more disturbing with time. The ownership of commercial media, communications channels and software platforms is becoming alarmingly concentrated. Besides, to what extent are the new media, such as games, an escape from reality? And for every dazzling new opening to knowledge and cultural expression in the new "gift economy" of the Internet (where content can be accessed for free)—and Google is a prime example of this—there are disturbing new possibilities for the invasion of privacy, cynically targeted advertising and control over knowledge sources and media (Kalantzis & Cope, 2008b).

Dimension 2: Divergence

What happens when you create space for agency? One of the first and most obvious things is that you discover a panoply of differences that the industrial-era workplace, the nationalistic state and modern ideas of personal normality had wanted to pretend did not exist.

Here's a catalog of differences which in an earlier modernity we tried to ignore, or if they could not be ignored, to separate onto another side of a geographical border, or institutional boundary, or a normative divide of "deviance": material differences (social class, locale, family circumstances); corporeal differences (age, race, sexual orientation, physical and mental abilities); and symbolic differences (culture, language, gender—an amalgam of gender and sexual identification and identity). All of these differences in our late modernity present themselves as insistent demographic realities. They have become living and normative realities too, supported by an expanded conception of human rights. However, as soon as we begin to negotiate these differences in good faith, we find ourselves confounded by the categories. We discover that the gross demographic groupings used in the first instance to acknowledge differences are too simple for our needs. We are instead dealing with an inexhaustible range of intersectional possibilities—where gender and race and class meet, for instance. We face real-world specificities which confound generalizations about people who formally fit the ostensible categorical norm. In fact, if you take any one the categories, you'll find that the variation within that group is greater than the average variation between groups. There are no norms. Rather, you find yourself in the presence of differences which can only be grasped at a level which defies categorization: different life narratives (experiences, places of belonging, networks), different personae (affinities, attachments, orientations, interests, stances, values, world views, dispositions, sensibilities); and different styles (epistemological, learning, discursive, interpersonal). The gross demographics might tell of larger historical forces, groupings and movements; they don't tell enough to provide a sufficiently subtle heuristic or guide for our everyday interactions. For history's sake, we need to do the gross demographics, but today a lot more.

The rebalancing of agency in our epoch brings with it a shift away from a fundamental logic of uniformity in an earlier modernity, to a logic of difference. And more: we don't just not have difference as a found object, legacies of lived experience that we can at last recognize. There is also today a tendency to diverge, or to become more different. Here is one of the great paradoxes of what is also an era of globalization, when we are undoubtedly becoming more closely interconnected in many respects: communications, media, trade, travel, capital flows, ideas flows (Steger, 2008). We also live in a time when the scope for agency allows us to make ourselves more different. And because we can, we do. Take for instance the rainbow of gender identifications and expressions of sexuality in the newly plastic body; or the shades of ethnic identity and the juxtapositions of identity which challenge our inherited conceptions of neighborhood; or the locale that highlights its peculiarities to tourists; or the bewildering range of products anticipating any number of consumer identities and product reconfigurations by consumers themselves.

The new media are one part of this mix, one of the many catalysts in the transition from an era of homogenization to an era of divergence. This is because the new media provide channels for differences to represent themselves. After an era in which every pressure was to create homogeneity (mass media, best-selling authors, mass-produced products, assimilating minorities), today's society and media provide spaces for divergence (the myriad of micropublishing opportunities on the web, from social networking sites to blogs to self-posted television, reflecting any and every shade of identity and timbre of voice).

Not only does difference come to light more vividly and poignantly. Differences can auto re-create. Individuals and groups can become more different. The cost of entry for different ways of speaking, seeing, thinking and acting is lower. You don't need specialist trade skills or heavy-duty infrastructure to be out there in your own voice—through the web, or in video, or using digital print.

The economies of scale of cultural production have been reversed. The logic of mass production (big-production TV; large print-run books) is being displaced at least in part by the logic of mass customization (tens of thousands of widely divergent messages in YouTube; books where a print-run of one costs the same per unit as a print run of 10 or 10,000). This is what makes it possible for discourse communities to diverge, to find and develop voices that are truer to their evolving selves—profession-speak, peer-speak, diaspora-speak, fad-speak, affinity-speak (Cope & Kalantzis, 2000). Knowledge and culture become more fluid, contestable and open. Discourses become less mutually intelligible, and we need to put more effort into cross-cultural dialogues in order to get things done.

After the sociological description of this moment, we may choose to add a layer of agenda-implying interest. Differences have historically been overlaid by patterns of injustice (Fraser, 2008; Fraser & Honneth, 2003). Recognition of differences requires some acknowledgment of injustice. And acknowledgment suggests redress. Greater scope for agency suggests autonomous spaces in which to be different, and to diverge. Agency plus difference/divergence prefigures a newly expanded conception of human rights.

Dimension 3: Multimodality

As for the means of production of meaning, one deceptively simple thing has produced enormous change. The digital world reduces the elementary modular unit for the production of textual meaning from the character to the pixel. Quite simply, this means that written language, sound and image are all made of the same stuff (Cope & Kalantzis, 2004).

Earlier modern technologies of representation found awkward ways of bolting one mode onto another. It was hard to print images and words on the same page, so images were isolated in a separate section of the book. It took several decades to achieve, but sound was finally attached to movie film stock, but only by means of a completely different, special purpose and expensive manufacturing technique. In the first centuries of print-literate modernity, we managed to put different representational modes together, but not comfortably, and at a cost.

This was one of the reasons why, in an earlier modernity, the modes of representation drifted apart. At times they were even dragged apart. The radical iconoclasts of Protestantism tore the stained glass windows and the statues out of churches in order to force upon supplicants an unmediated relationship with the Word. The printing press required different processes for text (the offset letterpress) and image (engraving) (Cope, 2001b), so if image and text were to be in the same book, for the most pragmatic of manufacturing purposes they had to be separated.

After half a millennium in which written text has been a pervasive source of knowledge and power, photographic means of representation (lithographic printing, cinema, analog television) began to afford greater power to create images and comfortably overlay images with written text. The digital accelerates this process as the elementary modular unit of manufacture of textual meaning is reduced from the character to the pixel. Images and fonts are now made of the same raw materials, and more easily overlaid—hence the television screens that stream more and more writing over images, and the magazines and newspapers which layer images and text in a way that was never easily achievable in the era of letterpress printing. Parallel to this is a revival of the aural, or the use of the oral as a representational means across distances previously dominated by writing. In the first instance, it was analog telephone and radio that allowed this possibility, then more closely overlaid in the digital era as sound is also made from the same bits and bytes as images and characters. New overlays of oral and written modes emerge as telegraph, telegram and then email stay more faithful to the fluid epistemes of speaking than the earlier literate forms of letters and memoranda. Then voice synthesis of digital text turns the readable into the hearable.

Now we have digital devices where we can put all of these together, but only because sound, written language, still image and moving image can all be made, stored and distributed—because they can all be reduced to the common platform that is the zeros and ones of the digital world. Hence multimodality, or, the capacity to mix modes.

New literacies centered on hybrid and multimodal text emerge. Modes of meaning that were relatively separate become ever-more closely intertwined. The practical consequences are enormous, as more written text appears in traditionally visual media (such as television) and truly integrated multimodal media emerge, even in traditional areas such as print. And at the creation end of the process, word processing and desktop publishing integrate the logistics of visual design into text construction, to the extent even of turning the once-obscure craft language of the typesetter into a universal language for text visualization—fonts, point sizes and the like—as a fundamental basis for "marking up" textual architectures (Kalantzis & Cope, 2008a).

From the mid-1990s, the Internet takes this even further, with its blurring of the boundaries and overlaying of written text, icon and image, as well as its extensive use of spatial and architectonic metaphors associated with site navigation (Castells, 2001; Gilster, 1997; Mitchell, 1995). Adding yet another layer of multimodality, the Internet and its earlier multimedia progenitors include the capacity to overlay audio because, ultimately, sound too can be made into the same digitally recordable stuff as pixels. The effect of all of these changes over the past half century, picking up pace with digitization, has been to reduce the privileged place of written text in Western culture, progressively bringing the visual and other modes to a par. In some contexts, even, other modes are now being privileged ahead of the written-textual (Kress, 2000, 2003).

Dimension 4: Conceptualization

To be a user of new media requires a kind of thinking which we will call "conceptualization." In the world of passive consumerism, you didn't need to know so much of what was inside the machine (mechanical, informational, socio-cultural). To be a player today and not just a viewer/reader/consumer, you need to get your head around new social and technical architectures. You need to be able to read and write representational designs. This creates a new cognitive load, not just to think in conceptual-design terms, but in order to monitor your thinking about your thinking, or metacognition. What are the skills and logics of navigation and discernment in a media environment of seemingly infinite extent and so demanding that we make hypertextual choices? How does one plan where one goes or recap where one has been? How are the social and informational networks to be mapped if one is to get a clearer view of their patterns of meaning?

Then there is the mechanics of communication and discovery, all of which require new forms of higher-order abstraction—ersatz identifications in the form of file names, thumbnails, menus and directories; semantic tagging, whether that be home-made folksonomies or the formal taxonomies and standards which are used to drive web feeds, to define database fields and identify document content; and using schemas or ontologies to structure information architectures and content for "semantic publishing." The new media needs a new, conceptualizing sensibility (Cope & Kalantzis, 2004).

New Learning

What does this mean for schools? Will the traditional classroom work, or even make sense, in the near future? Will the children of Nintendo, the web and video games find traditional classrooms engaging? Will the employers of the knowledge economy find good memory and good discipline sufficient or even adequate? (Gee, 2004).

Against each of the four dimensions of the new media, we will juxtapose four dimensions of the new learning.

Dimension 1: Designers

The balance of agency in heritage, didactic education was one in which teachers and textbooks told. For their part, students put up their hands and took tests in order to get the answers right or wrong. Knowledge was definitive. The direction of the knowledge flows was top-down. The moral lesson was to accept authoritative, universal knowledge as true and to comply with its "discipline."

This logic fitted well with the logic of the earlier modern media. It does not fit with the logic of the new media, or the commensurate shifts in the balance of agency in the everyday experiences of work, citizenship and personal life. If education is to be relevant to the contemporary social needs and personal dispositions, it has to do something different. Education has to conceive schools as knowledge-producing communities, and create in learners a sense that they themselves are knowledge producers.

In the case of teachers, digital media allow them to be designers of pedagogy and builders of learning content. Textbooks which followed the syllabus were designed to be followed by the teachers, and learners in turn followed these. "Turn to Chapter 7," was the extent of the teacher's intervention. Go to the next "digital learning object" is an instruction from a learning management system that is not much different. Like "Chapter 7," it is something that has been created by someone who can, and that's obviously not the teacher. However, given the accessibility of the digital world, what's to stop teachers and schools developing banks of learning resources and publishing them to the web—such as the Learning Elements of the "Learning by Design" project (http://L-by-D.com)—which are locally engaged and are expressions of their own professionalism and a culture of collaboration in the school as teachers share their work (Kalantzis & Cope, 2005)?

In the case of learners, why can't they draw on a variety of available resources—digitally accessible information, in their community and environment, amongst parents and peers—in which they actively make knowledge in its various modes and permutations (such as experiential, conceptual, analytical and applied)? They would not be reinventing the world any more or less than an expert does. They would be just as reliant on knowledge sources, but be rebuilding knowledge themselves in an active, engaged way as if they were an expert.

Once again, the digital will support this, providing as it does unprecedented means for accessing, recording, sharing, working collaboratively and publishing the knowledge that learners may have gained in their digital portfolios. The key shift, though, is not the medium, but the capacity of the medium to support learners to be knowledge producers rather than knowledge consumers (Kalantzis & Cope, 2008b).

Dimension 2: Learner Differences

The old, one-size-fits-all, on-the-same-page curriculum is no longer necessary in the context of new media. Nor is it such a good idea in a world of endemic divergence. Heritage modern schooling did all it could to remove or ignore differences, working on the foundational assumption that the learners in the classroom can be regarded as more or less the same, or can be sorted into groupings. With the teacher at the front of the room and the test at the end of the term, everyone had to be turning to "Chapter 7" at the same time. This was the communicative basis of its key technologies of homogenization—separatism (by age, "ability," culture, language, social destiny) and assimilation (remember this stuff, demonstrate you can think this way, become the kind of person we want you to be).

But look at all the differences in school today, so visible and so insistent: material (class, locale, family), corporeal (age, race, sex and sexuality, and physical and mental characteristics) and symbolic (culture, language, gender, family, affinity and persona). Today's education has little alternative but to recognize the social realities of pluralism and develop strategies for inclusion that are without prejudice to that diversity.

Using digital media, learners do not all have to be on the same page. At any one time, they can be doing what is best for them given what they already know. And how can a teacher know what a learner knows? A much more graphic, realistic and detailed view is possible in a digital environment in which actual performance is recorded in portfolios rather than bald test scores. Complex, multiperspectival assessment is possible, which continuously feeds back into the process of appropriate learning design for that student. If students are knowledge creators, they can be asked to link the particularities of their life experiences closely into the knowledge that is being made. By this means, their knowledge-making becomes revoicing, not replication. Students can also work together more readily in the digital environment. Lesser or greater contributions are visible for what they are (and this could be appropriate), and differential perspectives and knowledge can be valued as the basis for collective intelligence.

Here are some ways in which a more inclusive education, with and without the support of new media, can address learner differences:

1. Connect: Make points of contact with learners' lifeworlds. Create avenues for learners to say who they are, and to be who they are. Value what they already know by frequently asking what that is. Ask them to connect new experiences and knowledge with what they already know, think and feel. Do not second-guess the dimensions of difference—open out the curric-

ulum to embrace what learners bring to the learning experience, surprisingly perhaps. Open a window onto their identities and figure out what makes them "tick." By honoring their lifeworlds as places of valid and useful knowledge, a teacher creates the sense of belonging that is central to inclusive education. The new media provide no special path, but they do provide tools for self-identification and connecting with learners' lifeworld experiences by encouraging them to represent those experiences and encouraging them to connect these with the learning tasks at hand.

2. Value: Students need to be able to express themselves in the ways they feel most comfortable. They need to be able to create new knowledge in different kinds of ways, depending on what works best for them. Effective teaching and learning in the context of deep social diversity needs to involve multiple and varied pedagogical approaches. This entails different emphases and mixes of "knowledge processes" to suit different "learning orientations" and what a learner finds to be the most effective modalities of representation for them in the new media environment.
3. Engage: All-too-often our institutions and practices of schooling still reflect the knowledge transmission and personality frames of the command society, such as the communication patterns of classroom discourse, the information architectures of curriculum or the rigid expectations of "right" and "wrong" answers in testing regimes. These were all oriented to uniformity, or one-size-fits-all education. The more we take agency into account, however, the more multifarious its manifestations become—material, corporeal and symbolic—and the more complex the matrices and intersections. And to face all these agencies in one classroom! The solution of the command society was one teacher talking at the middle of the class, one textbook telling one narrative one chapter at a time, one test which told of one way of knowing. The result was assimilation to the middle way, or failure. A more inclusive approach will recruit learner agency, subjectivity and identity as an energy for learning. This means that the classroom must be very different to those to which we have become accustomed. It must allow alternative starting points for learning (what the learner perceives to be worth learning, what engages the particularities of their identity). It must allow for alternative forms of engagement (the varied experiences that need to be brought to bear on the learning, the different conceptual bents of learners, the different analytical perspectives the learner may have on the nature of cause, effect and human interest, and the different settings in which they may apply or enact their knowledge). It must allow for different learning orientations (preferences, for instance, for particular emphases in knowledge-making and patterns of engagement—experiential, conceptual, analytical or applied). It must allow for different modalities in meaning-making, embracing alternative expressive potentials for different learners. And it must allow for alternative pathways and destination points in learning. If we could allow this much scope to learner agency, we would allow a

thousand differences to flourish at the same time as creating a more powerful sense of inclusion and belonging. This would also mean that learners would have more opportunities to jump out of the rut of narrow lifeworld destinies, opening their horizons of possibility and their potentials for self-transformation. New media environments have the potential to make these ambitious aspirations practical possibilities.

4. Create knowledge ecologies: Centering educational energies on learner agency in all its variety will also create new dynamics, sociability and ethics of knowledge creation. Inclusive education changes the direction of knowledge flows so learners and teachers are more actively involved in the construction of knowledge. Learning is a matter of engagement, moving backward and forward between formally developed or scientific knowledge and the lifeworld. When learner–knower lifeworlds are so varied, diversity of perspective becomes a resource. Learning–knowing is most powerful when collaborative and diverse perspectives are brought to bear. Knowledge construction and learning, in other words, is all the more potent for its productive engagement of diversity. This is the basis for learning and knowledge ecologies are very different from traditional transmission models of pedagogy and broadcast models for communicating knowledge. New media environments make this a more manageable possibility—collaborative content creation environments such as wikis, personal journaling environments such as blogs, and digital imaging and video for the recording of content. The educational outcome is not just content knowledge, or at least not that primarily. It is the development of the kinds of people who have the capacity to learn and act in particular ways. They can navigate change, negotiate deep diversity and make and lead change rather than be knocked about by it. They can engage in sometimes difficult dialogues; they can compromise and create shared understandings; and they can comfortably extend their cultural and knowledge repertoires into new areas. They are tolerant, responsible and resilient in their differences. The key questions for educators, then, are how do these new "types of people" learn to be themselves, learn to relate with others and learn how to get things done in today's knowledge ecologies? And how can we use the new media to support these objectives?
5. Evaluate: Learner transformation is a central mission for education. This occurs through the extension of one's repertoire of knowledge and capacities. It involves boundary crossing, expanding one's horizons in a world of differences. This does not mean having to leave one's old self behind as was the case in the days of assimilation. Rather, a new equality of outcomes would be reflected not in sameness but in comparability, equivalent but not necessarily the same results. You don't have to be the same to be equal. How, then, do we create forms of assessment and evaluation which can tell us, in meaningful ways, how learners have grown through their learning experiences? The answer is only in part in conventional terms—test results which get you into certain educational sites and which

open up certain employment and life alternatives. It also means using innovative assessment and evaluation practices such as portfolio evaluation, peer review and the personal testimonies of learners. The new media environment is ideal for these kinds of complex and multifaceted learner assessment processes (Kalantzis & Cope, 2008b).

Dimension 3: Synesthesia

Heritage modern schooling divided modes of meaning neatly into different subjects. Language was for text; art was for visuals. Conventional modern schools stripped away the richly multimodal life of pre-school children by separating off the mechanics of handwriting or phonics. New learning uses synesthesia—or mode shifting—as a pedagogical device. The new media make this so much easier, and so much more excitingly close to the "realness" of television, video games and the Internet (Kress, 2000, 2003).

The process of shifting between modes and re-representing the same thing from one mode to another is called synesthesia. Traditional literacy does not by and large recognize or adequately use the meaning and learning potentials inherent in different modes, or the synesthesia involved in shifting between one mode and another. Rather, it tries to confine itself to the monomodal formalities of written language, as if the modality of written language could be isolated as a system unto itself. This was always a narrow agenda. Today, such narrowing is unrealistic, given the multimodal realities of the new media and broader changes in the communications environment.

However, the consequences of narrowing of representation and communication to the exclusive study of written language (sound–letter correspondences, parts of speech and the grammar of sentences, literary works and the like) are more serious than its still-powerful, though declining, relevance to contemporary conditions. Synesthesia is integral to representation. In a very ordinary, material sense, our bodily sensations are holistically integrated, even if our focus on meaning-making attentions in any particular moment might be one particular mode. Gestures may come with sound; images and text sit side by side on pages; architectural spaces are labeled with written signs. Much of our everyday representational experience is intrinsically multimodal. Indeed, some modes are naturally close to others, so close in fact that the one easily melds into the others in the multimodal actualities of everyday meaning. Written language is closely connected to the visual in its use of spacing, layout and typography. Spoken language is closely associated with the audio mode in the use of intonation, inflection, pitch, tempo and pause. Gesture may need to be planned or rehearsed, either in inner speech (talking to oneself), or by visualization. Children have natural synesthetic capacities, and instead of building upon and extending these, school literacy attempts, over a period of time, to separate them off, to the extent even of creating different subjects or disciplines, literacy in one cell of the class timetable and art in another (Kress, 1997).

In the face of the "back to basics" movement, we would put the case that synesthesia is a pedagogical move which makes for powerful learning in a number of ways. Some learners may be more comfortable in one mode than another. This may be their preferred mode of representation—what comes to them easiest, what they're good at, the mode in which they best express the world to themselves and themselves to the world. One person may prefer to conceive a project as a list of instructions; another as a flow diagram. The parallelism means that you can do a lot of the same things in one mode that you can do in the next, so a pedagogy which restricts learning to one artificially segregated mode will favor some types of learners over others. It also means that the starting point for meaning in one mode may be a way of extending one's representational repertoire by shifting from favored modes to less comfortable ones. If the words don't make sense, the diagram might, and then the words start to make sense. But the incommensurability of modes works pedagogically, too. The words make sense because the picture conveys meaning that words could never (quite or in a completely satisfactorily way) do. Conscious mode switching makes for more powerful learning (Kalantzis & Cope, 2008a).

Changes in the contemporary communications environment simply add urgency to the call to consciously deploy multimodality in learning. We are in the midst of a seismic shift in communications in which, as we have argued in this chapter, the new media are intrinsically multimodal. Word processing, web work, PowerPoint, blogging, making a wiki, creating image galleries, video-making and game-making and playing—all of these build upon and realize a wider and more powerful range of human meaning-making capacities than the heritage media of traditional school subjects. They also allow learners of different dispositions to drift in the direction of expressive forms with their comfort zones, while challenging them to transfer meanings into new and as yet unfamiliar forms.

Dimension 4: Metacognition

Didactic pedagogy taught facts assembled into disciplinary shape and unveiled to learners in theoretical sequence. In the 20th century, a less-abstract "authentic" pedagogy emphasized experiential learning—through doing, demonstration, experimentation or immersion. The new learning seeks to engage learners in more powerful conceptualizing and metacognizing processes. Some of this is reminiscent of didactic teaching—labels for things more finely defined than in the ambiguities of everyday language and theories which tie those labels together into patterns of explanation. But the new learning engages the learner as co-constructor of concepts—as definer, theory-maker, critic and analyst.

Specialized, disciplinary and deep knowledges are based on the finely tuned distinctions of concept and theory typical of those developed by expert communities of practice. Conceptualizing is not merely a matter of teacherly or textbook telling based on the legacy of academic disciplines, but a knowledge process in which the learners become active conceptualizers, making the tacit explicit and generalizing from the particular. This may involve drawing distinctions of similarity and difference, categorizing and naming. Here, learners give abstract names to things and develop concepts (Vygotsky, 1962). Or it may mean making generalizations and putting the key terms together into interpretative frameworks. Learners build mental models, abstract frameworks and transferable disciplinary schemas. In the same pedagogical territory, didactic pedagogy would lay out disciplinary schemas for the learners to acquire (the rules of literacy, the laws of physics and the like). Such conceptualizing requires that learners be active concept- and theory-makers. It also requires weaving between the experiential and the conceptual (Kalantzis & Cope, 2005). This kind of weaving is primarily cognitive, between Vygotsky's world of everyday or spontaneous knowledge and the world of science or systematic concepts, or between Piaget's concrete and abstract thinking (Cazden, 2006).

Some of the new learning is reminiscent of authentic education, when learners connect knowledge with personal experience, are immersed in new experiences and are asked to apply their learning in real-world contexts. But the new learning does more, by insisting on the higher-order conceptualizing. Insofar as navigation of the new media requires higher-order skills of conceptualization and abstraction, learning that engages students in and through new media environments will support pedagogical experiences appropriate to our moment, in and for its characteristic cartographies and its grammars.

Conclusion

The possibilities of the new media for education have as yet barely been explored. It may look as though we have adopted new media in the classroom. However, these media have a deceptive capacity to do to old things. In fact, we have often been weaned to the new media by metaphors from old representational and social practices. For these very reasons, we need to go back to an analysis of the fundamentals of the new media, and a reading of the affordances of the new media gives us a sense of their potentials to support a new learning.

References

Benjamin, W. (1970). The work of art in the age of mechanical reproduction. In Hannah Arendt (Ed.), *Illuminations* (pp. 219–254). London: Fontana.

Castells, M. (2001). *The Internet galaxy: Reflections on the Internet, business, and society.* Oxford: Oxford University Press.

Cazden, C. B. (2006, 18 January). *Connected learning: "Weaving" in classroom lessons.* Paper presented at the "Pedagogy in Practice 2006" Conference, University of Newcastle.

Cope, B. (2001a). Making and moving books in new ways, from the creator to the consumer. In B. Cope & D. Masons (Eds.), *Digital book production and supply chain management* (Vol. 2.3, pp. 1–20). Melbourne: Common Ground.

Cope, B. (2001b). New ways with words: Print and eText convergence. In B. Cope & D. Kalantzis (Eds.), *Print and electronic text convergence* (Vol. 2.1, pp. 1–15). Melbourne: Common Ground.

Cope, B., & Kalantzis, M. (1997). *Productive diversity: A new approach to work and management.* Sydney: Pluto Press.

Cope, B., & Kalantzis, M. (Eds.). (2000). *Multiliteracies: Literacy learning and the design of social futures.* London: Routledge.

Cope, B., & Kalantzis, M. (2004). Text-made text. *E-Learning,* 1(2), 198–282.

Cope, B., & Kalantzis, M. (2009). Ubiquitous learning: An agenda for educational transformation. In B. Cope & M. Kalantzis (Eds.), *Ubiquitous learning.* Champaign, IL: University of Illinois Press.

Cuban, L. (2001). *Oversold and underused: Computers in the classroom.* Cambridge, MA: Harvard University Press.

Eisenstein, E. L. (1979). *The printing press as an agent of change: Communications and cultural transformation in early-modern Europe.* Cambridge: Cambridge University Press.

Fraser, N. (2008). *Adding insult to injury: Nancy Fraser debates her critics.* London: Verso.

Fraser, N., & Honneth, A. (2003). *Redistribution or recognition: A political–philosophical exchange.* London: Verso.

Gee, J. (2004). *Situated language and learning: A critique of traditional schooling.* London: Routledge.

Gilster, P. (1997). *Digital literacy.* New York: John Wiley and Sons.

Grafton, A. (1997). *The footnote: A curious history.* London: Faber and Faber.

Kalantzis, M. (2006a). Changing subjectivities, new learning. *Pedagogies: An International Journal,* 1(1), 7–12.

Kalantzis, M. (2006b). Elements of a science of education. *Australian Educational Researcher,* 33(2), 15–42.

Kalantzis, M., & Cope, B. (2005). *Learning by design.* Melbourne: Victorian Schools Innovation Commission.

Kalantzis, M., & Cope, B. (2008a). Digital communications, multimodality and diversity: Towards a pedagogy of multiliteracies. *Scientia Paedagogica Experimentalis,* XLV(1), 15–50.

Kalantzis, M., & Cope, B. (2008b). *New learning: Elements of a science of education.* Cambridge: Cambridge University Press.

Kress, G. (1997). *Before writing: Rethinking the paths to literacy.* London: Routledge.

Kress, G. (2000). Multimodality. In B. Cope & M. Kalantzis (Eds.), *Multiliteracies: Literacy learning and the design of social futures* (pp. 182–202). Melbourne: Macmillan.

Kress, G. (2003). *Literacy in the new media age.* London: Routledge.

Mitchell, W. J. (1995). *City of bits: Space, place and the infobahn.* Cambridge, MA: MIT Press.

Steger, M. B. (2008). *The rise of the global imaginary: Political ideologies from the French revolution to the global war on terror.* Oxford: Oxford University Press.

Virilio, P. (1997). *Open sky.* London: Verso.

Vygotsky, L. (1962). *Thought and language.* Cambridge, MA: MIT Press.

6 Multiliteracies and the Agency Involved with Computer Operations in Education

David R. Cole, University of Technology, Sydney, and Darren L. Pullen, University of Tasmania

Introduction

This chapter is a critical discussion and approach to understanding agency in computer-mediated education. When students use computers to learn, they are simultaneously involved with various complicated processes of identity work (Luke & Luke, 2001). This identity work may be understood through the multiliteracies educational framework that has given us the notion of design as a central manner of organizing agency in learning (New London Group, 1996). However, the problem that this chapter grapples with is the socio-cultural consequences of understanding the agency of computers in education. The notion of design in multiliteracies must incorporate the formal and non-formal learning opportunities that computers facilitate (Street, 2000)—even though the "multimodality" of design when applied to contemporary text does give it emergent and multiple qualities that do go some way to account for the situation. The introduction of identity work through agency is the reason that curriculum designers and bureaucratic structures of educational systems may struggle with the non-linear and chaotic options that computer learning opens up (Cole, 2005a). To take account of the new ways in which social networks and technologically mediated desires and drives may be activated through computer use, the multiliteracies framework should be expanded to include connections to elements such as cyberpunk (Cole, 2005c)[1] and techno-tribalism. The former is an imaginary and literary manner of designating agency in a digitally mediated environment. The latter is a sociological platform whereby the movement of digitally mediated approaches to social organization may be understood as emergent properties that are being activated through education. The combination of cyberpunk and techno-tribalism as additive aspects to the multiliteracies framework—and with the explicit intent of exploring questions of agency—does take the educational package of multiliteracies into a new dimension. This move assumes that multiliteracies is flexible and open enough in order to absorb divergent through-lines present in any sociological context of education that are also saturated and transformed by digital technology. The organization of this chapter may by represented through Figure 6.1.

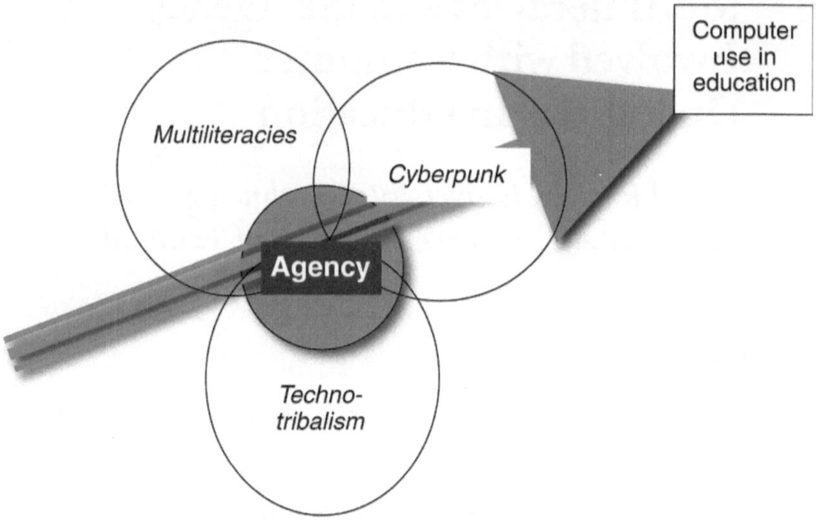

Figure 6.1 The Relationships between Agency, Multiliteracies, Cyberpunk and Techno-tribalism against a Backdrop of Computer Use in Education.

The Cyberpunk Agent in Multiliteracies

The notion of cyberpunk comes from films and literature in the 1980s that imagined a future where the institutions of civil society had broken down and technology had continued to evolve, but according to new and changing social conditions (Kahn & Kellner, 2005). An example of cyberpunk fiction is the movie *Blade Runner*, in which humanoid "replicants" live in fear of death as they have a finite life span written into their programming. These replicants are the most advanced technological forms in the *Blade Runner* society, and they are capable of destroying their creator. Such a capability is a non-predictive behavior, not permitted in machines. This cyberpunk landscape consequently opens up two primary questions for the multiliteracies framework:

1. What are the non-predictive behaviors encouraged by the notion of design as agency?
2. How does the multiliteracies approach incorporate radically changing social conditions into its programming (i.e., curriculum/knowledge/pedagogy)?

These questions point to the political realities of implementing social agendas that incorporate digital technology. An educational policy may designate computers as an effective means of teaching skills to students for future vocational choices (Bromley & Apple, 1998)—yet it is up to the students/teachers/schools to make effective use of the equipment (Apple, 1992). This usage involves the motivations and life choices of the students that are potentially open to design as agency—yet are also susceptible to fluctuations in work environments, opportunities and the social purposes of computer technology (Kellner, 2002). The tasks that one should consider when tackling the challenges to the multiliteracies framework that cyberpunk literature presents therefore include:

A Constructing knowledge, pedagogies and curricula that follow technological singularities, such as those presented by computers and cybernetic innovation in states of vital excitation; and attracting educational, commercial and governmental investment—yet doing so without falling into meta or grand narratives (Lyotard, 1984).

B Comprehending the agency of technological subjects as being in the "electronic palaver," or the ordered constraint of communicative complexity (Davis & Sumara, 2006), as an extension and explanation of digital design.

C Making explicit the relationships inherent in the differentials between micro–macro power relationships involved with recursive and emergent functioning (Waldrop, 1993) in education. These are the processes through which the cybernetics of learning with computers feeds back and new social and cultural forms become apparent.

These three tasks (A, B and C) to be completed by the educational multiliteracies framework when challenged by cyberpunk may be further illustrated through William Gibson's (1985) novel, *Mona Lisa Overdrive.* In this writing—a Japanese tourist called Kumiko has to go to the East End of London to find a data-thief called Tick. He conforms to the thin and nervous physiognomy of a console jockey who works outside of the law and mainstream society. However, the resources available to his milieu of English society do not define a narrow criminal underworld. Gibson's cyberpunk landscape envisages a convergent situation—involving the knowledge of Internet security codes, survival techniques and the social/cultural organization derived from living in a vast urban sprawl. Tick is part of a power structure that is able to take coordinated action in the data-world of cyberspace. This is in contrast to the lone cowboy, Case, who is an American anti-hero making his dysfunctional journey to a psychological and physical limit. Tick and his compatriot Slick do not live cosmopolitan lifestyles that match the corporate American dropout—yet through their ingenuity and innovation, they are able to access and work within the same cyberspace.

It could be said that the London underground of *Mona Lisa Overdrive* presents a virtual *Gemeinschaft*—or community—that excludes rigid hierarchies, status and promotional fears, appraisal and testing, deadlines and "clock-time" mentalities. Question 2 and Task A for this chapter ask whether the multiliteracies framework is sufficiently flexible to allow for such possibilities of agency that interrogates individualizing aspects of power and identity

(Marshall, 1996). It should be noted that the notion of community in this cyberpunk literary example arises from a different space to mainstream neoliberal capitalist endeavor and organization. As Deleuze and Guattari (1987) have explained, capitalism in its entirety now operates less by the striation of space and time that corresponds to the physiosocial concept of work, and more by a generalized "machinic enslavement" (p. 492). In effect, surplus value has become virtual value that is processed and used in capitalist exchange. For example: children, the retired, the unemployed and television audiences are brought into play by exchange and integrated processes of transportation, urbanization, the media, the entertainment industries, and ways of perceiving and feeling in semiotic systems (Jameson, 1991). One becomes an employee by simply turning on the television, or by booting up a computer at school. This is an entry point into a system of capital as surplus value, because one's agency is already operant as a user and buyer of technology and the products that this action engenders (Stoer & Amagalhaes, 2004) through, for example, advertising.

In a sense, machines themselves have become producers of surplus value, not just the controllers of the machines; furthermore, the global circulation of capital through technological conduits challenges the distinction between variable and constant capital (Castells, 1996, 1997). Deleuze and Guattari (1987) describe the integration of world capitalism with the operations of machines as constituting a "smooth space" where capital reaches an absolute speed in terms of the cybernetic transactions that move capital around the globe. This is where the cyberpunk heroes enact their raids (Clark, 1995)—and where one may perceive the greatest divergence between the educational framework of multiliteracies and the imagined world of cyberpunk. Multiliteracies enacts the heritage of critical pedagogy and critical literacy (Exley, 2008) in order to encourage a questioning attitude and thinking perspective to bear on commercial modes of operation in education. Cyberpunk accepts and subverts the tenets of late or fast capitalism, as long as they correspond to appropriate aspects of "cool"—such as fashion, music, literature and digital artifact.

The position of schools as liberal instruments in the democratic process was formalized in the US by the constructivist philosophy of John Dewey (1966); but constructivism is undermined by the functionality of schools as suppliers of human capital. The multiliteracies framework, with its underlying critical and emancipatory principles, rejects the imposition of human capital (Cope & Kalantzis, 2000). Yet the identification of agency with design allows for the exploitation of learning practices by capital through software packages and corporate learning communities. There is, therefore, an uneasy tension at the heart of the multiliteracies framework that points to the fact that design as agency can be used by corporations in order to introduce new products. For example, software manufacturers vie for business in the e-learning market; computer gaming companies take over youth movements to be "hip" (Cole, 2005b). The introduction of cyberpunk into the multiliteracies textual and educational mesh adds a darker edge to the framework and provides a critical crossover point for cultural transgression and specific curriculum content.

The literature of cyberpunk assumes that computers will be set into place in terms of the learning process, but contests the social functionalism of this placement as a means to enhanced, large-scale capitalist organization. *Neuromancer* (Gibson, 1984) gives us subcultures such as the Lo Teks; Zionites; Jack Draculas; Panther Moderns; Big Scientists; Gothicks; and Casuals. These groups indicate that the learning processes that are initiated in cyberpunk fiction do not attempt to unify fractured or disassembled individuals. Pierre Bourdieu (1980) has invoked the category of the *habitus* to explain the subordinate relationships inherent within worker–manager, student–school administration and child–parent complexes. He has spoken of symbolic violence as being a characteristic relation of pedagogic communication—and this is charged with the transmission of the "cultural arbitrary" (Bourdieu & Passeron, 1979, pp. 141–143)—or the special effect of symbolic relations in the reproduction of power relations within a framework of legitimate authority. Power according to Bourdieu (1980) is imposed by a system of social domination via symbolic means and through pedagogic authority, but its effectiveness in transmitting the culturally arbitrary is mediated by the strength of polarized classes and social movements. The relative strength and reinforcement given to the balance of powers between the groups or classes by symbolic relations expresses these power relations—it rises with the strength of various classes, and with the power of the market to confer higher value on the goods delivered by legitimate school authorities (Bourdieu & Passeron, 1979, pp. 150–170).

As such, economic power runs through schools, and reflexively disseminates its effects in the forms of qualifications, rewards, praise and jobs. Yet within a digitally mediated—or virtual—habitus, oppositional factors are subsumed and diverted by non-dialogic networks that are creating a world of experience that also raises questions about the reality of the political sign as Baudrillard (1994) has pointed out. Furthermore, this virtual habitus is present in the electronic arena of design that is central to agency for multiliteracies and by extension through "transformed practice" that indicates a "switching" between pedagogies to encourage agency as design (Cope & Kalantzis, 2000). This is because the symbolic violence that Bourdieu has theorized translates into digital networks through control and surveillance techniques, flaming, pornography and cyber-bullying. Multiliteracies endeavors to encourage social justice by promoting a balanced diet of activities and textual study skills involving the visual, audio, spatial, linguistic and gestural (New London Group, 1996). However, the content and focus of these areas are not pre-defined, and that leaves agency as design to be potentially filled by divergent value systems. This adds to the tension of the multiliteracies framework—especially as electronic networks are ambiguous in terms of their power affinities (Gee, 2005). On one hand, obvious "face-to-face" oppositional forces are mediated and complexified through digital technology as people do not meet. On the other hand, violence, danger and fear may be augmented through the camouflage and serendipity that digital technology permits in the virtual habitus.

The social critics, Kroker and Cook (1988), have presented a dramatic assessment of the current technological learning situation:

> We're living through a great story—an historical moment of implosion, cancellation and reversal; that moment where the will to the "techno-sphere"—or the dynamic expansion outwards of the technical mastery of social and non-social nature—traces a great arc of reversal, connecting us again to an almost mythic sense of primitivism as the primal of technological society.
>
> (p. 15)

This statement should be unpacked with respect to multiliteracies and cyberpunk. It could be stated that the development of high technology, such as the global Internet, also encourages an intensification of instinct and emotion (Ross, 1991) due to its connective and subconscious power. At the same time, populations are being flung into an unpredictable future of accelerated digital economics (Stoer & Amagalhaes, 2004); in this situation the past irrupts in the sense that the social vacuum that has been created through social economics may be plundered by residues of primitive energy not rendered useless by work or learning. In other words, energies that have been repressed through history by the construction of civil and democratic society with education now turn, in a Nietzschean moment of nihilism (Nietzsche, 1968), and are being dispersed through digital networks and in the virtual habitus. Kroker and Cook (1988) variously term these processes as "species-will" and the "DNA of post-modern psychology," displaying the "aesthetics of hyper-realism" (p. 113). Through these historical times, social life and education are being folded into dense mazes—agency is constituted by dead ends and bright horizons on a zero plane of digital envelopment.

Cyberpunk literature accepts such characterizations merely as the epoch of the real that we are living through—seen, for example, in *The Matrix*. The educational frame of multiliteracies challenges such a view, and contradicts the idea that civil society is breaking down due to the forces present in global accelerated capitalism. This framework puts its faith in critical pedagogies to heal the wounds that have been inflicted by intrusive and ubiquitous commercialism. McLuhan (1965) theorized this historical period as an extension of our nervous systems outside of the body. According to McLuhan (1965), information presents the ultimate in human use of tools—in that not only is physical work now done by machines, but that human activity can now be controlled electronically: "Electromagnetic technology requires utter human docility and quiescence of meditation such as befits an organism that now wears its brain outside its skull, and its nerves outside its hide" (p. 57). McLuhan's lively theorization concerns networks of electronic media and their subjugation of the populace. By extension, it could be stated that social organization has entered a digital phase through communication—as has been theorized by Wilden (1972)—which is by degrees ironic and reflexive.

Given this scenario, 1 and 0 on an electronic plane represent digital agency. The moment of rupture—when the subject becomes caught in swathes of technologically mediated thoughts and dreams—leads to a jumping between planes, and a consequent instability of the subject through oscillating agency (Wilden, 1972, p. 52). McLuhan's (1965) description of the modern classroom as a feudal dungeon—which must take account of the language of forms in the electronic media if it is to survive—has veracity in that this transformation is now happening in terms of the processing of new regimes of knowledge and curriculum, such as those contained in SMS messaging or multimodal literature on a digital plane.

Again, the educational frame of multiliteracies absorbs and distributes these points of contention through critical mores and by encouraging subjects to think about their positioning and textual practices (Cope & Kalantzis, 2000). Ironically, the transformed practice of multiliteracies is an attempt to allow educators to make their teaching approach flexible and open to digital oscillation (Wilden, 1972). Examples of cyberpunk literature, such as Gibson's early trilogy of cyberpunk novels, do not perform such an ironic oscillation, or attempt to make education better by increased engagement through electronic pedagogy or by re-energizing and integrating alienated youth. On the contrary, individuals and groups who have been "othered" by legitimate education populate Gibson's landscapes without any attempt to bring them back into the fold. In contrast, multiliteracies has been positioned as part of the fold, and as a way of bringing disillusioned groups back into the educational mainstream (New London Group, 1996) through a pedagogic and learning framework that is open to diversity.

Another way of understanding the fictional figures of cyberpunk and consequent agency is as "errant forces in the signs of capital" (Lyotard, 1993, p. 110). This translates to the idea that cyberpunk subjects are coded and fixed within regimes of capital—yet this procedure is mixed up due to subjective intensification and the social outcomes of this process. For example, cyberpunk hackers have rerouted shipments of Hagen Daas to the North Pole! Teacher hackers have sent back their training day electronic feedback questionnaires filled out with poetry and proverbs of wisdom! One objection to this cyberpunk stance is the simple rendition of the structures of domination that capitalist exchange has given rise to—this is proof of the social cohesive of exchange. It could be said that giving the systems of exchange value, even if we have the intention of subverting this value, still recognizes and valorizes the potential of exchange to create value. Multiliteracies suggests that we may question these processes of exchange in education through criticality and pedagogic switching. The model of exchange that one finds in cyberpunk literature locates "human–machine" or cyborg units as examples of flattened power relations in an accelerated environment (Csicsery-Ronay, 1991). Another possibility for challenging capitalist exchange lies in introducing discrete elements into the flows of analog society that constrain the continuum of reproduction (Wilden, 1972) with the immanent force of "on" and "off"—or the rupture of the digital as has been mentioned above. This conceptual strategy forms binary chains of, as Deleuze and Guattari (1984) have expressed it, "desiring-machines" (p. 232). The "desiring-machines" are a series which takes the multiplicity of social relations and subjects them to a recording plane, whereby the coupling may be understood. For example: a mouth as eating-machine or breathing-machine or speaking-machine. These actions are reproduced in and via education. The questions for multiliteracies and cyberpunk that surround these problems of exchange involve power, and more specifically: Where does the deepening of intensity occur in relations with technology? As Lyotard (1993) makes the point,

> the mad destruction of the organic body, the hysterical masochism, the decomposition of personal identity constructed by peasant traditions, the dissolution of the families and villages, the new monstrous anonymity of the suburbs and the pubs; these are all born and drawn out by *jouissance*, by the very enjoyment of their immolation.
>
> (p. 111)

Lyotard (1993) loaded his critical apparatus and writing with irony, and this is pertinent in the context of the agency of cyberpunk and multiliteracies as *jouissance* acts through self-reflection. The truth of the matter is that the current lifestyles, social choices and modes of organization in schools and universities will not be given up without a fight! Computers will be misused, the multiliteracies framework will be misapplied and students will become cyberpunks despite the best intentions of their mentors! All this happens because it is pleasurable to rebel. Yet beneath this normalized discourse about the domestic uses and misuses of power, there lies more serious questions that have recently served to animate behavior on a global scale. The questions that surround sophisticated, high-tech terrorism—or virtual terrorism (Cole, 2007a)—mark sites of resistance in the current field of human-machine and desiring-machine relations, and brings to the fore the issues of tactics and strategy that are to be played out in cyberpunk agency and in education with multiliteracies. Baudrillard's (1993) *Order of the Simulacra* is a sustained engagement with such an intersection of drives and the will to power.

As Baudrillard (1993) explains it, when the robot works, its functionality marks the end of the theatre and the beginning of human mechanics (p. 54). The entire industrial system of production radically opposes the principle of theatrical illusion, which supports an immanent logic of the principle of "operativity." Humans and machines can proliferate as automata. Freed from all semblance, humans and machines grow increasingly similar in a system of production. As the hegemony of the human-machines incurs cycles of production and (re)production, the counterfeit of the Renaissance, with its natural law and play of forms, is replaced by the market law of value and it calculations of forces—the unity of the processes of capital form in the sphere of simulacra and code, according to Baudrillard (1993, p. 55). Production itself has no meaning. Its social finality is lost in series, where the "real" message lies—and this is now called *simulation*. The capitalist code is realized scientifically through the "metaphysics of DNA" (Baudrillard, 1983, p. 57) and in the political sphere via the circularity of the media. Non-simulated response is impossible, given digital tactility (Baudrillard, 1983), where all communication is reduced to a 1 or 0—for example, the bi-partisan activities of the polling booths, and the way in which the media enhances the idea of *either–or* choices. The polling booth, which is supposedly private, is turned into a public event via the broadcast of exit polls. The production of a two-party system in Western democracies attests to binary regulation, which upholds a unitary market by *simulated opposition*. This is, according to Baudrillard (1994), the distribution of digital code as immanence. The binary series is reproduced and distributed as if it were a definitive model, as if it were a genetic code. Multiliteracies offers an alternative to these processes through the artificial construction of agency in design and the critical questioning of the power of the market through guided textual pedagogy. Cyberpunk literature denies the outward duality of the distribution of digital code through the media and in politics and consequent social control, because civil society has broken down in its fictional landscapes. The combination of cyberpunk with multiliteracies therefore acts as a pertinent device to constrain and act on the processes of digital duality that may be instigated by introducing computers into education.

The model of social control that one derives from Baudrillard (1993) is qualified by the "hyperrealism of simulation" (p. 198). The hyperreal works on the contradiction between the real and the imaginary—according to this idea, irreality no longer belongs to the dream or the phantasm or to a beyond or hidden interiority, but resides in the hallucinatory resemblance of the real itself. Science postulates that a process can be reproduced exactly within given conditions, with an industrial rationality that produces a universal system of equivalences. At the end of this process of reproducibility, the real is not only that which can be reproduced, but that which is already reproduced, i.e., the hyperreal. The hyperreal is analogous to the effect of an internal distance from a dream, allowing us to say that we are dreaming—hyperrealism is the play of censorship and the perpetuation of the dream, it is in the process of becoming an integral part of a coded reality that it perpetuates and leaves unaltered. Baudrillard (1993) speaks of the "aesthetic hallucination of reality which we are all living within" (p. 74). This is represented in cyberpunk literature and can be studied by using the multiliteracies framework to look at graphic novels or the presentation of videos on *YouTube*.

What is at stake in the theorization of the hyperreal by Baudrillard (1993) is parallel to the combined notion of agency in cyberpunk and multiliteracies. Baudrillard (1993) discusses the order of the technologically real, the aesthetic according to digital overload and submergence. This is the blind but brilliant ambience of the simulacra that sets up orders of existence, and becomes an effective "reality-diffractor" (Baudrillard, 1993, p. 78). Multiliteracies also requires an understanding of the ways in which multimodality acts to break up and redistribute reality—especially in the context of teaching and learning about text. Cyberpunk literature takes us on a journey through technologically mediated landscapes where orientation and freedom are intriguing and difficult to achieve.

The Story of Brithra

Brithra (a pseudonym) was a 15-year-old student at high school in the Midlands, UK when I met her during fieldwork for educational research. She was of north Indian descent, though she spoke with a heavy Midlands accent, and had been born and raised as a British-Indian girl. Brithra was part of the cohort that I was analyzing in terms of their literacy development and use of technology; she had been pointed out by an English teacher as being an exceptional student, who was also, however, "troubled." I spoke to her individually and was at once impressed by her articulation and curiosity. She was fascinated by my study, asked astute questions and gave in-depth answers to my questions, above and beyond the conjunction between identity development, literacy and the use of technology that I was exploring. Of all the students that I encountered in the research, I would like to suggest that she was the most "cyberpunk" and shows why the framework of multiliteracies should be expanded to include the types of agency that cyberpunk gives rise to.

Brithra described a moving story in one of our interviews covering her return to India and the social questions that this experience raised. This confrontation with poverty, disease and the masses of humanity on the Indian subcontinent had been an extremely powerful experience. The journey had caused Brithra to question many of the assumptions of life in the UK, and the previously comfortable nature of her existence. After this trip, she had become involved with homeless people, drug addicts and the unemployed. This young student wanted to help them and to change their lives. She spoke with disgust about individuals who were only driven by greed and the lust for money and power. Brithra had become politically active after her trip to India, and wanted to use technologies such as the Internet to get her message across. This usage was in contrast to the exercises that she was being set at school, which she found increasingly pointless and only useful in the competitive context of achieving qualifications to go on to further study at university. After my initial interview with Brithra and the group focus sessions, she disappeared from school for two weeks, sparking rumors amongst staff that she had overdosed on drugs.

Yet this was not the case. On her return to school, she presented me with a manuscript for a novella that she had been writing during her sojourn from organized educational life. She told me that a friend had a shed at the bottom of his garden and that she had used it as a writing den over the last fortnight. I had previously recommended Brithra extra curricula reading material (Conrad/Burroughs/J. G. Ballard, etc.) on her request that was far in advance of her designated literacy level. Perhaps these works had helped to inspire and encouraged her to write about her immediate reality, and had provided some ideas for the novella she had written. Brithra consequently sent the manuscript to a publisher and had it accepted, becoming the youngest female published author of Indian descent in the UK at the time.

Several years later I heard from Brithra again—by email. She had been enrolled to study at an exclusive woman's college at Oxford University. This exceptional individual shows how the conception of agency that one places at the heart of an educational framework needs to be open to perturbation. If multiliteracies is normalizing, it will exclude those who reach beyond everyday expectations—in particular those who change the rules by which social life is governed will be ostracized. Brithra may not have been consciously designing her social future through design, but she was heavily involved at a young age with powerful social forces, and she was able to express their confluence in language.

The Agency of Techno-tribalism and Multiliteracies

The society that we now live in is characterized by the use of digital technology at work, in schools and in our social lives. These dramatic changes in the ways that we communicate, learn, socialize and work are setting up new orders of emergence and instability, and the re-evaluation of values and digitally mediated "difference" (St. John, 2004). To understand how these comprehensive changes may be fed into relevant notions of agency for education, one may turn to sociologists such as Michel Maffesoli (1996), who has theorized the rise of tribal formations in modern society, and has used the idea of "proxemics" (p. 23)—proximate collective values. From the perspective of proxemics, societies share their values through social vitalism—in terms of technological development, the growth of urbanization has encouraged a "computerized palaver" (p. 25). Maffesoli (1996) has noted, ironically, that within the new urban settings there is a troublesome ambiguity; he has stated that although embracing the most sophisticated technology, the new urban societies remain nonetheless barbaric. The translation of desires into the construction of reality is not, however, a "one-to-one" translation (A-a, B-b, etc.), as the logic of the electronic networks within contemporary masses has also led to depersonalization and "disindividuation," which can only be analyzed from the general perspective of "ambience" or *Stimmung* (A-x, B-y, etc.) (Simmel, 1984, pp. 75–103). This is, to a certain extent, an "effect of composition" or *Zusammenschluss* of the complex networks, where individual intentionalities are mixed up in the process of interaction, the group coming to the fore through the *exis* and *habitus* as has been described by Mauss (1979).

Such an analysis of contemporary society has important consequences for the multiliteracies framework. Agency as design is not an individualizing notion, but should lead to the communal and social construction of meaning. Yet in a techno-tribal context, as theorized by Maffesoli (1996), the content of design is derived from a proximate web of connections and ambient crossover themes. For example, if a middle-school class are engaged in a project about urban renewal in their area, the ideas that they will produce will be mediated by the ways in which the group may use electronic technology and agree about their findings to construct urban growth. The students may view successful urban projects from around the world via the Internet, which may include a return to more ecological or environmental values. Yet the ways in which the group will represent these values will be transformed and adjusted to their own sets of imaginative recreations of the information that they have digested. Motifs from their sense of lifestyle taken from artificial "media-scapes" will be incorporated into their plans—for example, stage sets from music videos or popular films. As such, techno-tribalism will be represented through the agency of the project, and the ways in which the group are able to represent their combined identities during the course of constructing new ways of living.

Electronic tribalism was also theorized by Joshua Meyrowitz (1986). He characterized the social implications of electronic media as constituting "hunters and gatherers in an information age." It could be stated that his theorization of contemporary techno-tribal society is a qualified return to an age prior to the late Middle Ages that circumvents a fall into Romanticism that dominates many of the value systems of a sedentary and colonizing West (Meyrowitz, 1986, pp. 110–117). For example, in terms of the family unit, a lack of boundaries in the electronic universe and the hunter-gatherer tribes are in contrast to the (modernist) nuclear family. The nuclear family is constituted by restricted spaces, requiring an obedient wife to serve a patriarchal husband, who bring up children to be molded in similar double filiations. Literacy has played a large part in the maintenance and institutionalization of the nuclear family, as the ideology that it embodies requires linear progression from one word, phrase, paragraph or book to the next (Millard, 1997). The social consequences of literacy posits *sequence*, which is the binding power behind chains of command from "God-the-father" to "pagan children"; or from strong national leaders capable of wielding text as the law to malleable masses. Reading has separated and individualized a system of teaching and learning into its "educated parts," which show their distinctions through the ways in which they are able to communicate (Annadale, Bindon, Handley, Johnston, Lockett & Lynch, 2004). In contrast, in the present digital information era, with its multi-divergent communication options, the binding power of the literary pyramid is beginning to unravel. Boundary lines between systems such as the public and the private, the domestic and the political or the family and community, are being blurred by the inter-relation of media systems. This "crisis" of social breakdown is perhaps also the rediscovery of a different type of socialization that one may call the techno-tribe.

Multiliteracies absorbs the movement into techno-tribalism in terms of the ways in which it encourages social organization through the agency of design. As has been stated in the cyberpunk section, agency as design introduces a certain tension into this knowledge framework in terms of the allowances and affordances that design gives rise to. For example, fast capitalism will certainly vie to take over the agency of students learning through design by introducing products and services into streams of digital information and the exchange value that one might ascribe to any educational activity. Multiliteracies may counter this tendency with criticality and reflexive processes, yet even these may be packaged and redistributed as new ways to learn! In effect, the multiliteracies framework needs a sociological context and tendential marker in order that design as agency may be "steered." Techno-tribalism as theorized by Maffesoli (1996) and Meyrowitz (1986) may be used as such a steering device for multiliteracies, as they posit social characteristics into the educational frame. Techno-tribalism takes multiliteracies into a different space that is occupied by new ways of teaching and learning and consequently altered social organization.

The list of ways that society may change due to the influence of techno-tribalism is long, but may be clarified by the division of labor, which is less marked in hunter-gatherer societies. In these societies, women may hunt, men will tend the home, both men and women are expected to be gentle, mild-mannered and non-competitive (O'Kelly, 1980, pp. 82–100). A lack of privacy according to the tenets of techno-tribalism leads to communal control over private arguments. Children are not artificially isolated from adult activities; self-reliance is stressed rather than obedience to adults; physical punishment is not usually used (O'Kelly, 1980, p. 98). Play and work are not discretely separated, but merge in similar moments of mimicry, experimentation and fun. Electronic media also present the opportunity for work and play to be tightly woven. For example, computer hackers often turn out to be the best programmers; gamers may come up with the best ideas for designing new environments on the Internet. In terms of social and educational organization, leadership is set into the hunter-gatherer community as a whole, and it is not something "apart" from the everyday working of the community. Hunter-gatherer social and sexual instincts develop matrilineal and fluid social arrangements; marriage may break down as "social cement," and should be reinvented without the pertinence of permanent, binary attachment (Goodale, 1971).

An application of computer coding mechanisms that is relevant to the theory of techno-tribalism and a tendential marker for multiliteracies appears in the simulation of prehistoric hunter-gatherer societies. Simulations have been appearing since Thomas (1972), and are based on reconstructed hunter-gather environments—the probability of behavior may be modeled by using Markov transition matrices and data gathered from necessary food sources, weather factors and the predictability of the seasons. The simulation of extinct Pleistocene species such as the woolly mammoth or woolly rhinoceros do provide programmers with the challenge of incorporating archaeological evidence with behavior based on counterparts such as the modern-day elephant or rhinoceros. It has been argued that whole ecological communities of the

Pleistocene epoch, including fauna, hunter–game relationships and herd activities, are so different from the modern understanding of them that simulation is impossible, or at least subject to a zonation which has yet to be achieved (Guthrie, 1984). Amongst those simulations which have been tried, foraging efficiency is often used as the decision goal for simulated human forages (Reynolds, 1986; Aldenderfer, 1978; Mithen, 1990). Mithen (1990) makes it plain that his efficiency is based on Darwinian principles, in that being an efficient forager is a proximate means by which hunters gain reproductive success since it improves their capacity to compete for mates. The information flow is included in the movement algorithm by Aldenderfer (1978), which assumes that the foragers will internally know all that is necessary to gain maximal movement. Reynolds (1986) uses the notion of a "multigenerational memory" (p. 8) that selects strategies for the most efficient hunting and plant-collecting techniques. Thus, through time the foragers learn communally how best to adapt and survive in their environment. This expansive notion includes myth, the arts, ritual and story-telling, and in so doing prioritizes the flow of information in hunter-gather society as being central to foraging activities. Mithen (1990) does not employ such a notion, but integrates information flows into the ability of groups and individuals to estimate the previous day's foraging success. Based on the information gained from that excursion, the foragers will alter their behavior accordingly, and either continue with their previous activity, or revert to some other type of hunter-gatherer behavior. Consensus in this instance is predicated on success.

The challenge for the next generation of computer-generated hunter-gather societies is to make the processes of foraging and decision-making not just reactive to nature. The multi-generational memory of Reynolds (1986) would seem to offer one the best "engines" whereby the movements of human culture could be modeled; yet the complex nexus of libidinal leverage (Mithen, 1994), movement co-ordination (Aldenderfer, 1978) and cultural retrieval and dispersal (Reynolds, 1986) are an unstable patterning focus, not directly locatable in psychological or sociological study. As Shennan (1992) has argued, the modeling of group behavior depends upon the simulation of cultural transmission, so that the spread through time of the environmental, technological and material ideas may therefore be presented. The cultural transmission of prehistoric hunter-gather society also requires the analysis of ancient types of oral culture: e.g., shamanism, non-literal animisms, African religions such as the Dogon, Akan, Fon, Mende, Yoruba, Zande, Dinka, Nuere and Shilluk. With these types of transmission modeled, the flow of hunter-gatherer human beings may be more precisely modeled, and large portions of human history will become analyzable and useful in the present digitally mediated learning context that demarcates a transition to techno-tribalism and a knowledge base for multiliterate educational practice.

Free-party Organization in the Midlands, UK

I became aware during technological literacy research that many of the 15–18-year-old students that I was analyzing at school were also involved with free-parties. I found that outside of the institutional context, they were working together in coordinated teams to organize raves. These were "outlaw" events as the Conservative government of Margaret Thatcher had passed stringent laws that banned any gatherings of people and amplified repetitive-beat music not contained in licensed nightclubs. The free-party young people therefore used the Internet, mobile phones and pre-recorded messages to distribute the place of the rave, but only on the night that it was due to take place. This strategy was to avoid detection by the police, and any consequent disruption to the event. The organizers were also adept at finding "hidden" places in the English countryside that could accommodate the large gatherings of up to a thousand ravers.

The free-party organization included DJ music specialists, transport, lighting and decorations, music system technicians, marketing and security. The teams were blended groups of different ages, sexes and ethnicities. In contrast to the streamed and separate cohorts at school, the free-party units represented a convergent situation of technical skill and social force. The "youth" taking part in the free-parties, far from being virtually powerless players in a state-organized game of qualifications and jobs, were now in control of their activities. One should not, however, idealize the situation—arguments, power games and ego trips were also part of the free-party scene. Yet free party raves do serve as a way of understanding the type of techno-tribalism that is relevant as a social tendency and way of introducing content into the multiliteracies knowledge and pedagogic framework.

The techno-tribalism of free-party organization is essentially collective (Cole, 2007b). In contrast to achieving pre-tertiary qualifications, the skills necessary to be part of free-party structures cannot be found in textbooks. The ability to interpret and use codes is still prevalent in terms of making practical arrangements and using technology for celebratory purposes, yet one does not have to reproduce these skills to receive quantifiable results. Multiliteracies may be deployed in this context, as free-party organization is about designing social futures. The values, culture and emergent society that has developed around free-parties represent a purposeful deployment of technology to enhance social life. The agents taking part in the parties learn: to work together towards a definite goal, how group dynamics operate, and what conditions are necessary for a rave. These ranges of abilities do change the scope and direction of the civic orientation of the original multiliteracies formula (New London Group, 1996), but in a rapidly changing context of techno-tribalism, new social literacies of this kind may be the key to future success.

Conclusion

This chapter has explored how the embodiment of agency can be used to create meaningful literacy experiences. Through the notion of cyberpunk and techno-tribalism, new options for the agency of multiliteracies have been described. In particular, the chapter has provided examples of how individuals and groups of learners can use and appreciate the ability to personalize and adapt technologies to suit their own individual and cultural purposes—which in turn give new meanings to the technology and the literacy encounter. As such, the notion of agency in a multiliteracies framework enables the user or instructor to tailor the teaching and learning experiences to suit the particular requirements of the learning situation. In effect, the concept of agency allows individuals to act and react in a goal-directed fashion (Leslie, 1994). Within a communication system, the notion of language, whether that be written, spoken or tactile, is an ever-changing entity. For instance, the descriptions of cyberpunk and techno-tribalism in this chapter convey how the uses of language that are the synchronic (the conditions for existence of any language system) and the diachronic (the changes which take place in or to a language over time) change as a result of an individuals' agency.

In summary, the agency of multiliteracies enables literacy practice to be viewed as being embedded in social practice and cultural processes, as demonstrated by the entities of cyberpunks and techno-tribalism. This chapter has used the multiliteracies framework to illustrate how literacy learning is more than a focus on the individual attainment of "outcomes" to one where the emphasis is on embracing a participatory process that has relevance to the social community to which the learners belong. While we are not discounting the importance of schooling, we are merely pointing out that literacy acquisition is a lifelong process of acquisition, maintenance and transmission that can occur in any place and through any medium—digital or analog. So, the challenge for educators and schools is to teach in ways that are relevant and explicit to support all students, particularly those at risk, and pedagogies based on a multiliteracies framework provide an effective starting point for the development of literacies that are both critical and purposeful. Such an approach requires a reconsideration of personal and social agency, together with the recognition that the term "literate" is so much more than the ability to read and write. Rather, to be literate in the digital age requires experience and opportunities to actively engage with a number of literacy modes, as has been demonstrated in this chapter through the examples of cyberpunk and techno-tribalism.

Note

1. Sections of the arguments in this chapter have been taken from: Cole, D. R. (2005). Education and the politics of cyberpunk. *Review of Education Pedagogy and Cultural Studies*, 27(2), 159–170.

References

Aldenderfer, M. (1978). Creating assemblages by computer simulation: The development and uses of ABSIM. In J. Sabloff (Ed.), *Simulations in archaeology* (pp. 67–117). Albuquerque: University of New Mexico Press.

Annadale, K., Bindon, R., Handley, K., Johnston, A., Lockett, L., & Lynch, P. (2004). *Reading map of development: Second edition addressing current literacy challenges.* Port Melbourne: Reed International Books Australia Pty.

Apple, M. (1992). Is new technology part of the solution or part of the problem in education? In J. Beynon & H. Mackay (Eds.), *Technological literacy and the curriculum* (pp. 105–124). London: Falmer Press.

Baudrillard, J. (1983). *Simulations* (P. Foss, P. Patton & P. Beitchman, Trans.). New York: Semiotext(e).

Baudrillard, J. (1993). *Symbolic exchange and death* (I. H. Grant, Trans.). London: Sage Publications.

Baudrillard, J. (1994). *The illusion of the end.* Oxford: Polity Press.

Bourdieu, P. (1980). *Outline of a theory of practices* (R. Nice, Trans.). Cambridge: Cambridge University Press.

Bourdieu, P., & Passeron, J. C. (1979). *Reproduction in education: Society and culture.* Los Angeles: Sage Publications.

Bromley, H., & Apple, M. (Eds.). (1998). *Education/technology/power: Educational computing as social practice.* Albany: State University of New York Press.

Castells, M. (1996). *The rise of the network society: The information age: Economy, society and culture, Volume 1.* Cambridge, MA: Blackwell Publishers.

Castells, M. (1997). *The power of identity: The information age: Economy, society and culture, Volume 2.* Cambridge, MA: Blackwell Publishers.

Clark, N. (1995). The recursive generation of the cyberbody. In M. Featherstone & R. Burrows (Eds.), *Cyberspace/cyberbodies/cyberpunk* (pp. 159–170). London: Sage.

Cole, D. R. (2005a). Reading in the future: Literacy and the time of the Internet. *Reconstruction,* 5(2), EJ. Retrieved December 1, 2008 from http://reconstruction.eserver.org/052/cole.shtml.

Cole, D. R. (2005b). Learning through the virtual. *CTHEORY,* 1, EJ. Retrieved December 10, 2008, from www.ctheory.net/articles.aspx?id=445.

Cole, D. R. (2005c). Education and the politics of cyberpunk. *Review of Education Pedagogy and Cultural Studies,* 27(2), 159–170.

Cole, D. R. (2007a). Virtual terrorism and the Internet e-learning options. *E-Learning,* 4(2), 116–127.

Cole, D. R. (2007b). Techno-shamanism and educational research. *Ashe! Journal of Experimental Spirituality,* 6(1). Retrieved January 6, 2009, from http://ashejournal.com/index.php?id=277.

Cope, B., & Kalantzis, M. (Eds.). (2000). *Multiliteracies: Literacy learning and the design of social futures.* Victoria, Australia: Macmillan.

Csicsery-Ronay, I. (1991). Cyberpunk and neuromanticism. In L. McCaffrey (Ed.), *Storming the reality studio* (pp. 101–131). Durham: Duke University Press.

Davis, B., & Sumara, D. (2006). *Complexity and education: Inquiries into learning, teaching, and research.* Mahwah, NJ: Erlbaum.

Deleuze, G., & Guattari, F. (1984). *Anti-Oedipus: Capitalism and schizophrenia* (R. Hurley, M. Seem & H. R. Lane, Trans.). London: Athlone Press.

Deleuze, G., & Guattari, F. (1987). *A thousand plateaus: Capitalism and schizophrenia Part 2* (B. Massumi, Trans.). London: Athlone Press.
Dewey, J. (1966). *Education and democracy.* New York: The Free Press.
Exley, B. (2008). Communities of learners: Early years students, new learning pedagogy, and transformations. In A. Healy (Ed.), *Multiliteracies and diversity in education: New pedagogies for expanding landscapes* (pp. 126–144). South Melbourne: Oxford University Press.
Gee, J. (2005). Semiotic social spaces and affinity spaces: From the age of mythology to today's schools. In D. Barton & K. Tusting (Eds.), *Beyond communities of practice: Language, power, and social context* (pp. 214–232). Cambridge: Cambridge University Press.
Gibson, W. (1984). *Neuromancer.* London: HarperCollins.
Gibson, W. (1985). *Mona Lisa Overdrive.* London: HarperCollins.
Goodale, J. C. (1971). *Tiwi wives: A study of the women of Melville Island, North Australia.* Seattle: University of Washington Press.
Guthrie, R. D. (1984). Mosaics, allelochemicals and nutrients: An ecological theory of late Pleistocene extinctions. In P. S. Martin & R. G. Klein (Eds.), *Quaternary extinctions: A prehistoric revolution* (pp. 259–298). Tucson: University of Arizona Press.
Jameson, F. (1991). *Postmodernism: Or, the cultural logic of late capitalism.* London: Verso.
Kahn, R., & Kellner, D. (2005). Reconstructing technoliteracy: A multiple literacy approach. *E-Learning,* 2(3), EJ.
Kellner, D. (2002). Theorising globalisation. *Sociological theory,* 20(3), 285–305.
Kroker, A., & Cook, D. (1988). *The post-modern scene: Excremental culture and hyper-aesthetics.* London: Macmillan Education Ltd.
Leslie, A. (1994). ToMM, ToBy, and agency: Core architecture and domain specificity. In L. Hirschfeld & S. Gelman (Eds.), *Mapping the mind: Domain specificity in cognition and culture* (pp. 119–148). Cambridge: Cambridge University Press.
Luke, A., & Luke, C. (2001). Adolescence lost/childhood regained: On early intervention and the emergence of the techno-subject. *Journal of Early Childhood Literacy,* 1(1), 91–120.
Lyotard, J. F. (1984). *The post-modern condition: A report on knowledge* (G. Bennington & B. Massumi, Trans.). Minneapolis: University of Minnesota Press.
Lyotard, J. F. (1993). *Libidinal economy* (I. H. Grant, Trans.). London: Athlone Press.
McLuhan, M. (1965). *Understanding media: The extensions of man.* New York: McGraw-Hill.
Maffesoli, M. (1996). *The time of the tribes: The decline of individualism in mass society* (D. Smith, Trans.). London: Sage Publications.
Marshall, J. D. (1996). *Michel Foucault: Personal autonomy and education.* London: Kluwer Academic.
Mauss, M. (1979). *Sociology and psychology.* London: Routledge and Kegan Paul.
Meyrowitz, J. (1986). *No sense of place: The impact of electronic media on social behavior.* Oxford: Oxford University Press.
Millard, E. (1997). *Differently literate.* London: Falmer Press.
Mithen, S. J. (1990). *Thoughtful forages: A study of prehistoric decision making.* Cambridge: Cambridge University Press.
Mithen, S. J. (1994). Simulating prehistoric hunter-gatherer societies. In N. Gilbert & J. Doran (Eds.), *Simulating societies: The computer simulation of social phenomena* (pp. 165–195). London: University College London Press.

Nietzsche, F. (1968). *Twilight of the idols and the Anti-Christ* (R. J. Hollingdale, Trans.). London: Penguin Books.

New London Group. (1996). A pedagogy of multiliteracies: Designing social futures. *Harvard Educational Review*, 66, 60–92.

O'Kelly, C. G. (1980). *Women and men in society*. New York: Van Nostrand.

Reynolds, R. G. (1986). An adaptive computer model for the evolution of plant collecting and early agriculture in the Eastern Valley of Oaxaca, Mexico. In K. V. Flannery (Ed.), *Quila Naquitz: Archaic foraging and early agriculture in Oaxaca* (pp. 298–316). Mexico: Academic.

Ross, A. (1991). *Strange weather: Culture, science, and technology in the age of limits*. London: Verso Press.

St. John, G. (Ed.). (2004). *Rave culture and religion*. London and New York: Routledge.

Shennan, S. (1992). Tradition, rationality and cultural transmission. In R. Preucel (Ed.), *Processual & post-processual archaeology: The current debate* (pp. 197–208). Carbondale: Centre of Archaeological Investigations.

Simmel, G. (1984). Les problèmes de la philosophie de l'histoire. Paris: PUF.

Stoer, S. R., & Amagalhaes, A. M. (2004). Education, knowledge and the network society. *Globalisation, Societies and Education*. 2(3), 319–335.

Street, B. (2000). Literary events and literacy practices. In M. Martin-Jones & K. Jones (Eds.), *Multilingual literacies: Comparative perspectives on research and practice* (pp. 17–29). Amsterdam: John Benjamin's.

Thomas, D. (1972). A computer simulation model of Great Basin Shoshonean settlement patterns. In D. Clarke (Ed.), *Models in archaeology* (pp. 671–704). London: Methuen.

Waldrop, M. M. (1993). *Complexity*. London: Viking.

Wilden, A. (1972). *Systems and structure: Essays in communication & exchange*. London: Tavistock Publications.

7 Multiliteracies and the Politics of Desire

David R. Cole, University of Technology, Sydney

Introduction

The notion of multiliteracies (New London Group, 1996) was designed as a call for change in the field of literacy education. This was in part sparked by the push of media systems into education. These systems have in turn been driven by new digital technology that simultaneously acts as a divergent manner of communicating that extends literacy from simple reading and writing dualisms and into multimodality, and as a means of surveillance (Cole, 2007). This chapter deals with the second tendency in post-industrial civilization, that of cybernetic information distribution and retrieval. Computers in classrooms free students up in terms of their representational capacities. They also makes everything students do electronically "trackable." This control factor embedded in digital technology, combined with the spread of media into most aspects of everyday life, has given rise to a new form of moral perception. This chapter will explore this perception by building a perspective that deals with the moral perceptions of teachers' work in terms of the body and the processes inherent within a teacher's body under pressure from external surveillance and internal desire. The teacher's body in this chapter is a construction that is suitable for the contemporary politics of desire that allows for multiliterate pedagogy given the conception of bodily design.

"Sex Teacher Guilty"

The above heading was the front-page banner headline of a recent local newspaper in Australia. These words are also part of a global discourse that is appearing in the media about teachers having sexual relationships with students. On the same day, while waiting to have my hair cut, I read an article in *Marie Claire* (2007) that discussed and pictured specifically female teachers who have been accused of having affairs with their students. This chapter will not address the gender divide in public perception about teachers' sexual activity. Rather, it will look at this phenomenon as a contemporary cultural construction, and add to Elspeth Probyn's point that, "it's rare to find discussions of what concepts of body actually do within the classroom: rare, that is, outside of the pathological—'the lecherous professor' (O'Brien, 2000)" (Probyn, 2004, p. 33).

I will step around the pathological description of transgressive teachers (Gallop, 1994, 1995, 1997) and build a perspective that helps to explain the current hysterical enactment of teachers' desire within the context of multiliteracies. This perspective will address the affective nature of the educational body, and keep "the magic or chemistry that seems so elusive to any systemization," and that actually composes, "the bodies of teaching and learning" (Probyn, 2004, p. 37). Any passionate teacher will understand the emotional state when their body is tied to the rhythms and pulses of the assembled group. This is a state of animation and affective potential (Spivak, 1993) that I will draw on through this chapter in terms of constructing a "teacher's body" that works in the contemporary global context of media surveillance and situates the teacher within multiliterate desires—and not specific fears about sexual proclivity:

> at the same time the lapcourt schoolmaster was instructing the little villagers to mind their language and not to talk about all these (sexual) things aloud. But this was undoubtedly one of the conditions enabling the institutions of knowledge and power to overlay this everyday bit of theatre with their solemn discourse. So it was that our society—and it was doubtless the first in history to take such measures—assembled around these timeless gestures, these barely furtive pleasures between simple-minded adults and alert children, a whole machinery for "speechifying," analyzing and investigating. Incitements to speak were orchestrated from all quarters, apparatuses everywhere for listening and recording, procedures for observing, questioning and formulating. From this singular imperialism that compels everyone to transform their sexuality into a perpetual discourse, to the manifold mechanisms which, in the areas of economy, pedagogy, medicine, and justice; incite, extract, distribute, and institutionalize the sexual discourse, an immense verbosity is what our civilization has required and organized.
>
> (Foucault, 1978, pp. 32–33)

Moving Places—The Speeds of Multiliteracies

The mechanics of moral perceptivity of sexual behavior in educational situations is therefore not new. What is new is the speed and degree of access that digital technology enables in terms of surveillance of the body. To counteract these enabling conditions one requires a perspective that uses multiliteracies in order to regain the real body of the teacher—complete with their desires. Elizabeth Grosz (1994), in her *Volatile Bodies*, has composed a body that may be used for these purposes, and to more fully understand a teacher's body that can deal with contemporary affective pressures. This body is open to the dispersion of discontinuity, and to the distinct transformations that happen at the level of discourse (p. 34). It is a figure that is a discontinuous, non-totalizable series of processes, organs, flows, energies, corporeal substances and incorporeal events, speeds and durations. This body is outside of the binary oppositions that can be imposed on it, such as mind–body, nature–culture, subject–object and interior–exterior. This teacher's body may be understood specifically in terms of "what it can do"—the things which it can perform, the linkages it may establish, the transformations and becomings it undergoes, the machinic connections it forms with other bodies, what it links with, how it proliferates and its capacities. Grosz's (1994) body is a rare and affirmative understanding of the body, parallel in kind to the communicative cyborg of Haraway (1991), yet inscribed by education in terms of power and gender. This messy, moving picture of the teacher's body opens up the space into which heterogeneous elements may rush *around/through/in/on/out* of it. This body does not establish hierarchies away from a fixed position. It is not sexually neutral, as Braidotti (1991, p. 121) has argued, nor is it the projection and fantasy of woman's sexuality turned psychotic, as Irigaray (1985a, p. 141) has stated. Questions of sexuality are turned multiple through Grosz's body; these questions are fields of becoming, where the sexual norms are not directly approached. As Grosz (1994) puts it, this is a maneuver that "desexualizes and obfuscates one of the major features of phallocentric thought—its subsumption of two sexual symmetries under a single norm" (p. 163). The teacher's body in multiliterate situations takes on a chaotic sexuality, and is far from passive as it defies determination by actively following the powers of formation and the scattering of discourse (Cole, 2009).

Foucault's (1978) *History of Sexuality* looked at the body in terms of the censors that have impinged upon it. The various discourses and legal sanctions against minor perversions were multiplied, sexual irregularity was annexed to fit in with mental illness—from childhood to old age, a norm of sexual development was defined, and all the possible deviations were carefully described. Pedagogic controls and medical treatments were organized around the slightest fantasies, as Foucault (1978) terms it, they "brandished the whole emphatic vocabulary of abomination" (p. 36). As the powers of control advanced and multiplied their relays and effects, their target also expanded, subdivided and branched out, penetrating further into reality at the same pace. In appearance, we are dealing with a barrier system in terms of talking about teachers' sexuality, but in fact all around the child indefinite *lines of penetration* have been disposed to give access to the child's intimate thoughts (Foucault, 1978). Educational thinkers are caught in this matrix of dispersive functioning when examining the development of the child. For example, Aronowitz and Giroux (1985) have called for a critical psychology, which points to the way in which "un-freedom" reproduces itself in the human psyche.[1] Their hope is that this analysis will reveal how dominant ideologies have prevented the many-faceted needs of the oppressed from being realized, or, to understand how hegemonic ideologies function to exclude oppressed groups from creating needs that extend beyond the instrumental logic of the market. This call to arms around the needs of the oppressed has been previously theorized through Freire's (1972) *Pedagogy of the Oppressed.* In this work, the oppressed minorities are posited with the aim of releasing their capacities into the mainstream educational debate. The figure of the teacher's body is crucial in a perspective that could "make a difference"—but by constituting this body in terms of oppression, emancipation, freedom, resistance or struggle, one potentially sets up a locus of becoming which vibrates between the two poles of positive and negative enaction of liberation—and this is what I am arguing against in this chapter, as it is ineffective in a multiliterate environment. By theorizing the teacher's body as has been proposed by Grosz (1994), without fixed boundaries to describe it, we have a perspective that may avoid the oscillation between the rights of the weak and the manipulation of the strong. This plane of the teacher's body interacts with discourse through ruptures and bifurcation: it exists in the flux of pixels in multiliteracies and rides on waves of interference—it experiences a tempestuous and multidimensional journey in and out of education through the speeds contained in digital technology.

The Unknown Pleasures of Multiliteracies

The interactive game between discourse and the teacher's body that defines the focus of this chapter about multiliteracies and desire has been played with great intensity, especially since the intervention of psychoanalysis. Foucault (1978) has spoken about capture and seduction, confrontation and mutual reinforcement between educators and students, doctors and patients, the psychiatrist with his hysteric and his perverts (p. 45). These are the attractions and evasions, the circular incitements that have been traced around bodies and sexes that have not simply produced restricted boundaries, but spirals of power and pleasure. Thus are located sites of intensity in which regimes of discourse structure themselves. Furthermore, discourses themselves are pleasurable. The pleasure of tying up a teacher's body in educational parameters (even if they are multiliterate ones), of structuring the body's emergence with goals, targets, standards, mimetic loops, and channels of knowledge, freedom or the truth, locates and constructs the institutions within which these games are played out. The large populations of educational and psychiatric institutions—with their hierarchies, spatial arrangements and surveillance systems—have constituted alongside the family, other ways of distributing the interplay of power and pleasure. They also delineate areas of extreme saturation, with their privileged spaces and rituals—for example, the classroom, the dormitory, the visit, the consultation (Foucault, 1978, p. 46).

Luce Irigaray (1985b) has taken up the issue of pleasure and power through an analysis of Freud and Lacan. Freud (1953–1974, Vol. 22), who worked with concepts drawn from Goethe, set up the nature of the feminine as a riddle and as the ineffable (p. 113). Freud posits sexual difference in terms of that which is the object of investigation, yet it is mired in the infallible discrimination of the feminine. Irigaray (1985b) questions this infallible discrimination, this process of production and reproduction, and this expectation of a discovery of an unknown that defines the objectivity of scientific analysis in terms of anatomical discourse as far as sexual difference is concerned (p. 15). Freud worked to establish psychoanalysis as a scientific study that investigated the dynamics of sexual difference, laying hold of the unknown characteristic of the feminine. Irigaray (1985b) characterizes this as a type of "zoology" (p. 16), always looking for a counter example of behavior that would dissuade one of a former opinion—for example, a spider eating her mate, male lions rearing the young and the females hunting. In other words, the scientists are confused in their search for criteria about sexual difference. Yet they continue regardless, ignoring the rupture in their thinking—they substitute the pleasure of discourse for the pleasure of the subconscious. With all this sexual differentiation going on in nature, the only recourse for the scientists is to some micro-process that could salvage the project in terms of credible scientific investigation. Sexuality is thereafter aligned to the reproductive function. As a result of this alignment, the power of the patriarchal hegemony with all its deferrals and footnotes, and its "other" suggestions that define scientific validity—takes hold of the discourse, and by degrees, the reproductive function (Irigaray, 1985b, p. 19).

According to Irigaray (1985b), the economy of sexual reproduction creates mimes and stages plays. This aids the phallic order in its production of the same. The smoke screen of the reasoning defines the nexus of a bisexual pleasure center, notable for its masculine masochism—the following of the arguments of sexual differentiation is a perverse pleasure parameter, a constitution of power exactly on that which it tries to explain (heterosexuality). Strategies to avoid this heterosexual play of illusion include Butler's (1990) "subversive bodily acts" (pp. 79–141). She has used the writings of Kristeva (1980), Foucault (1978) and Wittig (1986) in order to displace the heterosexual matrix that dominates variations in sexual orientation. The tactics employed include the blurring and confusion of any sense of the term identity; this is in order to articulate the convergence of multiple sexual discourses on the site of identity, and thus to render it permanently problematic (as in multiliteracies). This, following on from the work of Lacan, where most categories are merged in the imaginary, is eminently achievable, yet with respect to the drives of Freud, perhaps does not serve as an adequate methodology for avoiding its reproductive and productive power relations, which assume the multiple variation of sexual identity from the start. The hierarchies which need to be avoided are those which would reinstitute sexual difference in another order, and in so doing retain the same mechanisms for institutionalization. Grosz (1994) has offered a potent critique in her theorization of the body, and the understanding of Freudian drives that takes the processes of the teacher's body as constituting an active plane of inscription in the contemporary multiliterate world.

Grosz (1994) has argued that Freud produces a series of displacements of the biological, modifying the ways in which biology is generally conceived, showing its susceptibility to the psychological rather than assuming a rift between them, as occurs in Cartesian notions of mind and body (p. 28). The surface of the teacher's body figured as a screen provides a ground for the articulation of orifices, erotogenic rims, cuts on the body's surface and the loci of exchange between the inside and the outside. These are sites not only for the reception and transmission of information, but also for bodily secretion, ongoing processes of sensory stimulation that require some form of signification and socio-cultural and psychical representation that is the autoeroticism of the body. These cuts on the teacher's body's surface create a type of landscape of that surface, which provides it with regions, zones, an uneven distribution of intensities and erotic investments in the teacher's body: i.e., the tendency towards body-art and markings (Grosz, 1994, p. 36). Freud's (1953–1974, Vol. 19) ego is an internal screen onto which the illuminated and projected images of the teacher's body's outer surface are directed (p. 25). It is the site for the gathering together and the unification of otherwise disparate and scattered sensations provided by the various sense organs. It is also a mapping of the teacher's body's inner surface, the surface of sensations, intensities and affects, the "subjective experience" of bodily sensations. The ego is derived from these two kinds of surfaces: the inner surface of psychical agencies and the outer surface of the projection or representation of the teacher's body's surface. Both surfaces are perceptual, and in the establishment of the ego, perceptual processes are sexualized and become a libidinal investment (Grosz, 1994, p. 38). The notion of the teacher's body as a whole is dependent on the recognition of the totality and autonomy of the teacher's body to "the other"—but not in a limited or singular sense as in Plato's cave. This cultural dimension implies that teachers' bodies, egos and subjectivities are not simply reflections of their cultural context and associated values, but are constituted as such by them marking teachers' bodies with "biological" configuration and socio-sexual inscriptions, as is happening in the media and through multiliteracies.

The ego, rather than representing the division between the feminine and the masculine in this schema, becomes the location for the contestation with the patriarchal formulation of the teacher's body. The reconstitution of the teacher's body through multiliteracies depends upon the throwing into relief of the processes that transcribe it. Freud's drives and instincts, which manifest an immense sexuality across every function of the body, cannot be diverted by the realignment of one or many of their distinctions, conjunctions, enactments or mergers. Irigaray (1985b) recognized this and looked at the discourse of psychoanalysis in terms of the ruptures and discontinuities that imply bodily process, and the connection between these processes and their reproduction. For example, she questioned the tying of anatomical references to the development of sexuality and the issue of reproduction. She asked, "What would happen when the sexual function is separated from the reproductive function?" (p. 71). Grosz (1994) looked at the rewriting of the female body, and by degrees the teacher's body, in multiliteracies in two ways:

(1) reorganizing and reframing the terms by which the body has been socially represented; and (2) challenging the discourses which claim to analyze and explain the body and subject scientifically: i.e., biology, psychology and sociology (Foucault, 1970).

Multiliterate Contiguity

Svi Shapiro (1995), in response to Alston's (1995) paper on multiculturalism, has positioned rationality as being no match for the raging, existentially hungry, desirous being of the body as it is presented in the media (p. 301) and by degrees through multiliteracies. This author looked forward to an educational discourse which embraces the desire of the teacher's body, and which sets up a space in which sensual language may live in education. Irigaray's (1985a, 1985b) language, still dancing in the psychoanalytic spectrum, alights on the skin of the teacher's body where fantasies abound, and where we find the locus of *contiguity*. According to Irigaray (1985b), the main theoretical concepts of psychoanalysis have taken no account of woman's desire, not even of her castrations (p. 55). The ways of psychoanalysis are derived from the history of male sexuality. Without knowing it, the woman is the place for the inscription of representations—she provides a basis for such fantasies as the amputation of her sex organ, and in a perverse deal, the anatomy of her body is put up as the security for reality. The images of her sex and organs, and her generalized body, are despoiled from the start by male-dominated discourse. The castration of the woman is taken back into the processes of the body undergoing psychoanalysis by the father of psychoanalysis (Freud). This censorship extends to all areas of sexual activity, masturbation coming in for particular attention, signification and sublimation (Irigaray, 1985b, p. 65).

The "fact of castration," as Freud (1953–1974, Vol. 19, p. 52) has termed it, has to be understood as a definitive prohibition against establishing a woman's own economy for the desire of origin. Hence the hole, the lack, the fault or the castration that greets the little girl as she enters as a subject into representative systems. This is the assumption governing her appearance upon the scene of presence, where neither her libido, nor her sex and organs have any right to truth, except the truth that casts her as a less than, or the other side of the equation. According to Irigaray (1985b), the desire for re-presentation, and for representing oneself in desire, is taken away by the *primary metaphorization* of the desire as a woman. Being caught up in the phallic metaphors of the same devours the desire for femininity—the origin of the woman in the phallic orders of the same produces a schizophrenia of desire. The prohibition of the Oedipus complex, the rule of the authority of the father or the parents and the construction of the super-ego are all justified in the same way—the securing from the return of the *libidinal cathexis* through identification (Irigaray, 1985b, p. 86). The phallic same, the little boy's penis, is protected by his narcissistic interest, which would be endangered by the discovery of the woman's castration. Judith Butler (1993) has offered the *lesbian phallus* as a critical response to the narcissistic Freudian theory, and in our context, the self same representation of the teacher's body in the media, multiliteracies and through the general practices of education (pp. 57–93).

Freud (1953–1974, Vol. 19) founded the ego with the externalized idea one has of one's own body and pain (pp. 1–66). Lacan (1985) read Freud in a similar way in that "the libidinal drive is centered on the function of the imaginary" (p. 122). Knowledge of one's own body becomes possible through an imaginary investiture: the Freudian "prototype" for this investiture was designated as the male genitals. Other *erotogenic zones* may act as substitutes for the genitals and behave analogously to them, yet the male genitals are, as Butler (1993) expresses it, "an originating idealization, as the symbolically encoded phallus" (p. 60). The metonymic trajectory of Freud's texts has, at their core, an ambivalence to the construction of the phallus, which is fundamentally erotogenically transferable and belongs to no one body part. The phallus rhetorically enacts the process of narcissistic investment and idealization that Freud seeks to document, overcoming ambivalence through the conjecturing of an ideal. Lacan (1977) rewrote Freud's theory of narcissism through the dynamics of projection and misrecognition. He established the morphology of the body as a psychically invested projection, an idealization or fiction of the teacher's body as a totality and locus of control in pedagogic action. He suggests that this narcissistic and idealizing projection that establishes morphology constitutes the condition for the generation of objects and the cognition of other examples of the body—it is the reserve of morph from which the contours of objects are produced (pp. 1–7).

Butler's lesbian phallus acts as an unexpected intervention and consequence of the Lacanian scheme, an apparently contradictory signifier which, through a critical mimesis, calls into question the ostensibly originating and controlling power of the Lacanian phallus—indeed, it is installed as the privileged signifier of the symbolic order. The move that is emblematized by the lesbian phallus contests the relationship between the logic of non-contradiction and the legislation of compulsory heterosexuality at the level of the symbolic and bodily morphogenesis. Consequently, the lesbian phallus seeks to open up a discursive site for reconsidering the tacit political relations that constitute and persist in the divisions between the teacher's body parts and wholes, anatomy and the imaginary, corporeality and the psyche (Butler, 1993, pp. 73–74). Butler (1993) envisaged that this imaginary phallus will tackle questions of femininity, desire and lesbian identification in a way that will not be caught in the legislative trap of controlling libidinal cathexis through repeated displacement, repression and symbolization. If the phallus is lesbian, it will not tend toward the masculine figures of power—its signification will be placed on a plane that is not attracted to the phallus, and opens up a site of "proliferate resignifications" (p. 89). Another way out of the Freudian specular game that could trap the teacher's body via its own desire in multiliteracies is through the work of Deleuze and Guattari (1984) and their understanding of the body.

The Synthetic Body in Multiliteracies

Gilles Deleuze (1990) took as his starting point the definition of partial objects (p. 196). Lacan (1977) associated the normalization of the phallus as partial object with the degradation of psychoanalysis (p. 77). However, Deleuze (1990) defined partial objects as having two senses: the first of the state of introjected objects and the corresponding state of the drives attached to these objects, and the second as being the elective body zones and the state of the drives which find in them a source of the zones (p. 200). It is in this sense that zones are facts of the *surface*, their organization implies the constitution, the discovery and the investment of a third dimension which is no longer either depth or height. One could say that the object of the zone is projected, but projection no longer signifies a mechanism of depth, it indicates a surface operation. Deleuze (1990) spreads this surface so that the libidinal drives may work on it. Action still happens in the depths, but the drives may free themselves from the constraint of the destructive drives by the production of new surfaces, and the involvement in relation with new objects. The twice-liberated libido is a veritable *superficial energy*, the object of the surface, projected over a zone in accordance with an entirely different mechanism: i.e., that of image and the consequent teacher's body in multiliteracies. The phallus does not play the role of an organ, but of a partial object, projected on the zone. The phallus may enter into a relationship with the privileged genital zone, as an image and in our case the multiliterate teacher's body; yet the status of a partial object assures the transitory nature of this relationship. It traces a line at the surface, interfacing with all the erogenous zones, bringing together partial surfaces on the body of the child (Deleuze, 1990, p. 201). Yet the Oedipal game is not so easily won. The real test of the ego lies in the autoeroticism of partial surfaces, the phallic coordination, where the super-ego invests the libido as superficial energy in a "secondary narcissism" (Deleuze, 1990, p. 203). The line that the phallus has traced at the surface, across every partial surface, is now the trace of castration, where the phallus and the penis are dissipated. This Oedipal tragedy is the site for action, which Deleuze calls a metaphysical or transcendental surface. The castration of the mother and the death of the father preserve the Oedipus complex, and organizes a definitive sexuality on its own surface—it is also the origin of what Freud called "de-sexualized energy," where energy reinvests the destructive drives on its new metaphysical surface, or the surface of pure thought. This second process corresponds to sublimation and symbolization, and the Freudian idea that the death instinct is an affair of speculation that corresponds to and augments the representation of the teacher's body as a repeated media event in multiliteracies.

Melanie Klein (1970, p. 290) remarked that symbolism is the foundation of every phantasm, and that the development of the "phantasmic" life is hindered by the persistence of the schizoid and depressive positions. The phantasm finds its origins in the secondary narcissism, and is inseparable not only from grammatical transformations, but also from the ideational material of these transformations. Deleuze and Guattari (1984) took these transformations further in their work, *Anti-Oedipus*.[2] Here, the evolution of the drives is questioned: there is no direction for them to progress as an integrated whole, neither is there an original totality from which they are derived. Partial objects have a sufficient charge to demolish the Oedipal triangle when they connect with desiring-production and group fantasy and they establish non-familial relations: i.e., "the unconscious as orphan" (Deleuze & Guattari, 1984, p. 49). The Oedipal triangulation fails to see the nature of desiring-production, buts acts as a recording process for power and education, thereby trapping the child, the neurotic, the psychopath, sexuality (especially that of the teacher), and the schizophrenic in its dissipated net. Deleuze and Guattari (1984) wondered if it wouldn't be better to "schizophrenise" the domain of the unconscious as well as the socio-historical domain to shatter the iron collar of Oedipus and to rediscover everywhere the force of desiring-production (p. 53). Psychoanalysis crushes desiring-production in representation—the productive unconscious is hereafter expressed in dream, myth and tragedy. Deleuze and Guattari (1984) expressed the notion that desire cannot be defined in terms of lack, and this is especially apposite in terms of the politics of desire that surround the teacher's body. It could be said that desire needs its own reproduction, otherwise the teacher or the colonel or the instructor are reduced to mommy/daddy—they are figures of *familial reproduction*, whereby desire is plugged into the system. The child finds daddy in the teacher, is dependent on recognition, loses its own desiring-production and does not participate in the desires of the real teacher's body through multiliteracies—which may be subsequently seen as subversive or perverse.

To implement the desiring-production of the multiliterate teacher's body, Deleuze and Guattari (1984) proposed three syntheses. Connective synthesis involves the libido and is the joining of territories in a flux, and could be said to be an analog form of production. Disjunctive synthesis is digital in that it involves code, it is production which expresses surplus, recording processes and the transmission of messages. Conjunctive synthesis is intensive, revolving around types of consumption and consummation. It tends to individualize and to sexualize:

1. In **connective synthesis**, partial objects can join with anything, which confronts the recording processes of the Oedipal as they figure the pairing of people in familial reproduction (Deleuze & Guattari, 1984, p. 71). To avoid this pairing, the teacher's body should not deal with persons in terms of closed dual connections. The non-personal flows of connective synthesis do not designate persons as abstract quantities, but rather they figure the global and specific uses of transversal forms of sedimentation or *strata*.
2. **Disjunctive synthesis** has two uses, one immanent, the other transcendental (Deleuze & Guattari, 1984, p. 78). Psychoanalysis uses the

transcendental to impose exclusions and restrictions, making the unconscious swing over into Oedipus. The immanent use of disjunctive synthesis is one that remains disjunctive, it is no longer exclusive or restrictive, but it is fully affirmative, non-restrictive and inclusive. It is not that the teacher's body resolves paradoxes or contradictions, but that it does not closet itself in its own terms in multiliteracies (Deleuze & Guattari, 1984, p. 77).

3. In **conjunctive synthesis**, a great intermingling takes place of intense becomings, passages and migrations that drift in flows of time, countries, races, families, geographical and historical designations: even miscellaneous news items may partake in this immense passage (Deleuze & Guattari, 1984, p. 85). It is a matter of relationships of intensities through which the subject passes on the body without organs—also known as the synthetic or partial body, or the multiliteracies teacher's body in time. This is a process that engages the subject in rises and falls, displacements and journeys. The races and cultures designate regions on this teacher's body. They are zones of intensity, where the phenomena of individualization and sexuality are produced. Here the schizophrenic delirium is set free. All the names in history (Nietzsche's *Ecco Homo*) are gathered together, and they participate in their settings, becomings and stories. It carries the real beyond its principle to the point where it is effectively produced by the desiring-machine. This is the point where the copy ceases to be a copy in order to become the Real and its artifice. Freudian psychoanalysis made intensive use of the family, yet it distorted the nature of the intensive quantities in the unconscious. The *familial* reproduced itself through the institutions of Lacanian analysis by stressing the imaginary and intensive qualities of their origination (Deleuze & Guattari, 1984, p. 94). The unconscious is to this extent immensely powerful—conjunctive syntheses have the potential to raise every type of national, racial or religious sentiment. Questions about groups, individuals, societies or origins all have their communicative apparatus wrapped in the establishment of their processes in the unconscious, and this may be clarified and surmounted in contemporary education as the emergence of the representation of the multiliterate teacher's body.

Deleuze and Guattari (1984) produced these three syntheses so that they might be used as machinery for the analysis of desire and, in this context, the reconstruction of the teacher's body through multiliterate discourse. This immanent mechanism takes us toward the understanding of teachers, without social power structures adopting the discourses of psychoanalysis as state science and a static apparatus. Rather, this chapter sets the debate adrift into the folds of the contemporary teacher's body. It acts as a non-containment strategy for desire in education, or as Foucault (1970) expressed it: "when Desire reigns in the wild state, as if the rigor of its rule had leveled all opposition" (p. 375). Such a pragmatics of education is a step to making discourse work, and also a commentary on the ground of educational freedom—where we may experience the full teacher's body in multiliteracies, or the body without organs as a partial object that is set up as a designation in discourse through time and the comprehension of the objectivity of desire. Or, as Irigaray (1985a) has stated:

> If we keep on speaking sameness, if we speak to each other as men have been doing for centuries, as we have been taught to speak, we'll miss each other, fail ourselves. Again.... Words will pass through our bodies, above our heads. They'll vanish, and we'll be lost. Far off, up high. Absent from ourselves: we'll be spoken machines, speaking machines. Enveloped in proper skins, but not our own. Withdrawn into proper names, violated by them. Not yours, not mine. We don't have any. We change names as men exchange us, as they use us, use us up. It would be frivolous of us, exchanged by them, to be so changeable.
>
> (p. 205)

Conclusion

It has been pleasing to note that teachers' bodies are recently being recognized as sites for serious sociological exploration, and books such as *The Teacher's Body* by Freedman and Holmes (2003) have shown how qualitative analysis may be used to express the physical reality of teachers as bodies. I hope to add to this multifaceted examination through the writing of this chapter in order to alleviate some of the affective pressure on teachers' bodies in society. This may be achieved by implementing strategies from Grosz (1994) and Deleuze and Guattari (1984)—locating the power structures that play upon the body in the educational context through the design of multiliteracies, and setting them into a lateral or planar direction so that further presentation, representation and designation does not set up an order of bodily categorization or system of exclusion. Such processes have already been enacted through the work of Lather (1991) and McWilliam (1994), and they have indexed sites for lateral thinking about the varied types of desiring-production that are proliferating in a global multiliterate climate.

This spreadsheet for cultural investigation cannot be played out without certain forces rearranging its conditions, translating its codes or reversing its tendencies: this constitutes the reality of the desires and moral perception that we are examining. The leading edge of multiliterate educational practice opens up difference, and combines the types of synthesis (Deleuze & Guattari, 1984) involved with the processes of the teacher's body. That is, the distinctions, concepts or ideas about the teacher's body do not constitute intensive fields that act as centralizing modes of production. Contrastingly, desire acts through multiple linkages, heterogeneous separations and virtual becomings. Deleuze and Guattari (1987) have elsewhere termed this process as being "rhizomatics."[3] Such a scattering of discourse is a positive tactical maneuver to keep desire alive in the classroom. It is a social transformation that should not serve as singular and authoritative, "knowledge," "method," or the "truth," as change in the field of education is immanent, and marks channels of experience and the super-mediation of multiliterate teachers' bodies that we find on the Internet and through the media.

Notes

1. The collection of essays by Aronowitz and Giroux (1985) dealt with various theories of radical education, but includes the formulation of the teacher as intellectual, which limits analysis of the body and multiliterate discourse by siding too far on the side of rationality—the forces of production that are therefore located in education are resolved into an emancipated critical framework. Such a framework will inevitably be patriarchal in terms of not reproducing its own sexual codes, and this could reinforce the binary distinctions that need to be eliminated in terms of understanding the teacher's body for the purposes of this chapter: i.e., this multiliterate body may also be irrational or imaginary. Perhaps the limitations of critical pedagogy are highlighted through the sexuality of the teacher's body as the constant attention to educational reform works to drain the body of actual sexual charge by transforming it into protest that shapes the politics of institutional life. Henry A. Giroux's (1994) *Disturbing Pleasures: Learning Popular Culture* did take into account popular elements of educational practice, yet the tendency to strengthen rational pedagogy is still apparent, and the arguments about the position of the teacher belies a deep-seated reinforcement of (his) power and not the position of the teacher's body that I wish to pursue.
2. In addition to Elizabeth Grosz's ideas about the body, the major impetus for the notion of the teacher's body that I have presented comes from the movement on the plane of the full body in *Anti-Oedipus*, where it is termed as the "body without organs." I have presented a straightforward summary of the central tenets of *Anti-Oedipus* in order to demonstrate the type of synthesis that I am constructing through the writing of this chapter on body politics and multiliteracies.
3. In Deleuze and Guattari's (1987) *A Thousand Plateaus*, the term "rhizomatics" appears as a process that makes connections via structures which are strata and not arboreal. This "growth" of linkages is a highly flexible and mobile type of investigative paradigm in that the surprising and often unforeseen consequences of its operations lead to the dissolution of its former parts, rather than a strengthening of its hegemony. This works in this chapter through the connectivity with educational ideology, and the way in which the teacher's body may be used to understand the power complexes that have gathered around the actual physical presence of the teacher in the classroom, such as multiliteracies.

References

Alston, K. (1995). The difference we make: Philosophy of education and the tower of Babel. In W. Kohli (Ed.), *Critical conversations in philosophy of education* (pp. 278–297). New York: Routledge.

Aronowitz, S., & Giroux, H. (1985). *Education under siege.* Massachusetts: Bergin & Garvey Publishers, Inc.

Braidotti, R. (1991). *Patterns of dissonance.* Oxford: Polity Press.

Butler, J. (1990). *Gender trouble: Feminism and the subversion of identity.* New York: Routledge.

Butler, J. (1993). *Bodies that matter*. New York: Routledge.

Cole, D. R. (2007). Virtual terrorism and the Internet e-learning options. *E-Learning*, 4(2), 116–127.

Cole, D. R. (2009). The power of emotional factors in English teaching. *Power and Education*, 1(1), 57–70.

Deleuze, G. (1990). *The logic of sense* (M. Lester, Trans.). New York: Columbia University Press.

Deleuze, G., & Guattari, F. (1984). *Anti-Oedipus: Capitalism and schizophrenia* (R. Hurley, M. Seem & H. R. Lane, Trans.). London: Athlone Press.

Deleuze, G., & Guattari, F. (1987). *A thousand plateaus: Capitalism and schizophrenia: Part Two* (B. Massumi, Trans.). Minneapolis: University of Minnesota Press.

Foucault, M. (1970). *The order of things*. London: Routledge.

Foucault, M. (1978). *The history of sexuality*. London: Penguin Books.

Freedman, D. P., & Holmes, M. S. (Eds.). (2003). *The teacher's body: Embodiment, authority, and identity in the academy*. New York: State University of New York Press.

Freire, P. (1972). *Pedagogy of the oppressed*. New York: Herder and Herder.

Freud, S. (1953–1974). *The standard edition of the complete psychological works of Sigmund Freud*. London: Hogarth Press.

Gallop, J. (1994). The teacher's breasts. In J. J. Matthews (Ed.), *Jane Gallop seminar papers* (pp. 1–17). Canberra: HRC and the Australian National University.

Gallop, J. (Ed.). (1995). *Pedagogy: The question of impersonation*. Bloomington: Indiana University Press.

Gallop, J. (1997). *Feminist accused of sexual harassment*. Durham, NC: Duke University Press.

Giroux, H. A. (1994). *Disturbing pleasures: Learning popular culture*. New York: Routledge.

Grosz, E. (1994). *Volatile bodies: Toward a corporeal feminism*. Bloomington: Indiana University Press.

Haraway, D. J. (1991). *Simians, cyborgs, and women: The reinvention of nature*. London: Free Association Books.

Irigaray, L. (1985a). *This sex which is not one* (C. Porter, Trans.). Ithaca: Cornell University Press.

Irigaray, L. (1985b). *Speculum of the other woman* (G. C. Gill, Trans.). Ithaca: Cornell University Press.

Klein, M. (1970). *Developments in psychoanalysis*. London: Hogarth Press.

Kristeva, J. (1980). *Desire in language*. New York: Columbia University Press.

Lacan, J. (1977). *Écrits: A selection* (A. Sheridan, Trans.). London: Routledge.

Lacan, J. (1985). *The seminar of Jacques Lacan: Book 1—Freud's papers on technique, 1953–54*. New York: Norton.

Lather, P. (1991). *Getting smart: Feminist research and pedagogy with/in the post-modern*. New York: Routledge.

McWilliam, E. (1994). *In broken images: Feminist tales for a different teacher education*. New York: Teacher College Press.

New London Group. (1996). A pedagogy of multiliteracies: Designing social futures. *Harvard Educational Review*, 66, 60–92.

O'Brien, S. (2000). The lecherous teacher: "An explosive thriller about naked lust, perverted justice and obsession beyond control." In C. O'Farrell, D. Meadmore, E. McWilliam and C. Symes (Eds.), *Taught bodies* (pp. 39–56). New York: Peter Lang.

Probyn, E. (2004). Teaching bodies: Affects in the classroom. *Body & Society*, 10(4), 21–43.
Shapiro, S. (1995). Post-modern dilemmas. In W. Kohli (Ed.), *Critical conversations in philosophy of education* (pp. 278–297). New York: Routledge.
Spivak, G. C. (1993). *Outside in the teaching machine.* New York: Routledge.
Wittig, M. (1986). *The lesbian body.* Boston: Beacon Books.

Part III

The Pedagogy of Multiliteracies in Motion

8 Using the Principles of Multiliteracies to Inform Pedagogical Change

Geoff Bull and Michèle Anstey, Anstey & Bull Consultants in Education

Introduction

Over the past decade the areas of educational theory, literacy and leadership have focused upon the issue of responding to rapid and significant change. The concept of "multiliteracies," first coined in 1996, arose from the concerns of a group of literacy educators about developing appropriate pedagogical responses for teaching literacy in a world undergoing significant economic, social and technological change. Soon after 1996, the literature on educational leadership began addressing the issue of assisting teachers to respond to the educational demands that resulted from such rapid change.

This chapter reports on the successful implementation of a professional development program that focused on multiliteracies and produced pedagogical change at individual, year and school levels. The program, implemented at primary and secondary level, embodied beliefs and principles from the literature on multiliteracies and educational leadership. It engaged teachers in an action-learning model of professional development based on the principles of action research that has a history of supporting teachers to implement change successfully in literacy education in Australia (see Comber & Hill, 2000; Comber, 2005; Comber & Kamler, 2005; Kamler & Comber, 2008). As it has been implemented throughout Queensland in various educational sectors and systems at individual, regional and whole-school levels, it is now possible to draw conclusions on how implementation of professional development around a multiliterate pedagogy can produce successful long-term outcomes and contribute to school renewal.

The Multiliteracies Professional Development Program was based on a definition of multiliteracies that includes a focus on pedagogy. Therefore the chapter will commence with a review of the relationship between multiliteracies and pedagogy and the development of the term "multiliteracies" since its origin in 1996.

Following this, the chapter will describe how the structure of the program evolved and the theoretical constructs that informed it. The program had three main foci:

1. Defining multiliteracies and identifying the participants' current understandings and practices around it;
2. Developing strategies for analyzing and changing participants' individual classroom pedagogies;
3. Responding to and managing change as an individual and in the broader school context.

Defining and Understanding a Multiliterate Pedagogy

Our beliefs about quality literacy education derive from the concept of multiliteracies (Anstey, 2002; Anstey & Bull, 2004, 2006; Bull & Anstey, 2005; Cope & Kalantzis, 2000; Kalantzis & Cope, 2005; New London Group, 1996). We construct multiliteracies as a term that goes beyond the discipline area of English. It is essential to, and an integral part of, all disciplines from science and mathematics to the arts, since all disciplines rely on their own particular forms of literacy. It is socio-culturally derived, yet influenced by psychological factors. Literacy education addressed from a multiliteracies perspective concerns both literacy and pedagogy, making the role of pedagogy in the teaching of literacy explicit.

Too often, literacy education becomes entrenched in debates about "Should it be about literacy or English?" and "What is the relationship between the two?" These two questions are reminiscent of many similar debates we have had in literacy education, for example, between the "whole language" or "genre" approaches. The veracity of these debates encourages teachers to take sides or ignore—rather than take responsibility for—moving literacy education forward through their teaching practices. A larger and more important question is "What is the pedagogy that informs better literacy education?" If we accept that literacy education is about multiliteracies and the broader concept of curriculum rather than debating which discipline it "belongs in," then we can focus on the pedagogy and how to do it better (Anstey & Bull, 2004; Edwards-Groves 2003; Lingard, Hayes & Mills, 2003a; Lingard, Hayes, Mills & Christie, 2003b). We take the position that while being passionate about teaching literacy is important, being critically reflective and knowledgeable about pedagogy and practice is essential. As we have worked with many teachers through the "research in context" approach that is embodied in the various multiliteracies projects that we have jointly developed, it has been continually demonstrated that the link between multiliteracies and pedagogy is very strong. In these projects, we (as facilitators of the process) and teachers (as the action learners) have come to realize that the literacy curriculum supplies the "what" of the teaching, while learning process and pedagogy supplies the "how." In this way we have come to see literacy and pedagogy as co-dependent.

The bases of our ideas about the co-dependency of literacy and pedagogy go back over 30 years. The work of Bernstein (1973), who conceptualized formal education as realized through three message systems: curriculum (what counts as valid knowledge), pedagogy (what counts as valid transmission of knowledge) and evaluation (what counts as a valid realization of this knowledge on the part of the taught) has assisted us to explore the relationship of learning and pedagogy. More recently the work of Lingard et al. (2003b) and Lingard et al. (2003a) further developed our ideas about the alignment of pedagogy and student learning during their research for the Queensland Schools Reform Longitudinal Study. In pointing out that teachers' talk about pedagogy should be at the core of the professional culture of schools, Young (1998) has convinced us that schools must be learning communities where both teachers and students are engaged in learning through talk. We have summarized our position on the inter-relation of literacy, multiliteracies and pedagogy in Figure 8.1.

We have indicated what we believe are the characteristics of a literate and multiliterate person and how these characteristics determine a multiliterate curriculum. We have then used the relationships presented to derive what a multiliterate pedagogy might encompass. For us, the crucial feature of Figure 8.1 is that it represents the co-dependency of literacy, multiliteracy and pedagogy. It was on this basis that we designed the multiliteracies project in order to use the principles of multiliteracies to affect pedagogical change in pre-school, primary and secondary classrooms.

Developing Strategies for Affecting Pedagogical Change

The multiliteracies project was designed with the aim of supporting teachers as they changed their professional practice. In order to achieve this, the project was based on a number of beliefs that we felt would promote a focus on literacy and pedagogy and encourage pedagogical change in classrooms:

- Literacy education is as much about pedagogy as it is about literacy.
- Successful professional development needs to be based on action learning and encourage collegial and self-reflective conversations.
- Validation of learning and change in practice and pedagogy is essential to success.
- Change in practice and pedagogy requires knowledge of the change process.
- Literacy education is not advanced in a culture of blame where stakeholders such as parents, students or teachers are blamed for deficiencies or lack of progress. Rather, advancement occurs where there is mutual acceptance of responsibility.

Responding to and Managing Change

The five belief statements became the underlying tenets on which all the subsequent projects were based. We then used these beliefs to determine the goals of the project, drawing on the work of Fullan (2001, 2002, 2004, 2005). From

A literate person is able to:	A multiliterate person is able to:	Therefore a multiliterate curriculum should include:
• be strategically responsive to changing literacies. • reformulate existing literacy knowledge and practices. • access and learn new literacy knowledge and practices. • use a repertoire of literate practices and strategies appropriately. • use traditional paper and live technologies. • use multimodal texts and new digital-electronic technologies.	• understand the influence of diversity on literacy and literate practices. • use critical literacy practices. • use literacy and literate practices in socially responsible ways. • use literacy and literate practices in diverse contexts. • use literacy and literate practices as an active and informed citizen. • understand and use a range of texts and technologies.	• the consumption, production and transformation of knowledge about literacy and literate practices. • investigation of how literacy and literate practices operate in a variety of contexts. • understandings about, and the use of, critical literacy. • understandings about how literate practices relate to all aspects of society. • knowledge about and use of all semiotic systems. • knowledge about and use of paper, digital-electronic and live technologies.
↓	↓	↓

Therefore the following characteristics are desirable in a multiliterate pedagogy:

1. **Characteristics of classroom interaction**
   - Match interaction to desired learning outcomes.
   - Use explicit talk that balances informative, process and utility functions.
   - Use of accurate and consistent metalanguage.
   - Model and practice metacognitive processes.
   - Balance the use of Initiation Response Feedback (IRF) models, substantive conversation and classroom narratives (oral and written) as ways of exploring and learning literacy and literate practices.
2. **Construction and realisation of literacy and literate practices through pedagogy**
   - Acknowledge that literacies and literate practices will continue to change.
   - Use of real and simulated contexts.
   - Use of authentic texts and tasks.
   - Learn and apply the literacies and literate practices of all disciplines.
   - View literacy as a strategic problem-solving activity.
   - Engage in the consumption, production and transformation of knowledge about literacy and literate practices.
3. **Expectations and responsibilities**
   - The locus of control and responsibility between students and teachers changes with regard to selection of content, and nature of participation.
   - Self regulation is expected and supported.
   - Expectations and learning outcomes are specified.
   - Student diversity is recognized and cultural safety practiced.
   - Each student's unique literacy identity is explored in terms of how it affects his or her literacies and literate practices.

Figure 8.1 Identifying and Defining a Multiliterate Pedagogy.
Source: Adapted from Anstey & Bull, 2004, p. 314 and Anstey & Bull, 2006, p. 57.

Fullan's work we identified the concepts of capability, sustainability and "thriveability" to give direction to the project and also provide a means of establishing whether it was succeeding. In the early stages of the project the goal was to increase the capacity of individual teachers by developing their knowledge about literacy and their ability to change pedagogy in their classroom. In this way teachers would have increased capability. Sustainability was addressed first by encouraging teachers to implement the project from an action research perspective that was designed to change existing pedagogy rather than add extra dimensions to an already-crowded curriculum. Second, suggestions regarding creating and maintaining support for capability were made to school leadership and to other teacher leaders. This was designed to create a whole-school focus that would lead to sustainability and resilience. The involvement of school leadership and a school-wide focus proved to be key ingredients for promoting all three goals. Thriveability, or the potential to continue to grow and create new knowledge and further develop literacy education in the school, was taken to be a measure of the success of a project. For example, if a project continued to thrive beyond the initial action research project and led to further change in pedagogy in the classroom, then the school and community would deem the original project successful.

Key Features of the Multiliteracies Project

1. Duration of the Project

Duration of the project was seen to be critical. The two authors share a strong belief that significant and lasting pedagogical change can only be attained over time. The project was therefore designed to run for a minimum of six months, up to a maximum of two or three years, depending on the wishes of individual schools or networks. We believe that effective PD (and by this we mean "professional development" and "professional dialogue") needs time to develop and flourish. This allows participants time to develop and trial ideas and approaches so that follow-up can become a feature of the process of change in pedagogy.

2. "Tailored" Professional Development and Professional Dialogue

The conditions for PD require that teachers have a shared knowledge in a particular area of the curriculum—in this case multiliteracies and pedagogical change. For this reason the introduction to the multiliteracies project included a minimum of two days specific PD based on jointly identified needs plus regular follow-up. We found that the relationship between PD and shared knowledge developed best when it was conducted around needs that had been identified by the teachers concerned. The ongoing PD was therefore always specific to a particular project, although each project had some commonalities with others.

3. Knowledge about Change Management

Because one of the main belief statements that drives the multiliteracies project involves change in pedagogy and practice, there is an expectation that significant change will take place at the classroom and school level. We have found that this change is more likely to take place, and is less likely to produce undue anxiety, if teachers have knowledge of the change process and understand that there are some predictable reactions to the process that are experienced by many individuals. Teachers need to appreciate that there will be highs and lows in the change process, and also plateaus where little change occurs. For these reasons, the research of Michael Fullan on working in a culture of change forms an important component of the project.

4. Role of Leadership Team

The participation of the leadership team, including the principal, is particularly important to the success of the multiliteracies project. In our research into what makes an effective project, a consistent finding has been that completion rates and satisfaction with the outcomes of the project are related to the participation of teacher leaders. Such participation is central to success within a particular school, and is a noticeable factor in distinguishing progress between schools when the project is run in a network of schools. When a network of schools participate in a project, a special PD day is provided for teacher leaders to introduce them to the variety of changes that are likely to occur in their schools.

5. Multiliteracies Matrix and Reflection Tool

The authors designed the multiliteracies matrix (to be explored fully later in this chapter) specifically for use in the multiliteracies project. Participants engaged with the matrix a number of times during a project, depending on the purpose at the time. Initially, the matrix was used to define the concept of multiliteracies through the 24 items that were contained in it. It was then used as a self-reflection tool for participants to reflect on their classroom pedagogy through the use of rating scales. Reflection was also encouraged through the use of a reflection journal, which was used as a daily diary to record ideas, and as a record of professional reading around the topic under investigation. Finally, participants selected items from the matrix that were then transferred to an action plan to form the basis of ongoing, classroom-based action research. Successful engagement with the matrix depended on participants having a shared knowledge about multiliteracies that made the PD outlined (in point 2, above) essential.

6. Action Plans

The matrix proved very useful in assisting participants to develop their action plans, and allowed them to self-select the area that they wanted to research. This enabled participants to begin their research at a level they were comfortable with and to proceed at a pace that was suitable for their level of expertise. Because participants were able to self-select their preferred area for research, it was quite common for teachers of different year levels to select the same area. This enabled participants to become aware of what was happening across the school. In some cases this meant that the primary section of the school was working closely with the secondary section. In all cases the project encouraged a whole-school approach to multiliteracies teaching and learning. From the outset, the action plans were to focus on changing teacher practice and pedagogy rather than student behavior. Participants were also required to collect evidence for all the changes that they identified had taken place in their classrooms. The teacher focus and the evidence-based focus on pedagogical change became a feature of the multiliteracies project.

7. Pedagogical Analyses

As part of implementing action plans, participants were required to audiotape a 30-minute lesson and prepare a transcript. The transcripts were analyzed to identify the different phases of lessons present and the types of teacher talk. (For further detail on this analysis, see Bull & Anstey, 2003.) While this proved to be a time-consuming activity that caused some stress to participants, it was frequently identified as one of the most useful parts of the project in identifying features of pedagogy that needed to be changed. Many participants prepared a second or third transcript once they had identified the phase or phases of the lessons they wished to focus on. These later transcripts allowed comparisons about teacher talk or use of phases to be made over time.

8. Follow-up Support

Regular follow-up sessions were incorporated into the project to allow for clarification and feedback to occur. Participants also used these sessions to negotiate modifications to action plans. These sessions were also used by the authors to re-focus participants on up-coming tasks and to meet identified needs as they arose. Participants found these sessions to be invaluable and often remarked that they provided the time and space for them to step back and reflect on their practice and the chance to talk with fellow teachers. Participants also had access to the authors through telephone and email contact, although this option was not taken up very often because face-to-face contact was preferred.

9. Validation Day

At the conclusion to the project, a validation or sharing day was organized. Participants were asked to make a 15–20-minute oral presentation on a feature of their action research that they felt was noteworthy. These sessions were aimed at providing validation of their study through the evidence they had collected. These sessions proved to be a very powerful way of recognizing and sharing the progress that participants had made and were highly valued by the teachers.

10. Reports

At the conclusion of the multiliteracies project, participants submitted an evidence-based written report on their action research. This report was initially used as the basis for their oral presentation on validation day. It fulfilled the objective of being a record of the progress and pedagogical change in a classroom. It was also a record of further questions to be explored that had arisen during the initial study. Participants then used these questions to embark on further action research. This proved to be a very common response deriving from the written report, and possibly accounts for the high levels of sustainability and thriveability present in schools that the authors have noted long after the completion of the various multiliteracies projects. The written report was also structured into sections so that it was in an appropriate form to submit to a university faculty as part of an independent study in an undergraduate or postgraduate degree program. A number of participants in the multiliteracies projects have reported submitting their written reports to a university faculty (University of Southern Queensland and James Cook University) and receiving credit for their research.

Tools Specifically Developed for the Multiliteracies Project

The Multiliteracies Matrix

We developed two tools, the multiliteracies matrix and the action plan, specifically for the multiliteracies projects. The multiliteracies matrix is a self-reflective tool of 24 items about multiliteracies. It was designed to assist teachers in determining their current literacy knowledge and practice in the three domains of text, context and pedagogy. Teachers used a five-point self-rating scale to rate their level of knowledge in each of the 24 items. They then had to justify the rating they had chosen and, where possible, propose a strategy for action. The matrix was used at the beginning of the projects to identify the areas in which participants might need specific PD, and to stimulate professional conversation among participants. Teachers selected two or three items as goals for change and developed an action plan that specified the actions to be taken and data collection methods for validating change in their knowledge, pedagogy and practice. Action plans were incorporated into their normal classroom program. Figure 8.2 illustrates six of the 24 items from the matrix—numbers 1, 2 and 6 from the text domain, 8 from the context domain, and 13 and 14 from the pedagogy domain.

Each item in the matrix contained a statement of a feature of a multiliterate classroom (e.g., students use, interpret, and produce paper, live and electronic texts) followed by an italicized section that was meant to illustrate a possible response by a student if these features were present. This second (italicized) section was intended to focus participants' attention on what students should be able to do if the feature of the classroom was operating successfully. When earlier versions of the matrix did not contain this statement, participants tended to rate themselves highly on an item, giving justifications like "I cover this in a number of lessons." When the italicized statements were added then participants were more likely to say, "Well I may have covered it but I don't think the students would be able to say that." By making these modifications we felt that teacher ratings were more realistic, particularly when they had to justify their ratings in the third column of the matrix. It was important that the teacher statement in the justification column reflected actual *practice* rather than just a *belief.*

The "Scale for Rating Personal Knowledge Planning and Practice" section was included to provide further support to participants to complete the five-point rating scale. Each of the five statements contained two parts, the first part being a statement about teacher knowledge, while the second part described teacher practice. Knowing about a particular item on the matrix was not sufficient unless it was accompanied by actual classroom practice.

The Action Plan Proforma

The action plan proforma was developed to support teachers in planning toward the achievement of their personal goals. This proforma provided a structure to assist teachers in identifying their goal, the actions to be taken and how they would collect data to measure change in their knowledge, pedagogy and practice. The focus on validating any action that they took as a result of self-rating on the matrix was a key component. The proforma is illustrated in Figure 8.3.

The proforma is divided into two sections, the first of which, comprising the first two columns, is focused on what action is to be taken in the action research (or action learning) project, and the second section, comprising the second two columns, focuses on validating the action taken. Our approach to the use of the proforma was that for every action a teacher planned to take in the classroom, there needed to be a corresponding validation. In each of the four columns there is a set of italicized questions that is meant to give direction to the project. Each of the participants was meant to take some action in professional reading, pedagogy and practice, planning and resources. The emphasis in the Action Research Projects was always on collecting evidence to

Literacy Knowledge: Personal Matrix Name: ____________________ Year ________ School ______________________________							
My understandings about multiliteracies and reading	*1*	*2*	*3*	*4*	*5*	*Justification and comment differentiate between belief and practice*	*Possible strategy for action*
1. Students use, interpret, and produce • **paper,** • **live, and** • **electronic texts.** *For this purpose and in this context it would be better to conduct a conversation face to face rather than send an email because…*							
2. Students know, understand and use **individual and combined semiotic systems:** • linguistic (e.g., vocabulary, grammar) • visual (e.g., still and moving images, page and screen layouts) • auditory (e.g., music, sound effects, silence) • gestural (e.g., facial expression and body language) • spatial (e.g., environmental and architectural spaces and layouts) *As I watched this video I could see that the character was being developed not only by the way the plot dictated his actions but through the costuming, soft lighting and close-up camera shots. This was achieved by…*							
6. Students explore and develop understandings about **how and why institutions produce and distribute texts.** *We explored mobile phone brochures and found that mobile phones are marketed as a form of entertainment. This was evident because … Mobile phone manufacturers do this because…*							

8. Students explore and develop understandings about how **social practices shape texts and behaviors with texts.** *Today we looked at places where we do not always use correct spelling and grammar (such as SMS messages and shopping lists) and then we talked about why this was acceptable in these contexts but not in others. We concluded that…*							
13. The class literacy learning and teaching program is informed by reference to the **Four Resource Model**. There is not only a **balance** between the four reading practices, but the program clearly articulates what each practice looks like in **different disciplines** and year levels. *When I am planning I ensure that students are engaged in all four reading practices across all disciplines. I am also careful to select appropriate materials and teaching strategies for the reading practice I am focusing upon.*							
14. Teachers and students have a **metalanguag**e for exploring and talking about texts and their semiotic systems *When we discuss texts the students and I use the correct terminology, so for example we talk about technical codes, parallel cutting and close-ups when we deconstruct or construct moving images.*							

Scale for Rating Personal Knowledge Planning and Practice.

- This is a **new concept** to me and I have **no understanding** of it.
- I have **some understanding** of this concept but have **not attempted to apply** it in my classroom planning and practice.
- I **understand** this concept and have **begun** exploring ways I can implement this as part of my classroom planning and practice.
- I **fully understand** this concept and it is an **important part** of my classroom planning and practice.
- This concept is **fully embedded** in my understanding and **consistently implemented** in my classroom planning and practice.

Figure 8.2 Sample Items from the Multiliteracies Matrix Reflection Tool.

Title of Project______	Investigator ______	School ______	
Action		Validation	
Aim or goal	Method (focus on action)	Method (focus on validation)*	Data collection, analysis and reporting*
What are the items identified for change? What is your desired outcome?	How will you go about achieving this? What will you do?	What would you expect to see as evidence of change or improvement? Where would you look for this evidence? How would you recognize it? What would it look like?	How would you collect this evidence? How would you collate it? How will you analyze it and report it?
Items	Professional reading, visits, conversations		
	Pedagogy and practice		
Desired outcomes	Planning		
	Resources		

* **Examples:** Reflection journals about reading/experiences; observations of your work by critical friend; discussions with critical friend; field notes about sessions with teachers; samples of your planning (before, during, after); samples of lesson analyses or teacher talk (before, during, after).

Figure 8.3 Proforma for Action Plan and Validation.

validate any desired outcome, and the focus was always on investigating the change in teacher pedagogy. The action research projects were therefore all about change in teacher behavior rather than change in student behavior (although the two are obviously related). Initially, participants had some difficulty with this approach because their natural inclination was to focus on students. However, the recording of a 30-minute lesson and the construction of a transcript reinforced the concept of pedagogical change and enabled participants to re-orient their approach. For the authors, the crucial advantages brought about by the use of the proforma centered on evidence-based research and validation of change. The use of the proforma allowed participants to answer many questions about pedagogy and multiliteracies, but also discover new questions to follow up in future projects.

Outcomes of Multiliteracies Projects

1. One of the positive features of the multiliteracies projects overall was the willingness of teachers to participate in the projects. All of the projects met their quota of participants, and in a number of cases the entire school staff took part. There was a relatively low drop-out rate among participating teachers, although there was an expected attrition caused by teacher transfer and illness. When teachers did withdraw from a project we found that administrators or teacher leaders often related this to participation. Where participation rates for teacher leaders were high, then completion rates for teachers were high. Conversely, when participation rates were low for teacher leaders, then completion rates for teachers tended to be lower. This trend was identified early in the first three multiliteracies projects and proved to be constant through all the projects.
2. Another key factor was the opportunities provided for teacher PD. Where a whole school staff, or a major proportion of the staff, participated in a project, there were many opportunities for professional talk among the participants. Such talk provided support for participants as they conducted their action research and learning projects. Where a project involved a network of schools, the feedback from teachers who were part of a group from a particular school reported that they derived crucial support throughout the project from their fellow participants by constantly talking about issues raised by the project. Where a participant was the sole teacher from a particular school, the feedback consistently mentioned the lack of opportunity to talk with colleagues back at the school. While the talk at shared sessions during the multiliteracies project was seen as a positive feature, the less formal, opportunistic talk back at school was seen as a great advantage. Similar feedback was obtained from any participant who was the sole representative from a school. This trend indicated the necessity of provision for PD during professional development sessions.

3. One of the methods that was used to test the effectiveness of the multiliteracies matrix was to compare the ratings that teachers gave themselves when rating their knowledge about, and implementation of, the 24 items about multiliteracies. Table 8.1 shows a comparison of teacher self-ratings in two multiliteracies projects, one in an independent school and one in a government school.

   Table 8.1 illustrates the consistency of the teachers' self-ratings across education systems. While this comparison was not drawn for every multiliteracies project, a similar one was undertaken in a Catholic school with similar results. Of further interest in Table 8.1 is the difference in the rating for the independent school in the pedagogy domain. The government school had entry to a large-scale, long-term, state-wide professional development program that focused on literacy pedagogy, which the independent school was not able to access. Interestingly, the Catholic school was able to take up the opportunity for the professional development, and their self-ratings were at a similar level to the government school. We found it encouraging that the matrix appeared to be consistent across schools and systems. The effectiveness of the professional development in raising teachers' self-ratings may have been due to the long-term nature of the program.
4. Due to space limitations, it is not possible to provide examples of entire action plans prepared by the teachers. However, the following extracts illustrate the professional level at which the teachers were working. The extracts serve to illustrate the range of strategies teachers used to collect evidence-based data, the range of methods they used to validate change and what they judged to be appropriate evidence to indicate that change had taken place.

   Extract 1: Method of Collecting Data

   Invite a colleague into my classroom to give specific feedback on whether or not my planning is resulting in the practice of metacognition in my classroom. Identify how often I ask the students "how" and "why."

   Reflection log—as I apply the different strategies, consider how effective I have found them in terms of achieving a reflective classroom. This will involve qualitative data from both my own evaluation/reflection as well as feedback from students.

Table 8.1 Percentage Rating for each Domain of the Matrix for Two Multiliteracies Projects

Domain of matrix	*Percentage of teachers' ratings at three or below for Multiliteracies Project 1*	*Percentage of teachers' ratings at three or below for Multiliteracies Project 2*
Text domain	63	63
Context domain	71	70
Pedagogy domain	70	33

Extract 2: Method of Validating Pedagogical Change

Provide colleague/s with a feedback proforma to complete with some guided questions, some open feedback opportunities. If repeated several times over a period of time, I can use quantitative and qualitative data to analyze whether there is improvement evident in the explicitness of my talk/pedagogical strategies chosen.

Reflection log—allows me to consider my perceptions of the success or otherwise of different strategies for different purposes. Could tabulate findings across time and task, perhaps? Should be able to analyze student talk and questioning from transcripts and see an increase in invited and uninvited observations as to how a particular understanding could be reached

Extract 3: Use of Evidence to Indicate Change in Pedagogy

Excerpts of transcripts of three audiotaped lessons will be analyzed for the language which I use, and encourage my students to use, at the commencement and conclusion of my lessons. It is envisaged that evidence of an increase in the metacognitive language use by my students and myself will be analyzed in terms of the number of utterances that they constitute and this can be recorded over three lessons. This will be analyzed in terms of a percentage of total utterances for those two phases. Where my professional reading has led to successful implementation of strategies and types of talk will be referenced in my final written report.

5. The extracts from the action plans in point 4 give some idea of the goals that a range of participants aspired to at the *beginning* of a multiliteracies project. The following extracts are from the written reports that the participants submitted on validation day at the conclusion to the project. The most pleasing features of these comments are that they are overwhelmingly positive, and that they demonstrate that participants were able to achieve the goals they had set themselves. It is also interesting to note that while the multiliteracies projects require a considerable amount of work, the participants remain very positive and appear to have enjoyed the process of change. What is also of interest is that the participants have tended to identify the same elements of the projects as successful that the authors have regarded as the strengths of the project.

> This project has been highly significant to my teaching practice. It has been an exhilarating experience for me as a professional. I found it valuable because of its sheer practicality and I feel that I have grown as a teacher in so many ways. The paradigm shift I have made as a result of taking part in this project has provided enormously enhanced learning for my students. I have made positive growth and change as a teacher and a learner.
>
> I felt that the biggest gain I have made is in professional discourse

> with my colleagues from a P-12 basis. In our busy working lives there is rarely any time to sit and discuss educational matters, especially with people who work outside my area of the school. By being part of this project I have been given this time and have really appreciated learning more about how others work, their amazing ideas and pedagogy and feel more part of the "whole" school than was previously the case.
>
> I have struggled from the beginning to understand what the actual project was, how it was relevant to teaching, how I would go about implementing strategies and gathering data in order to reflect on and improve my teaching practice. It is only in the latter few months, at this reflection stage of writing a report and preparing for the Validation Day that I have come to acknowledge what it is that I have trialed, what has worked for me and my students, what has been achieved and how I have gained from the experience.

This final extract is from administrators/school leaders who were commenting on the change in the school staff as a whole.

> One of the most pleasing outcomes of this project has not been "literacy" based. It has been the development of collegiality and the palpable respect for one another, and the work done in each sector of the school. Group members have been impressed by the knowledge, experience, expertise and enthusiasm they possess as a group, and are immensely respectful of their different roles in the education chain. They are interested in, and supportive of the teachers, the students and the learning that occurs outside of their own area.

The following points represent a summary of the strengths identified by participants across all of the multiliteracies projects. The projects:

- focused on development of professional knowledge about teaching in general and literacy in particular.
- focused on change in teacher behavior and classroom practice.
- highlighted the value of transcript analysis on change in pedagogy and practice.
- foregrounded the role of teacher talk in supporting interaction in the classroom and promoting different learnings.
- emphasized the impact of explicit teaching on student learning and teacher practice.
- valued the interaction between metacognition and teacher and student thinking and learning.
- highlighted the role that reflection plays in student and teacher learning.
- encouraged and supported the development of collegiality within the group.

6. Both teachers and teacher leaders were asked a series of questions at the conclusion to the multiliteracies projects relating to what they identified as positive outcomes from the teachers' action research projects. Table 8.2 presents a summary of the outcomes identified by teacher leaders in one project that is typical of the responses that were obtained across all of the projects.

What is of interest in these responses is the range of changes in teacher behaviors that have been identified. In comparing this range of responses to the 24 items on the multiliteracies matrix, it becomes evident that teachers took up many of the suggested areas for study mentioned in the matrix. This highlights the usefulness of the matrix in guiding teachers in their choice of study in their action research projects.

When teachers were asked to identify the benefits of the multiliteracies projects, they selected a smaller range of outcomes that nevertheless had much in common with those suggested by their teacher leaders. In Tables 8.3, 8.4 and 8.5 are presented the responses from the teachers in the same multiliteracies project as those described in Table 8.2.

Table 8.2 Changes Identified by Administrators/Teacher Leaders on Evaluation Form

Items	*Focus of administrator comments*
Change in teacher talk about multiliteracies	• More aware of the need for different strategies • Increase in teacher knowledge • Deeper understanding of student empowerment. • More risk taking by teachers • Development of collegiality
Changes to classroom practice, pedagogy and planning	• Increased teacher confidence • More explicit teaching • An ability to explain teaching practice • A greater focus on professional reading • Improved student listening • Changes to belief systems • The importance of reflection • More focused instructions • Increased student responses • Student articulation of concepts • Increased student engagement in discussion

Table 8.3 Teachers' Responses to Question 1 on Evaluation Form: What have you learned that is of interest and benefit to you during the project?

Area identified by teachers	*% of teachers identifying this area*
Types of teacher talk	23
Metacognition	23
Strategies across discipline areas	31
Explicitness in teacher talk	31

Table 8.4 Teachers' Responses to Question 2 on Evaluation Form: What changes to classroom practice, planning and pedagogy have you made as a result of the project

Area identified by teachers	*% of teachers identifying this area*
Types of teacher talk	31
Different approaches to teaching strategies	31
New approaches to planning	38
Explicitness in teacher talk	46
Changes in phases of lessons	46

Table 8.5 Teachers' Responses to Question 3 on Evaluation Form: What do you need to know more about and what issues will you explore in the future?

Area identified by teachers	*% of teachers identifying this area*
Teacher reflection strategies	31
New pedagogies to support student learning	54

In comparing the responses of teacher leaders with teachers (Tables 8.2–8.5), it can be seen that both groups have identified strategies, teacher talk and explicit teaching as areas of major benefit. The teachers also identified strategies and pedagogies as areas that they wished to follow up in the future. This is a very encouraging feature of the feedback about the success of the process of teacher learning that took place, since these areas formed the major emphases of the multiliteracies projects.

Conclusion

This chapter reported on the successful implementation of a professional development program that focused on multiliteracies and produced pedagogical change at individual, year and school level at both primary and secondary level. We have shown how implementation of professional development around a multiliterate pedagogy can produce successful long-term outcomes and contribute to school renewal. The analyses that we have undertaken indicate that specific characteristics of the multiliteracies project contributed to the successful attainment and sustainability of participants' goals. The focus on pedagogy in particular contributed to considerable change in participants' classroom practices and the implementation of a multiliterate pedagogy.

References

Anstey, M. (2002). *Literate futures: Reading.* Coorparoo, Australia: Queensland Department of Education.

Anstey, M., & Bull, G. (2004). *The literacy labyrinth* (2nd ed.). Sydney: Pearson.

Anstey, M., & Bull, G. (2006). Responding to rapid change: Multiliteracies and ICT. *EQ Australia*, Winter, 17–18.

Bernstein, B. (1973). Class and pedagogy visible and invisible. In *Class, Codes and Control* (Vol. 3) (pp. 86–102). London: Routledge and Kegan Paul.

Bull, G., & Anstey, M. (2004). *Inala multiliteracies project report*, submitted to Mark Campling, Principal, Forest Lakes State School for Inala Cluster of Schools, Brisbane: Authors.

Bull, G., & Anstey, M. (2005). *Townsville multiliteracies project report*, submitted to Janelle Pepperdene, Co-ordinator Townsville LDC (Literacy) and Melinda Webb, Education Advisor, Literacy-Productive pedagogies, Townsville: Authors.

Comber, B. (2005). Making use of theories about literacy and justice: Teachers researching practice. *Educational Action Research*, 13(1), 43–55.

Comber, B., & Hill, S. (2000). Socio-economic disadvantage, literacy and social justice; Learning from longitudinal case study research. *Australian Education Researcher*, 27(3), 151–166.

Comber, B., & Kamler, B. (Eds.). (2005). *Turn-around pedagogies: Literacy interventions for at-risk students*. Primary English Teachers Association: Newtown.

Cope, B., & Kalantzis, M. (2000). *Multiliteracies: Literacy learning and the design of social futures*. South Yarra: Macmillan.

Edwards-Groves, C. (2003). Building an inclusive classroom through explicit pedagogy: A focus on the language of teaching. In G. Bull & M. Anstey (Eds.), *The literacy lexicon* (2nd ed.) (pp. 83–101). Sydney: Pearson.

Fullan, M. (2001). *Leading in a culture of change*. San Francisco: Jossey-Bass.

Fullan, M. (2002). Leadership and sustainability. *Principal Leadership*, 3(4), 1–9.

Fullan, M. (2004). *Leadership and sustainability*. Thousand Oaks, CA: Corwin Press.

Fullan, M. (2005). Resiliency and sustainability. *The School Administrator*, February, 16–18.

Kalantzis, M., & Cope, B. (2005). *Learning by design*. Melbourne: Victorian Schools Commission in association with Common Ground.

Kamler, B., & Comber, B. (2008). Making a difference: Early career English teachers research their practice. *Changing English*, 15(1), 65–76.

Lingard, B., Hayes, D., & Mills, M. (2003a). Teachers and productive pedagogies: Contextualising, conceptualising, utilising. *Pedagogy Culture and Society*, 11(3), 399–424.

Lingard, B., Hayes, D., Mills, M., & Christie, P. (2003b). *Leading learning: Making hope practical in schools*. Buckingham: Open University Press.

New London Group. (1996). A pedagogy of multiliteracies: Designing social futures. *Harvard Educational Review*, 66(1), 60–92.

Young, M. (1998). *The curriculum of the future from the "new sociology of education" to a critical theory of learning*. London: Falmer.

9 Disrupting Traditions

Teachers Negotiating Multiliteracies and Digital Technologies

Elizabeth Petroelje Stolle, Grand Valley State University, and Gustavo E. Fischman, Arizona State University

Introduction

Recently we saw a striking photograph in the *New York Times*[1] that illustrates Prensky's (2001) notions of digital natives and digital immigrants. This photograph visualized a family of four spending a quiet evening at home reading. The father sat in his chair reading a print-based newspaper, while the mother sat in her chair reading a print-based novel. The children, two teenagers, sat on the couch reading their laptops. This image portrays a dichotomy in our society. Many students today are digital natives—ones who have lived with digital technologies and personal computers all of their lives and tend not to choose print-based resources, but instead often choose to read and socialize online. On the other hand, the parents of those students may learn and adapt to the digital environment, but they always retain the "digital immigrant accent" (Prensky, 2001). One accent may be their preference for traditional, print-based texts as seen in the image of one family reading. Prensky argues: "The single biggest problem facing education today is that our digital immigrant instructors, who speak an outdated language (that of the pre-digital age), are struggling to teach a population that speaks an entirely new language." Acknowledging Prensky's argument, we set out to explore to what extent, and in what forms, the problems noted by Prensky were manifested in two US high schools.

In this study, we specifically seek to understand how 16 teachers negotiated power dynamics within their classrooms when multiliteracies and digital-based technologies were used. Our goal for this chapter is to present evidence and a conceptual perspective that could expand current teaching approaches in relationship to: (a) power relations among digitally native students and digitally migrant teachers; and (b) literacy/multiliteracies resources displayed in the classroom.

Methods

Data for this chapter were taken from a larger qualitative study Elizabeth conducted looking at secondary content area teachers' conceptualizations of technology and literacy (Stolle, 2007). Sixteen teachers, both male and female, from two high schools within a high-achieving school district (as evidenced by test scores above state and national averages) voluntarily participated in this study. Their teaching assignments included ninth through twelfth grade English, social studies, and science, and their professional experiences varied from one year to 31 years. The teachers were divided into two categories: primary participants and secondary participants.

Four teachers became the primary participants of the study, and each was observed for a total of 25–30 hours during the spring 2006 semester. Observation schedules varied from week to week, but each teacher was observed for 1–4 hours per day, 1 or 2 days per week. Teachers were observed during different periods of the day, capturing a complete picture of their lives in the classroom. The observations followed Werner and Schoepfle's (1987) systematic approach in naturalistic settings, keeping detailed observational notes. This approach progresses through three types of observations—descriptive, focused, and selective—to gain a comprehensive depiction of the setting. The observations were complemented with three in-depth, semi-structured interviews with each teacher. The interviews followed an interactive, situational, and generative approach by posing open-ended questions that initiated dialogue (Burgess, 1984; Fontana & Frey, 2000). As ideas and stories emerged, further questions were asked, helping teachers elaborate, explore, and describe their thinking and experiences. Furthermore, response data (St. Pierre, 1997) was gathered from these four teachers by conducting one final interview. All of the primary participants' interviews were audio-recorded and transcribed for analysis.

In addition to the observations and interviews, four focus groups were conducted, with another 12 teachers labeled as secondary participants. During the focus group meetings, the discussions followed a structured approach, centered on questions from a prepared discussion outline. This was done to keep the discussion concentrated on the topics of interest (Morgan, 1997) and to address similar topics between the two high schools. All of the focus group interviews were audio-recorded and transcribed for analysis.

Finally, a researcher's journal was kept throughout the project (Richardson, 2000). In it memos were written to: (1) record the concrete details of what was seen and heard while in the teachers' classrooms; (2) articulate the data collection process; (3) connect what was being seen and heard with what was being read professionally; (4) encourage the use of multiple perspectives to navigate, shift, relocate, and renegotiate the thinking and analysis; and (5) record the raw feelings and emotions experienced as a researcher.

During the data collection process, the classroom observations were used to create focus group questions, and the focus group discussions were used to guide and direct the observations. Additionally, themes and conceptualizations observed during the classroom observations were compared and contrasted to the themes and conceptualizations noted in the focus groups. The researcher's journal provided a space to explore the interplay between the data sources and to see how the themes and ideas noted during classroom observations and in-depth interviews were then corroborated during the focus group interviews. Finally, the response data interviews were used to move the analysis "toward the unthought" (St. Pierre, 1997, p. 410).

Data Analysis

For the purposes of this chapter, we went back to the original data, specifically analyzing: (1) the dynamics associated with "native" and/or "immigrant" perspectives related to multiliteracies and digital technologies manifested within the classroom; and (2) to what extent, and in what forms, power dynamics were negotiated within the classroom when multiliteracies and digital technologies were being used.

We took up Richardson's (2000) notion that writing is a "way of *knowing*" (p. 923), and analyzed the "pivotal moments" by writing poems, narratives, lists, and reflections using the teachers' words, sometimes juxtaposing conflicting thoughts in order to see the complexity within the moment. These writings pared down the data so we could analyze specific moments and situations in concrete, explicit ways. Writing was not just an end activity, a way to write up the findings, but rather an integral part of the understandings.'The majority of the analysis, in fact, occurred within the writing process.

Findings

The data analyzed indicates that when multiliteracies and digital technologies are allowed into a classroom, there is a tendency to disrupt, or unsettle, traditional power structures. Traditional power structures within a classroom position the teacher as the one in authority over the student. That is, the teacher is in-the-know, or the "depositor," while the students are the "depositories" (Freire, 1970, p. 72). The disruptions are particularly noticeable when the digitally immigrant teachers lack adequate knowledge for the task at hand, and attempt to use digital technologies in new and unfamiliar ways.

Our analysis identified the presence of four main "approaches/strategies" developed by teachers to negotiate the *digital disruptions*: (1) refusing to invite students' advanced knowledge of technology into the classroom; (2) only using familiar technology in familiar ways; (3) attempting to take control in different ways in the classroom; and (4) abandoning multiliteracies and digital technologies.

Disruptions

In order to understand the digital disruptions identified in these classrooms, we frame our critical analysis within Street's (1984, 2005) perspectives about ideological and autonomous models of literacy and the importance of understanding the cultural meanings and power dimensions of literacy. Street notes that the autonomous model assumes that "literacy" in and of itself is an independent entity. With this view, literacy alone can create positive effects on cognitive and social practices. However, the autonomous model ignores individuality, cultural understandings, and the ever-present negotiation of power in classrooms. The autonomous model holds to traditional power structures within the classroom, thus perpetuating the banking model of education, treating all students the same, as empty vessels ready to be filled by the teacher's knowledge (Freire, 1970). Alternately, the ideological model is more culturally sensitive, positing that literacy is a social practice, not just a technical and neutral skill. Recognizing literacy as a social act, we understand that power relationships will be negotiated within any given social context.

When multiliteracies and digital technologies are present in the classroom, traditional power structures will necessarily be affected. That is, disruptions will occur because new dynamics affect the traditional notions of "teacher in authority." Here we wrote a poem to illustrate a disruption as noted by one of the secondary participants, a first-year teacher taking her ninth grade English class to the computer lab to find resources for a research paper.

Freshman, students, online, oh my!

Freshman English class in the library,
On computers
Online...
30 kids
30 different computers
How do I monitor all of the kids at once?
I'm peeking, trying to check
To make sure students are on task.

Freshman, students, online, oh my!

What are students doing?
Where are they going?
They're very comfortable with technology.
I never really learned like the kids are learning now.
Things are just like snap to them.
Not me.

Freshman, students, online, oh my!

This teacher expressed her feelings about how new digital technologies disrupted the previously well-known norms. Many of the teachers conceptualized that print-based texts gave them a sense of control over what students read. Although students still made choices while researching in regard to which texts to read or not to read, they had clear boundaries based on the available, preapproved texts within the library or classroom. With the Internet, the boundaries are not as well defined, creating a sense of ambiguity in the classrooms.

To minimize ambiguity, this English teacher monitored the class, "peeking" at the computer screens with a sentiment of surveillance. Students made choices to stay on the task or move beyond the boundaries. The teacher told us that during this time in the computer lab, she found two students on myspace.com. It appears that teachers do not have complete authority over how students navigate texts using the Internet. Instead, students can use the Internet to negotiate the power structure, making their own choices regarding which texts to read or not read, thus disrupting the traditional power structure.

Our data shows that most of the disruptions are particularly noticeable when teachers lacked adequate knowledge for the task. A common disruption seen and acknowledged by almost all of the teachers in the study occurred when something went wrong with the digital technology. The teachers articulated that they seek students' help when the technology fails to cooperate. For example, one secondary participant shared,

> If I'm stuck at the computer, and I can't figure out how to copy this into that or PowerPoint, or whatever else, I say, "Okay, who are my computer people? Come on up." … They feel like they're teaching; they're being a resource for you.

In these types of situations, traditional notions of authority and power relationships are disrupted, and to some extent reversed, as the teacher invites the student into the authoritative position, to be the one in-the-know.

Other teachers shared similar examples of using students as resources. The teachers perceive students as more knowledgeable in the "how-to" category of multiliteracies because the students "have grown up with it." This statement draws us back to Prensky's (2001) notions of digital natives and digital immigrants. The teachers in this study conceptualize the students as digital natives and themselves as digital immigrants. For example, one primary participant, Rich (pseudonym), an advanced placement English teacher, explained his rationale for not teaching PowerPoint extensively: "Most of them would be bored to death because most of them can run circles around me. They bring stuff in here that's wonderful that I could never put together." A secondary participant shared the same sentiment: "It's not anything new [to the students]. It just keeps changing, and they learn a little bit more each time. So, it's not like us starting over with a new kind of thing." Once again, in these teachers' statements, students are being positioned as the ones in-the-know, a concept that has implications for understanding power relationships in the classroom.

To better comprehend classrooms as social contexts in which knowing about multiliteracies and digital technologies shape and reshape the literacy practices of students (Karchmer, Mallette, Kara-Soteriou, & Leu, 2005), we pay attention to the Foucauldian notion that knowledge is dynamically involved in the relationship of power (Gordon, 1980). That is, students, acting as natives, fully socialized in multiliteracies and digital technologies, engage in different social practices than their teachers, the digital immigrants. This shaping and reshaping emphasizes the connection Lankshear and Knobel (2002, 2003) make between literacy and technology: engaging in the new literacy practices associated with multiliteracies and technology is a social act. In the end, this shaping and reshaping impacts the power relationships between teachers and students, positioning the students as the ones in-the-know.

Still, understanding this perceived shift based on knowledge levels is more nuanced and complex. Although the teachers in this study believe students know more about multiliteracies and digital technologies, they also think the opposite. This contradiction came out specifically in the words of Rich. While talking about his students using editing tools in writing, he stated, "There are huge gaps sometimes in what they [students] know how to do." The focus groups corroborated this concept as they discussed the students' abilities to effectively navigate the Internet. One ninth grade science teacher shared her observations of students using the Internet to research earthquakes, "I have a lot [of students] who get there [search result page] and just go click, one by one, and don't know how to look and see what they want." Teachers shared that although students can act as a resource in the classroom when technology doesn't cooperate, they still lack academic knowledge about multiliteracies and digital technologies such as formatting a word document, writing a professional email, or researching effectively and efficiently. The next poem aims at capturing Rich's thoughts more in-depth regarding the students' knowledge levels.

Students, technology, and writing

I cannot imagine how I ever wrote papers without a word processor.
I really don't know.
I don't know how I did that, now.
It seems odd that that was even possible to get a paper,
A term paper,
Written on a type-writer.
I don't know.

To what degree have things like word processors improved writing?
They definitely improved my writing,
But I'm a writer.
So, I use the editing tools a lot.
But I don't have time,
You know,
In my class curriculum,
To really teach kids how to use the editing tools.
That's getting in the way of me teaching Faulkner or something else that I should be doing,
That I consider more important and more relevant to my content area.

This poem highlights the "gaps" troubling teachers, placing them back in the traditional role of authority, or the one in-the-know. So, although multiliteracies and digital technologies can disrupt established structures of authority within the classroom, they also can reinforce the traditional dynamics as well. This poem also highlights the teachers' notions of what is important in the classroom—Faulkner, or classic texts from the canon. Here, multiliteracies are not equated with traditional literacy based on printed texts. With this valuing comes a positioning of multiliteracies and digital technologies as something second to traditional print-based texts, thus perpetuating the traditional power structure in the classroom.

Relationships and Negotiations

The teachers in this study negotiated dynamics of authority and power within the classroom when multiliteracies and digital technologies were being used by using four main approaches/strategies: (1) refusing to invite students' advanced knowledge of technology into the classroom; (2) only using familiar technology in familiar ways; (3) attempting to take control in different ways in the classroom; and (4) abandoning multiliteracies and digital technologies. The teachers used these approaches/strategies to maintain traditional power structures, or to enact Street's (1984, 2005) autonomous model that places teachers in the authoritative role within the classroom.

Refusing Acknowledgment

Although all of the teachers in this study acknowledged the students' advanced knowledge of multiliteracies and digital technologies, their comfort level varied regarding how that advanced knowledge would be invited, or not invited, into the classroom. As discussed before, some teachers valued the students as a knowledgeable resource and allowed students to teach them new how-to tips. However, other teachers refused to invite students' knowledge into the classroom.

One example of this refusal stems from the classroom of one of the primary participants, Lynne (pseudonym), who taught on-level ninth grade English. Lynne attempted to use an unfamiliar type of technology in her classroom—podcasts. She wanted to show her students a few podcasts in class and then have them create podcasts on their own. However, she didn't know how to teach students how to create a podcast. Standing in front of the class, she admitted her lack of knowledge regarding podcast production. Here, she allowed a disruption in traditional power structures. With this opening, one student raised his hand to share that he knew how to create a podcast. Lynne allowed him to come to her computer to show her a comprehensive website about podcast production. In this instance, Lynne yielded her position of authority, or her position of being the one in-the-know, to her student. In this sense, Lynne took up the ideological model, understanding that her students bring knowledge and meaning to the classroom—they had knowledge of podcasts. Her willingness to diverge from traditional roles of teacher and students opened the door for new ways Lynne could engage her students with multiliteracies and digital technologies. This yielding provided Lynne with the opportunity to transform, and to grow in knowledge.

Lynne recognized the tension she experienced based on her limited knowledge, and she negotiated the power structure within the classroom to ease some of this tension. However, Lynne fell back on the strategy of refusal by shutting down the exchange with her student. After viewing the website on podcast production, she asked the student to return to his desk. Instead of committing to podcasts and learning from her student, she simply showed the class a few examples and then filed the idea away for a different day when she had the necessary knowledge. We cannot help but wonder if this avoidance was fed by a fear of the unfamiliar shift in power dynamics. If Lynne knew more about podcasts, that is, if she was the expert on podcast production, would she have had the confidence to use them effectively with students?

Constrained Acknowledgment

The second strategy the teachers in this study administered was to only use digital technologies in familiar ways. Instead of branching out and experimenting with multiliteracies and digital technologies, the teachers tended to stick with that which they felt most comfortable, constraining the tools and pedagogical options. One of the primary participants, Ben (pseudonym), who taught ninth and tenth grade social studies, provides a good example of how this strategy is implemented in his classroom.

Ben was positioned by others, such as the principal, as an innovative teacher who engaged his students with the multiliteracies and used digital technologies effectively with students. Based on the principal's positioning, Ben was given a SMART board. With the SMART board, the principal and other teachers further positioned Ben as an innovative teacher with technology. However, after observation in Ben's classroom, it appeared he was limited in scope. Ben equated technology with multimedia and believed innovative practice was showing movie clips with a DVD player and the data projector. Although visual literacy can be incorporated in the multiliteracies scope, and movie clips enhance student learning, judging from the research regarding the new trends in new literacies (Karchmer et al., 2005; Kist, 2005), his practices involving technology and multiliteracies lacked innovation.

But why the lack of innovation when a teacher has an innovative piece of technology? Ben talked specifically about not being more proficient with the SMART board because he did not have time to learn alternative ways to use it. So, based on limited knowledge and time, Ben chose to use the SMART board in less than innovative ways instead of disrupting the power structure within the classroom. Ben was a teacher who always appeared to be in-the-know.

He was quick-witted, intelligent, and well-liked among the students. From the observations, students looked to Ben for advice, new knowledge, and novel insights. With this image, Ben seemed reluctant to test out an alternative power structure between the students and himself by experimenting with the SMART board. So, instead of appearing less knowledgeable, Ben chose to use the technology in familiar ways that placed him in a particular role, the position of the expert (Davies & Harre, 2001).

This strategy of constraining multiliteracies was demonstrated by other teachers in the study as well. For example, Lynne used a recording to read a novel as a class. Instead of using a tape recorder or CD, she chose to listen to the novel on her ipod. In this situation, although using an ipod with students could be innovative and engage them in multiliteracies, this use of an ipod resembled the "old wine in new bottles syndrome," where long-standing school literacy routines simply have a new technology tacked on, but the substance of the practice has not changed (Lankshear & Knobel, 2003, p. 29). That is, teachers continue to do what they've always done while technology is seen as "an add-on, or a tool, to support forms of practice that are well-rehearsed circuits that travel along deep grooves" (Leander, 2007, p. 47).

Taming Acknowledgment

The third strategy teachers in this study employed to negotiate authority structures around multiliteracies and digital technologies was to take control in different ways in the classroom. This strategy was seen most frequently when the teachers had the students using the Internet in school. The fear factor discussed previously around students and the Internet was a common feeling among the teachers in this study. The freedom students have on the Internet makes the teachers uncomfortable and puts them in a position with only limited authority.

This strategy is most evident in Lynne's classroom as she engaged her students in a Web Scavenger Hunt. In this assignment, students were brought to the computer lab where they were directed to search five specific, pre-selected, teacher-censored websites. Each student had a worksheet with specific questions they were to answer based on the information found on these websites. This assignment was Lynne's attempt to resume control over her students' surfing while using the Internet. Through this assignment, she felt assured that her students would spend their time on meaningful, informational websites learning the predetermined knowledge base. With this assurance, Lynne's strategy maintained her authority within the classroom. Because she determined the sites, she not only was the one in-the-know, but she was also the one in control.

The concerns the teachers raised in this study are not unique. In Leander's (2007) study, he found that teacher discourse imagines the Internet as a space filled with danger, while also constructing the Internet as a distraction that "disrupts schooled assumptions about containment and surveillance of individual activity" (p. 35). These ideas of the Internet resonate with the teachers in this study, as they negotiated the power structures within the classroom by seeking to control student activities on the Internet. Teachers feared where students might go, with whom the students might speak, and what the students might see in cyberspace. They also feared students would engage in off-task behaviors while online.

An incident in Ben's classroom provides some justification for the teachers' tamed acknowledgment. Ben was using an educational website to engage the students in a geography review game when an inappropriate advertisement popped-up on the screen. Ben quickly clicked away from the advertisement, but the damage was already done—the class was disrupted and in an uproar. Ben acknowledged his lack of control when using a commercial website. Although he could control the game content, selecting categories and quiz questions, he could not control what advertisements the webmaster allowed on the site.

Although Ben recognized he could not control all that his students would see on the Internet, he confidently negotiated this tension to retain authority by previewing sites before he asked students to use them. He explained, saying

> I'm on that site prior to giving it to kids. I know what I'm sending the kids to because I use it with the kids. I use the site myself if I send them to it. I look at the website and determine its credibility. If it's something that we can learn from, then I'll send the kids there. Otherwise, I won't use it.

Similar to Lynne, Ben found an alternative way to control the students' online behavior and maintain authority—he assigned specific, teacher-approved websites instead of homework that required searches.

Rejective Acknowledgment

The final strategy the teachers took up to maintain traditional power structures in the classroom when using multiliteracies and digital technologies was to reject multiliteracies and digital technologies. Although the teachers conceptualized a shift in literacy practices to include multiliteracies, the negotiation of power structures drove their classroom practices as they continued to valorize and solidify traditional literacy practices by requiring students to read print-based texts and write with pen and paper. One secondary participant described it, saying,

> I think technology almost deters kids from wanting to enhance their literacy skills. For example, I told students, "We're going to sit down and start drafting a rough draft of an essay." The students said, "We're just going to type it at home." I said, "Well, no. We're going to sit here, and we're going to physically write on a piece of paper with an old-style pencil." They're so used to hopping right on the computer.

This teacher's comment illustrates that teachers are comfortable with traditional literacies; they use traditional literacy practices. Therefore, the teachers in this study position traditional literacy practices ahead of new literacy practices, thus positioning themselves as experts within the classroom.

Teachers are not the only ones positioning traditional literacy practices ahead of new literacy practices. This tension between traditional literacy practices and multiliteracies is also rooted in the practical realities of legislation and the standardized testing movement in the United States of America. Although the No Child Left Behind legislation requires that schools "assist every student in crossing the digital divide by ensuring that every student is technologically literate by the time the student finishes the 8th grade" (U.S. Department of Education, 2001), the standardized tests require that students use traditional literacy practices such as writing an essay with paper and pen or using correct grammar and spelling without a dictionary or spell check. As Leu (2006) notes, the test does not assess whether students can search online for information, critically evaluate online information, synthesize online information, or communicate online. In this sense, the standardized assessment is congruent with the teachers' comfort level, valorizing and assessing traditional literacy practices, positioning them ahead of new literacy practices. Another secondary participant articulates this idea, saying,

> [Students] have to be able to write in the classroom setting. They have to be able to do that. They're not going to be able to go to the computer [during a standardized test], period. They can't. So, if for nothing else, just for the test purposes, they better be able to practice writing a rough draft here, even if it's not the final draft.

The teachers can look to legislation to find justification for their abandonment strategy. They can, and should, emphasize traditional literacies in class because the standardized tests assess these traditional literacy practices. They can and should maintain the authoritative position given to them in traditional literacy because of legislation and standardized tests.

Implications

This study highlights some of the complex issues secondary teachers face as they use multiliteracies and digital technologies to enhance literacy practices and learning. Specifically, our findings suggest the likelihood of a changing scenario in classrooms due to the increased presence of multiliteracies and digital technologies and their disruptive effects on traditional structures of authority. Although the teachers may like to ignore the changes associated with multiliteracies and digital technologies because they often expose the teachers' limited knowledge, thus impacting the authority structures of classrooms, it seems they cannot. Teachers are forced to struggle to make sense of the new scenarios, negotiating the disruptions occurring in their classrooms.

As seen in the data, the teachers are more comfortable with what they already know, the traditional literacies (which it is presumed that teachers have mastered). Although most teachers believe in the importance of teaching and using digital technologies as part of the new literacy skills of the 21st century, they are not as knowledgeable as their digitally native students. This shift in knowledge disrupts traditional relationships of authority and power, and many teachers deal with that fundamental disruption of their "traditional" role by simply skimming the surface of multiliteracies and digital technologies in order to preserve traditional power relationships within their classrooms. Although some of the teachers allow students to position themselves as the ones in-the-know on certain occasions, they never bring this new dynamic of authority to fruition. Instead, teachers employ the "acknowledgment strategies" noted in this study, hoping to do two contradictory actions simultaneously: acknowledging the "authority" based on the mastery of knowledge and skills of their students, while maintaining themselves as the "authority" within their classrooms.

We do not believe the teachers in this study are alone in this desire to retain traditional power relationships within their classrooms. We would like to suggest that teachers around the world are using "acknowledgment strategies." However, in order to move toward a more collaborative learning environment where multiliteracies and digital technologies are explored and fully learned, teachers need to realize that it is healthy and beneficial to allow for other relationships of authority in their classrooms, including the feared situation in which the "students are the ones in-the-know."

Note

1. www.nytimes.com/2008/07/27/books/27reading.html?_r=1&pagewanted=all&oref=slogin.

References

Burgess, R. G. (1984). *In the field: An introduction to field research.* London: Allen & Unwin.

Davies, B., & Harre, R. (2001). Positioning: The discursive production of selves. In M. Wetherell, S. Taylor, & S. J. Yates (Eds.), *Discourse theory and practice* (pp. 261–271). Thousand Oaks, CA: Sage.

Fontana, A., & Frey, J. H. (2000). The interview: From structured questions to negotiated text. In N. K. Denzin & Y. S. Lincoln (Eds.), *Handbook of qualitative research* (2nd ed.) (pp. 645–672). Thousand Oaks, CA: Sage.

Freire, P. (1970). *Pedagogy of the oppressed.* New York: Continuum.

Gordon, C. (Ed.). (1980). *Power/knowledge: Selected interviews & other writings by Michel Foucault.* New York: Pantheon Books.

Karchmer, R. A., Mallette, M. H., Kara-Soteriou, J., & Leu, D. J., Jr. (Eds.). (2005). *Innovative approaches to literacy education: Using the internet to support new literacies.* Newark, DE: International Reading Association.

Kist, W. (2005). *New literacies in action: Teaching and learning in multiple media.* New York: Teachers College.

Lankshear, C., & Knobel, M. (2002). Do we have your attention? New literacies, digital technologies and the education of adolescents. In D. Alvermann (Ed.), *Adolescents and literacies in a digital world* (pp. 19–39). New York: Peter Lang.

Lankshear, C., & Knobel, M. (2003). *New literacies: Changing knowledge and classroom learning.* Buckingham: Open University Press.

Leander, K. M. (2007). "You won't be needing your laptops today": Wired bodies in the wireless classroom. In M. Knobel & C. Lankshear (Eds.), *A new literacies sampler* (pp. 25–48). New York: Peter Lang.

Leu, D. J., Jr. (2006). New literacies, reading research, and the challenges of change: A deictic perspective. In J. V. Hoffman, D. L. Schallert, C. M. Fairbanks, J. Worth, & B. Malock (Eds.), *55th Yearbook of the National Reading Conference* (pp. 1–42). Oak Creek, WI: National Reading Conference.

Morgan, D. L. (1997). *Focus groups as qualitative research* (2nd ed.). Thousands Oak, CA: Sage.

Prensky, M. (2001). Digital natives, digital immigrants. *On the Horizon,* 9(5): EJ. Retrieved October 10, 2007 from http://pre2005.flexiblelearning.net.au/projects/resources/Digital_Natives_Digital_Immigrants.pdf.

Richardson, L. (2000). Writing: A method of inquiry. In N. K. Denzin & Y. S. Lincoln (Eds.), *Handbook of qualitative research* (2nd ed.) (pp. 923–948). Thousand Oaks, CA: Sage.

St. Pierre, E. A. (1997). Methodology in the fold and the irruption of transgressive data. In S. B. Merriam and associates (Eds.), *Qualitative research in practice: Examples for discussion and analysis* (pp. 399–416). San Francisco: Jossey-Bass.

Stolle, E. P. (2007). *Secondary content area teachers speak about literacy and technology: Tensions, complexities, conceptualizations, and practices* (Doctoral dissertation, Arizona State University, 2007). ProQuest, 3258046.

Street, B. V. (1984). *Literacy in theory and practice.* Cambridge: Cambridge University Press.

Street, B. V. (2005). Recent application of new literacy studies in educational contexts. *Research in the Teaching of English,* 39(4), 417–423.

U.S. Department of Education. (2001). *The No Child Left Behind act of 2001: Enhancing education through technology.* Retrieved July 27, 2005, from www.ed.gov/policy/elsec/leg/esea02/pg34.html.

Werner, O., & Schoepfle, G. M. (1987). *Systematic fieldwork: Vol. 1. Foundations of ethnography and interviewing.* Newbury Park, CA: Sage.

10 Using Multiliteracies to Facilitate Culturally Relevant Pedagogy in the Classroom

Louanne Ione Smolin, National-Louis University, and Kimberly Lawless, University of Illinois at Chicago

Introduction

Today's students comprise a range of cultures, ethnicities, languages, gender and social class, and they bring these rich characteristics with them into the classroom. Yet often, the content of the curriculum, the materials integrated within academic lessons, and the pedagogical interactions between students and teachers do not reflect these assets. This creates an unfortunate mismatch between the lives of students outside of the classroom and what is expected of them inside the classroom. In the process, a potential resource for student learning remains untapped: using students' multifaceted personal and cultural assets to maximize learning in the classroom. A focus on these assets opens up possibilities for variability in the language of academics, enhancing opportunities for the content of the curriculum to be more accessible to students. Since multiliteracies represent the multiple modes through which students can communicate and learn, they foster diversity as a resource for learning. In this chapter, we explore the potential for multiliteracies to enhance culturally responsive approaches to classroom instruction.

Culturally Relevant Pedagogy

One construct that many have explored as a means of bridging the classroom environment and the social and cultural identities that students bring from home is culturally relevant pedagogy (Gay, 2000; Ladson-Billings, 1994; Moll, Amanti, Neff & Gonzalez, 1992; Villegas, 1991). Ladson-Billings (1994) has defined culturally relevant pedagogy as that "which empowers students intellectually, socially, emotionally, and politically by using cultural referents to foster knowledge, skills & attitude" (p. 18). Instead of marginalizing or even homogenizing student differences, it capitalizes upon the unique backgrounds, knowledge and experiences of the students to inform a teacher's lessons and methodology. As such, culturally relevant practices are "not merely vehicles for bridging or explaining the dominant culture, they are aspects of the curriculum in their own right" (Ladson-Billings, 2004, p. 18). This enables students to succeed in formalized academic tasks such as reading and writing, while at the same time not alienating them from their familial and cultural histories.

Culturally relevant pedagogy involves more for teachers than developing an understanding of how a particular culture learns and then teaching in a specific way to that specific culture. Rather, it is about inviting students' cultures to be a part of the social practices of the classroom (Gay, 2000). In other words, culturally relevant pedagogy is not about leveraging resources to teach a particular culture, but rather leveraging culture as a resource for teaching. Doing so changes the focal point of traditional curriculum by de-centering and enlarging it. For example, a traditional approach to the study of the civil war at the high-school level might include a focus on battles, generals and soldiers and the notion that Lincoln emancipated the slaves. A culturally relevant approach might shift the focus of such a unit along two distinctive veins. Through one approach, rather than learning about the Emancipation Proclamation as a historical fact, students might explore the notion of freedom through contradictions such as the reality that while the Emancipation Proclamation occurred in the 1800s, African Americans did not gain civil rights in America until the 1960s. Through their own cultural referents students are developing insights into historical ideas. Another potential focus of the curriculum might incorporate unique and particular social issues experienced by diverse communities that are not necessarily represented in traditional curricular materials. For example, there is little information about the Sand Creek Massacre of "hundreds of Indian villagers in Colorado just as 'emancipation' was proclaimed for black people by Lincoln's administration" (Zinn, 2008, p. 5). The irony of one population being emancipated while another is being destroyed adds a seldom-explored perspective, enlarging the focus to those communities traditionally not represented in the curriculum. These scenarios exemplify two ways in which the focal point of curriculum can be enlarged to foster student learning. The curriculum can center on the lives of students, leveraging their histories as a classroom resource, and at the same time can provide students with alternative and multiple perspectives surrounding a curricular topic.

As teachers construct learning opportunities, they can examine key attributes to shift and expand the focus of the curriculum. When examining a learning environment for its cultural attributes, an educator must ask: "In what ways is or can culture be represented?" A critical perspective enables students and teachers to explore, examine and critique assumptions related to the status quo through the lenses of race, ethnicity, gender, class, and special needs. A culturally relevant learning environment offers students rich intellectual possibilities, facilitating their development of content-rich "habits of mind," engaging them in higher-order cognitive processes. Based upon the notion that learning is a social endeavor, culturally relevant academic environments help students establish learning relationships through collaborative interactions with each other, their teachers and, importantly, the wider community.

Technology and Multiliteracies

While culturally relevant teaching enlarges the focus and perspectives of the curriculum, the concept of cultural identity also continues to broaden in our contemporary society. Alongside race, ethnicity, language and gender, another important dimension of culture is digital identity. Teachers and students often have markedly different digital experiences. Prensky (2001a, 2001b) has defined individuals as being either "digital natives" (students) or "digital immigrants" (teachers). Because students today have grown up with technology, Prensky (2001) maintains that they "think and process information fundamentally differently from their predecessors" (p. 1). Digital natives and digital immigrants have contrastive experiences, with students not only incorporating technology in their lives outside school more than inside school (Gewertz, 2007), but using it differently (Hird, 2000). At home, students use technology to expand their social network as well using multimedia tools to represent aspects of their identity on various social networking websites. In school, studies indicate that college students are using technology to communicate with classmates and professors, thereby extending the classroom walls. This involvement "basically supplements to the curriculum" (Burbules, 2007, p. 212; see also Jones, Johnson-Yale, Perez & Schuler, 2007). A culturally relevant approach to curriculum should incorporate students' digital experiences and identities, as their technology practice outside of school represents a unique fund of knowledge that we must explore to meet their educational needs and better understand what their futures might be (Smolin & Lawless, 2003). If we educators do not build bridges between students' cultural experiences in and out of school, we run the grave risk of "school becoming less and less relevant" (Prensky, in Gewertz, 2007).

Through this expanded notion of culture, inclusive of digital identity, classrooms must shift away from traditional notions of literacy that focus on language only, moving toward a multiliterate perspective. Multiliteracies are defined in a various ways. The New London Group (1996) discusses two important concepts: the multiple modes of representation that, through their affordances, help shape meaning; and the expanding contextual boundaries in which we use these modes to communicate. Cope and Kalantzis (2000) maintain that multiliteracies include both the "increasing multiplicity and integration of significant modes of meaning making, where the textual is also related to the visual, the audio, the spatial, the behavioral, and so on" (p. 5). Globalization provides a contextual necessity for us to become multiliterate. The multiple literacies that are important to student learning are described by Cope and Kalantzis (2000): "Effective citizenship and productive work now require that we interact effectively using multiple languages, multiple Englishes, and communication patterns that more frequently cross cultural, community and national boundaries" (also see Unsworth, 2001). These include the

> visual literacies that afford meaning-making in written texts with visual images; curriculum literacies, or those illiteracies particular to the various

> academic disciplines, such as language, arts or science; computer or cyberliteracies, such as effectively navigating hyperlinked texts; and critical literacies, or the link between texts and the social contexts in which they function.
>
> (p. 16)

Unsworth (2001) advocates that schools play a central role in facilitating students' development of these multiliteracies so that they can *become* fully literate. He maintains that "in order to become *effective participants* in emerging multiliteracies, students need to understand how the resources of language, image and digital rhetorics can be employed independently and interactively to construct different kinds of meaning" (p. 8). In so doing, students can prepare themselves for their future civic and professional lives.

A pedagogy of multiliteracies goes beyond engaging in separate literacy activities, and means more than using "more than one mode of representation at a time" (Enciso, Katz, Kiefer, Price-Dennis & Wilson, 2006, p. 8). Rather, multiliteracies are combined *in a social practice* that "animates social life and social actions" (Enciso et al., 2006, p. 8). Using information and communication technologies (ICT) greatly facilitates students' abilities to engage multiliteracies, and provides a rich learning environment in which students can engage and *practice* participating and shaping their present and future roles in a multidimensional, global society. These properties enable students to access a variety of media and provide new avenues in order to direct their learning in novel ways (MacKinnon, McFadden & Forsythe, 2002). As such, technology offers both a qualitatively and quantitatively different learning environment than a traditional print-centered curriculum (Leu, 2002; New London Group, 1996; Smolin & Lawless, 2003; Unsworth, 2001).

The definitions of multiliteracies that we build upon in this chapter are reflective of the above, and share a common framework based upon the realities of using multiple modalities for information access and production. Our *working* definition, influenced by the above sources, is fundamentally conceived through our work in classrooms with teachers and students (Smolin & Lawless, 2003). Multiliteracies encompass issues of visual literacy, technological or cyberliteracies, information or media literacy, and critical literacies. When engaged in visual literacy, students make meaning out of visual resources, in addition to those that are text-based. For example, when analyzing advertising campaigns, students must examine how the visual aspects of a message impact what is communicated and potentially understood. Further, visual literacy is also a critical component of the artifacts that students produce. When creating multimedia slideshows documenting stages of a scientific experiment, for instance, students must evaluate which of the images they have taken best portray a scientific principle they wish to describe. Students exhibit technological literacy when they seamlessly integrate a variety of technologies to accomplish an academic goal. To create the multimedia presentation described in the above example, students must know how to operate traditional or digital cameras, capture their images via a scanner or export them to a computer, and then place these images into the multimedia software application they are using to create their presentation. These abilities enhance student learning and expand the audience with which they can communicate, because through digital formats student artifacts can be more readily shared with, and accessed by, a wider audience.

Because access to ICT provides students with an ever-expanding amount of information that has been posted in an open, uncontrolled environment, it is imperative for students to analyze, evaluate and synthesize this information so that they can transform it into knowledge. In a classroom that stresses information literacy, teachers provide students with tools to analyze information for its inherent bias, its currency and its credibility. Finally, as students explore how information and ideas are constructed and conveyed through different media, such as visual images or hypertext, they are encouraged to critique how these multimodal artifacts affect people's (e.g., their) understandings and use of information. To do this, students must explore the relationship between text and context, thereby participating *with* a text rather than having a text define who they are and what they think. As such, they have the opportunity to deconstruct issues of power that occur when readers accept the written word without examination. They learn to "read the world," deconstructing the meaning of a text through understandings of their experiences and their world (Freire & Macedo, 1987). This process is called critical literacy.

The possibilities for student achievement brought about by this more broadened vision of literacy instruction have been documented (Bialo, Sivin-Kachala & Langford, 1997; Kress, 2003; Scardamalia & Bereiter, 1996), yet ironically the adoption of ICT as a classroom teaching tool is often a slow and difficult process (Cuban, 1986, 1996). Teachers are challenged by national, state and local standards to use ICT as a medium for teaching the core subject areas (e.g., National Council of Teachers of Mathematics, 2000; National Research Council, 1998), while at the same time they are being held accountable to strict evaluation of student outcomes which greatly restricts their control over curriculum planning, time and the necessary experimentation that curricular innovation requires. As a result, teachers often provide *access* to technology without an articulated philosophy for its *use*, compromising quality instruction. Students often engage in unprotected, unguided information searches or drill-and-skill remediation that mirror traditional paper and pencil worksheet activity. These approaches merely change the media rather than the pedagogy: i.e., rather than using paper and pencil, students use a computer. They do not see technology as a tool for their academic growth, nor develop a sense of how technology fits into their future in a digital-information-based world. They are not served well by this approach, which merely co-opts ICT into the traditional notion of literacy.

Culturally Relevant Pedagogy and Multiliteracies

Teachers must create conditions for students to participate in technology experiences that build upon their cultural and social realities. They need to involve students in technology-infused curriculum that exemplifies *how* technology can be used in an information-rich society, facilitating their understandings of concepts and domains that a traditional curriculum won't help them achieve. Using multiliteracies as a basis for defining what it means to think, to learn and to know also facilitates culturally relevant pedagogy. As we help students learn through media, we become much more culturally relevant because we leverage their digital "funds of knowledge" (Moll et al., 1992) in order to facilitate their learning. By appropriating multiliteracies to facilitate culturally relevant pedagogy, teachers can also build a curriculum based upon difference, "recruiting rather than ignoring and erasing the different intersubjectivities, interests, intentions, commitments and purposes that students bring to learning" (Cope & Kalantzis, 2000, p. 18). This enriches and expands the context of the curriculum. Therefore students have more opportunities to see themselves represented in the text and images they access rather then attempting to find a fit between themselves and the contexts represented by textbook publishers. When using the Internet, students can follow hypertext links that are driven, in part, by their personal histories and interests. Using multiliteracies to facilitate culturally relevant pedagogy invites students to engage in a technology-mediated social practice that requires them to establish a relationship with technology and see its use not only as important for inside school in the here-and-now, but outside school for now and for their future.

Multiliteracies and culturally relevant pedagogy are mutually supportive. Both are student-centered, and are driven by students' inquiries and concerns. Using multiliteracies facilitates culturally relevant pedagogy because they enable teachers to soften the boundaries between school and community; personal identity and disciplinary modes of thinking; academic work and life skills. Finally, a focus on multiliteracies enables students to become more than consumers of knowledge, but producers of it as well, building their knowledge from what is relevant to them and enabling them to contribute their knowledge to the growth of their communities and their future place in the world. This chapter explores how multiliteracies can be used to enhance culturally responsive approaches to classroom instruction through an analysis of two curriculum projects implemented by teachers with their students in two classrooms, and provides implications for classroom practice and research.

Curricular Cases

Example 1: What Does It Mean to be Bilingual?

Ms. Dennis and her second grade students used digital technologies, such as digital still and video cameras to interview bilingual business owners in the community surrounding their culturally diverse urban school. The purpose underlying the interviews was to discover insights to the question: "What does it mean to be bilingual?" Together students wrote interview questions, practiced them on one another, took walking field trips into the community and, armed with digital cameras, video cameras and audio tapes, carried out the interviews. Upon returning to their classroom, the students reviewed their pictures, audiotapes and videotapes. They then used the five classroom computers to analyze and synthesize their information to create a digital slide show they were to share with their school community. They also e-mailed these slide shows to e-pals with whom they had been tele-communicating.

The learning context exemplified above is rich in multiliteracies. Students are using a variety of media to communicate with an audience beyond the classroom as they engage in this project. They take digital photos, export them into their school computers and combine them into a digital slideshow, an example of technological literacy. By examining their photographs, students are making meaning of their experiences and deciding which pictures best communicate their message: an important component of visual literacy. Students are learning to use multiple technologies in the context of an authentic project, similar to broadcast and journalism professionals, rather than in a decontextualized computer lab course. They are also collaborating on many tasks, including multimedia design. Through these activities students are being apprenticed because they are interacting as professionals do. Therefore, students are developing lifelong skills that will not only serve them now, but well into the future.

These multiliteracies also facilitate students' engagement in culturally relevant experiences in a number of ways. In this project, Ms. Denis went beyond adding more culturally relevant content or technology to an existing course of study. She *merged* both in order to organize a course of study that built upon the students' own lifeworlds. Students can develop their literacy through a rich *social network* rather than through text-only resources. Student peers collaborate to manage technology resources and design multimedia slideshows. The primary sources of information for these students are the people living in their community. In order to develop the content for their presentations, students interact with their community members and actively integrate all of these intertextual resources to develop their understandings of bilingualism and to communicate these ideas to others.

Students go beyond using audiotape recorders, digital cameras, video camcorders and Internet technologies to complete a school assignment. The technology tools enable students to actively engage with members of their Mexican culture and create a living text using their own cultural referents. Through ICT, students manipulate text and images taken from the interviews and arrange and rearrange these resources in a variety of ways. This helps them to reflect on and make meaning of their community-based experience. In the process, they are using critical literacy. Their text runs counter to the deficit assumptions underlying many school approaches to bilingual students. In the end, the students revealed an important, implicit message: there are advantages to being bilingual. For them, being bilingual means that *you have two languages*, not that you are "less than" your English-speaking classmates who speak the dominant language of the classroom.

Example 2: Community Learning Center

Mr. Padron teaches eighth grade in a middle school north west of a downtown area in an urban school district. Ninety-five percent of the students are from low-income families, and 90% of the students are Latino. Academic achievement is an issue in this community, yet overcrowding in the elementary schools was a concern that community members voiced as a barrier to student success. This middle school was built as a solution to relieve the overcrowding. This was a grassroots community effort. The school emphasizes a "small school" concept characterized by smaller class size, a more personalized learning environment, and a cohesive vision among teachers. This vision includes a strong desire to collaborate in the development of interdisciplinary, thematic curriculum that integrates technology.

The rich history of community participation and school-wide vision provided Mr. Padron with academic resources for building the curriculum. He and his eighth-grade students received a grant to start a community learning center within the school. To gauge the needs of the community, his students surveyed members of their surrounding community. They began by looking at sample surveys on the Internet, and then constructed their own. They tested their surveys on one another and on their family members. Since all the parents were not from the city or country in which they currently live, a discussion of demographic patterns and changes in the community emerged, along with a sharing of ideas concerning how these patterns impact community need. Students used these ideas to revise the surveys as necessary before moving into the community. For a period of a week, students went out in the community in groups of five, with a parent mentor in each group, and conducted the survey, collecting data door-to-door. They also documented various community artifacts by taking digital pictures. When they returned to school the students entered the survey data into a Microsoft Excel spreadsheet. In groups, students analyzed the data to make community-based recommendations. They incorporated the results of this analysis, along with digital images they had taken, into a digital proposal for a community learning center. Finally, they presented their work to community members.

This project provides a powerful model for how students can be apprenticed for participation in an information society replete with multiple literacies. By appropriating technology to engage in high-level data collection and analysis, students are learning about data-driven decision-making, a skill important to many professions. They are also developing important future communication skills. They must present themselves in a professional manner to the adults in their community while they collect data and when they present their final recommendations. As they engage in multiliteracies, students are steeped in culturally relevant learning. They are not only learning *from* their community members, but are directly *impacting* the community in which they live. By authentically contributing to their community, they are *challenging* prevailing notions of "inner-city" youth as problematic.

The nature of this project requires students to use their academic skills beyond the classroom to impact social change. Students engaged in intensive planning and used information literacy processes for producing multimedia presentations. They had to collaborate in order to synthesize the great amount of data they received during the community data collection phase. They analyzed their findings, negotiating with one another to develop shared understandings of what the data suggested. Finally, they had to develop an interactive report that could support community members' informed decision-making. The report required students to seamlessly combine multimodal resources, integrating images and text as well as sequencing images in order to effectively tell a story. When choosing multimodal resources, students were problem solving and learning important media communications skills. Taken together, students are developing academic proficiency through alternative forms of meaning-making that are flexible and generative rather than through static rote memorization or repetition.

Students were empowered to challenge the status quo by actively *changing* it. They interacted with community members in new and different ways: gathering information; learning from one another; and collaborating in order to support their learning. Mr. Padron recounted: "In middle school, students found that they never expected to be so well received by the people in the houses." Students said that "these people actually listened to me, they're paying attention, they're answering my questions, also, I'm the one in charge, I control the situation and they're okay with it. That was really good!"

Both of these projects exemplify two important roles technology can play in creating culturally relevant learning environments rich in multiliteracies. First, students are using multiple technologies such as audio tape recorders, digital cameras, video cameras and the Internet for authentic purposes similar to the ways in which historians, mathematicians and writers use them for their work. They are gaining comfort and familiarity with important tools and are using them in ways that reflect everyday, situated uses as opposed to using such tools for formalized, traditional school instruction only. Second, technology serves as a bridge connecting the classroom and the community, supporting culturally relevant teaching and learning. Technology becomes a documentation device that enables teachers and students to make the community a part of the content of the curriculum. Therefore, students can learn formal academic content through learning activities that are situated in their unique personal experiences and lives.

Implications

For Practice

Developing comfort and familiarity with the technology tools necessary to incorporate multiliteracies for culturally relevant learning is a hands-on endeavor, and growth in this area is very personal: there is not one right way. There are an overwhelming amount of ideas and resources available to teachers and students. We as teachers can easily run the risk of using digital tools without a plan, or worse, not use them at all. Articulating a vision for how multiliteracies can be used to create culturally relevant curriculum is an important first step. For example, Ms. Denis wanted her students to develop their literacy skills from the vibrant business community that they see as they walk to school everyday. Mr. Padron wanted his students to make decisions based upon authentic, "everyday" data. Both of these ideas have clear academic goals that can be made more accessible through the use of technology.

Another important implication for teachers is that they take on an inquiring stance as they design curriculum, focusing on the "whole child" and asking what is culturally relevant for each of them. Rather than focusing on a particular content area theme, Ms. Denis and Mr. Padron began with issues important to the students: i.e., their language and their communities. A student-centered stance provides a useful focus for accessing the vast technology resources available. For example, Ms. Denis and her students gravitated towards multimedia tools; Mr. Padron and his students appropriated data collection technologies.

The technologies we use are continually changing, and therefore our notions of literacy are dynamic as well (Cope & Kalantzis, 2000; Leu, 2002). Using multiliteracies for culturally relevant approaches requires teachers to engage in ongoing formal and informal professional development. In addition to the variety of formalized school and web-based professional development networks, teachers can begin to explore digital tools and multimedia outside of school, not only for their professional growth, but for their personal growth as well. In this way, teachers are developing abilities with technology in ways similar to their students.

A multiliteracies approach to culturally relevant curriculum requires teachers to incorporate a classroom practice of "improvisation" rather than "performance" (Sawyer, 2004). In direct-instruction pedagogical approaches, the teacher performs a script she has created or one offered through standardized curriculum. Teaching as "improvisation" emphasizes the "interactional and responsive creativity of a teacher working together with a unique group of students," in which "the flow of the class is unpredictable and emerges from the actions of all participants, both teachers and students" (Sawyer, 2004, p. 13). To incorporate multiple sources of information, perspectives, voices and activities, a culturally relevant approach requires teachers to *orchestrate* a multi-dimensional learning environment. As such, teachers must *improvise,* leveraging resources in emergent ways, as well as tailoring their scaffolds and classroom discourse to the ideas generated by the students.

While there are many advantages to incorporating multiliteracies and culturally relevant pedagogy, there are also challenges. Because multiliteracies rely heavily on technology, and technology is rarely ubiquitous in schools, teachers often encounter barriers. Therefore, they must be persistent and resilient. Curriculum design must not only take into account students interests and perspectives, but the technology resources that are realistically available. This begins with a comparison of what technology resources are required to implement a project against an inventory of what is actually available to students. For example, Mr. Padron knew that his project initially needed his classroom computer and that multiple visits to the lab were required once the students analyzed their data and were ready to create their multimedia presentations. While their data input and analysis could be achieved with the single classroom computer, they required an LCD projection device to look at the pooled data in small groups or as an entire class. Mr. Padron requested a long-term loan from the school's media specialist. On days when this was not possible, he had to organize activities in a different way to accommodate smaller groups of students and use another means to share their work. While students could still access the community spreadsheet, they had to share their results and interpretations with the entire class using overhead transparencies. Mr. Padron made similar accommodations for the computer lab. In addition, he wanted his students to use a multimedia software program with which he wasn't familiar. He therefore invited the technology coordinator to collaborate with him on the project. Had Mr. Padron not had this human resource available, he would have incorporated a different, more familiar multimedia program that he could teach his students to use.

For Research

Although there is a great deal of agreement in the literature that culturally relevant pedagogy and technology are important aspects that must be incorporated into contemporary instructional practices, the empirical research base informing their connections remains relatively sparse (Brenner, 1998; Ladson-Billings, 1995; Lawless & Schrader, 2008; Patchen & Cox-Petersen, 2008). As a research community, we must endeavor to deepen our knowledge of what works, why it works and for whom if we are to have a larger impact on the education experiences provided to students in schools today. We conclude this chapter by highlighting a few areas that need to be expanded as we strive to make educational experiences meaningful, productive and inclusive for all students.

First and foremost, it is important that we begin to document what teachers are doing in classrooms that purport to enact a culturally relevant, technology-immersive instructional perspective. What do teachers consider to be inherent in a student's cultural identity? How are teachers leveraging these existing funds of cultural knowledge? Are students' out-of-classroom identities and their educational experiences becoming leveled? Documenting a well-sampled survey of the universe of instructional approaches taken by teachers has the ability to inform our knowledge of effective practice and direct appropriate curricular reform. This line of research, however, is one that is bound by the contextual affordances that make each classroom a unique entity. As such, whatever research is conducted in this area must situate practices within the community in which they are expressed. This means that this research must not only look at the student constituency of the classroom, but also simultaneously examine the teacher, the school and the surrounding community. Therefore, this research must employ some level of ethnographic technique to unearth the rich base of data required to understand a complex, situated system.

Further, research on culturally relevant pedagogy and technology must incorporate some principles of action research, emanating from teacher concerns and incorporating principles of design-based research. As described by Wang and Hannafin (2005), design-based research is "a systematic but flexible methodology aimed to improve educational practices through iterative analysis, design, development, and implementation, based on collaboration among researchers and practitioners in real-world settings, and leading to contextually-sensitive design principles and theories" (p. 6). Because the culture of each classroom context is so unique, other, more static research approaches are unlikely to yield results that are generalizable outside of the initial research site. The careful documentation required by action- and design-based research will allow other researchers and practitioner researchers alike to ascertain similarities and differences across contexts with their own classrooms. As such, replication of practices will yield greater fidelity and the possibility for similar outcomes.

Finally, research seeking to leverage the links between culturally relevant pedagogy and technology must take a multidisciplinary approach (Lee, 2005). A student's culture and use of technology as conduits for meaning-making may shift across instructional domains. A student's cultural background may privilege one content area over other areas. Similarly, technology facilitates affordances across varying academic disciplines, some distinctive and some similar. Moreover, some core interdisciplinary skills, such as accessing information from text or communicating acquired knowledge through visual means, may be more favorably scaffolded by certain characteristics of culturally relevant pedagogy or technology than others. As such, we need to understand the variance for *when* such approaches work, not just *that* they work.

Concluding Remarks

As exemplified in the curricular cases discussed in this chapter, multiliteracies and culturally relevant practices can be brought to bear by teachers to create academically rich learning environments with their students in mind, expanding learning in ways that a traditional curriculum cannot. As teachers integrate these mutually supportive practices, they actually have the potential to transform the status quo related to teaching and learning. These approaches to teaching and learning are student-centered, facilitate diversity of thought, and invite multiple perspectives. By appropriating a culturally relevant stance that is enacted through a multiliteracies lens, teachers can de-center and expand the content of the curriculum. In doing so, the curriculum becomes more reflective of students' lives and inclusive of the multiple perspectives that a more traditional curriculum does not address. Students therefore have greater potential to see themselves in the curriculum, to develop their academic identities and to contribute their voices to academic discourses.

These approaches facilitate ongoing learning, breaking down the barriers between students' in-school and out-of-school experiences. The technological capabilities students informally develop outside of school, such as texting, blogging and podcasting, can be incorporated into the formal academic space within school. Students' use of multiliteracies within the school curricula also has the potential to impact their standing in the community. In both cases examined within this chapter, students saw themselves as a part of their communities because their neighbors were in awe of their technological facility, and these adults saw them as potential advocates. Therefore, rather than homogenizing students, multiliteracies enabled them to deepen their own cultural connections. As barriers between in-school and out-of-school learning are reduced, students will continue to value learning and see it as relevant to their lives.

References

Bialo, E., Sivin-Kachala, J., & Langford, J. (1997). The effectiveness of technology in schools, '90–'97 report. Washington, DC: Software Publishers of America. (ERIC Document Reproduction Service No. ED 413 875).

Brenner, M. E. (1998). Adding cognition to the formula for culturally relevant instruction in mathematics. *Anthropology & Education Quarterly*, 29, 214–244.

Burbules, N. (2007). E-lessons learned. In L. Smolin, K. Lawless & N. Burbules (Eds.), *Information and communication technologies: Considerations of practice for teachers and teacher educators* (pp. 207–216). Malden, MA: Blackwell Publishing.

Cope, B., & Kalantzis, M. (2000). Introduction: Multiliteracies: The beginnings of an idea. In B. Cope & M. Kalantzis (Eds.), *Multiliteracies: Literacy learning and the design of social futures* (pp. 3–8). New York, NY: Routledge.

Cuban, L. (1986). *Teachers and machines: The classroom use of technology since 1920.* New York, NY: Teachers College Press.

Cuban, L. (1996). Computers in the classroom: Revolutions that fizzled. *Washington Post.* Washington, DC: R01.

Enciso, P., Katz, L., Kiefer B., Price-Dennis, D., & Wilson, M. (2006). Words, signs, and social relations. *Language Arts*, 84(1), 8–9.

Freire, P., & Macedo, D. (1987). *Literacy: Reading the word and the world.* Westport, CT: Bergin & Garvey.

Gay, G. (2000). *Culturally responsive teaching: Theory, research, & practice.* New York, NY: Teachers College Press.

Gewertz, C. (2007). Outside interests: Young people typically plug in to new technology far more often on their own time than in school. *Education Week*, Technology Counts 2007. Downloaded November, 2008 from: www.edweek.org/ew/articles/2007/03/29/30tcstudent.h26.html.

Hird, A. (2000). *Learning from cyber-savvy students: How internet age kids impact classroom teaching.* Sterling, VA: Stylus Publishing.

Jones, S., Johnson-Yale, C., Perez, F., & Schuler, J. (2007). The internet landscape in college. In L. Smolin, K. Lawless & N. Burbules (Eds.), *Information and communication technologies: Considerations of practice for teachers and teacher educators* (pp. 39–51). Malden, MA: Blackwell Publishing.

Kress, G. (2003). *Literacy in the new media age.* New York, NY: Routledge.

Ladson-Billings, G. (1994). *The Dreamkeepers: Successful teachers of African American children.* San Francisco, CA: Jossey Bass.

Ladson-Billings, G. (1995). Toward a theory of culturally relevant pedagogy. *American Educational Research Journal*, 32(3), 465–491.

Lawless, K. A., & Schrader, P. G. (2008). Where do we go now? Understanding research on navigation in complex digital environments. In J. Coiro, M. Knobel, C. Lankshear & D. J. Leu (Eds.), *Handbook of new literacies* (pp. 267–296). Hillsdale, NJ: Lawrence Erlbaum Associates.

Lee, O. (2005). Science education and English language learners: Synthesis and research agenda. *Review of Educational Research*, 75(4), 491–530.

Leu, Donald J. (2002). The new literacies: Research on reading instruction with the internet and other digital technologies. In J. Samuels & A. E. Farstrup (Eds.), *What research has to say about reading instruction* (pp. 310–336). Newark, DE: International Reading Association.

MacKinnon, G. R., McFadden, C., & Forsythe, T. (2002). The tension between hypertext environments and science learning. *Electronic Journal of Science Education*, 6(3), EJ, downloaded November 2008 from: http://unr.edu/homepage/crowther/ejse/mackinnonetal.pdf.

Moll, L. C., Amanti, C., Neff, D., & Gonzalez, N. (1992). Funds of knowledge for teaching: Using a qualitative approach to connect homes and classrooms. *Theory into Practice*, 31(2), 132–141.

National Council of Teachers of Mathematics. (2000). *Principles and standards for school mathematics.* Reston, VA. Downloaded November 2008 from: http://standards.nctm.org/document.

National Research Council. (1998). *National science education standards.* Washington, DC: National Academy Press.

New London Group. (1996). A pedagogy of multiliteracies: Designing social futures. *Harvard Educational Review*, 66, 60–92.

Patchen, T., & Cox-Petersen, A. (2008). Constructing cultural relevance in science: A case study of two elementary teachers. *Science Education*, 92(6), 994–1014.

Prensky, M. (2001a). Digital natives, digital immigrants. *On The Horizon*, 9(5), Downloaded November 2008 from: http://74.125.95.132/search?q=cache:Yvdyw3gWkxwJ:www.marcprensky.com/writing/Prensky%2520-%2520Digital%2520Natives,%2520Digital%2520Immigrants%2520-%2520Part1.pdf+prensky+digital+natives&hl=en&ct=clnk&cd=1&gl=us.

Prensky, M. (2001b). Digital natives, digital immigrants, Part II: Do they think differently? *On the Horizon*, 9(6). Downloaded November 2008 from: http://74.125.95.132/search?q=cache:Yvdyw3gWkxwJ:www.marcprensky.com/writing/Prensky%2520-%2520Digital%2520Natives,%2520Digital%2520Immigrants%2520-%2520Part2.pdf+prensky+digital+natives&hl=en&ct=clnk&cd=1&gl=us.

Sawyer, K. (2004). Creative teaching: Collaborative discussion as disciplined improvisation. *Educational Researcher*, 33(2), 12–20.

Scardamalia, M., & Bereiter, C. (1996). Engaging students in a knowledge society. *Educational Leadership*, 54(3), 6–10.

Smolin, L., & Lawless, K. (2003). Becoming literate in the technological age: New responsibilities and tools for teachers. *The Reading Teacher*, 56(6), 570–577.

Unsworth, L. (2001). *Teaching multiliteracies across the curriculum: Changing contexts of text and image in classroom practice.* Maidenhead: Open University Press.

Villegas, A. M. (1991). *Culturally responsive pedagogy for the 1990s and beyond.* Washington, DC: ERIC Clearinghouse on Teacher Education. Downloaded April 2009 from: www.eric.ed.gov/ERICWebPortal/custom/portlets/recordDetails/detailmini.jsp?_nfpb=true&_&ERICExtSearch_SearchValue_0=ED339698&ERICExtSearch_SearchType_0=no&accno=ED339698.

Wang, F., & Hannafin, M. J. (2005). Design-based research and technology enhanced learning environments. *Educational Technology Research & Development*, 53(4), 5–23.

Zinn, H. (2008). Empire or humanity: What the classroom didn't teach me about the American Empire. *Rethinking Schools Online*, 22(4), downloaded December 2008 from: www.rethinkingschools.org/archive/22_04/empi224.shtml.

Part IV

Multiliteracies in Practice

11 Multiliteracies and Assessment Practice

Ian Brown and Lori Lockyer, Faculty of Education, University of Wollongong, and Peter Caputi, School of Psychology, Faculty of Health and Behavioral Sciences, University of Wollongong

Introduction: Multiliteracies and Multimodal Learning

As the nature of learning has changed, so too has our notion of literacy. While educators recognize the transformative nature of education in the 21st century, the how and why of assessment still eludes curriculum developers, educational policy-makers and classroom practitioners. Many of the current assessment practices are too narrow, too limited to cater for the oral, critical, linguistic, visual and technological understandings required by today's learners. While teachers are adjusting their pedagogies to match the real-world practice, they are struggling to respond with appropriate assessment techniques. To fully grasp the complexities associated with assessment of these new ways of learning, one must examine the origins, practices and shift to multimodal learning and the impact of this on assessment practices.

The nature of teaching and learning is becoming increasingly complex and learners can no longer rely on a single learning design. Today, most effective learning designs include a variety of media, combinations of modalities, levels of interactivity, learner characteristics and pedagogy based on a complex set of circumstances (Metiri Group, 2008).

As with the nature of learning, the nature of literacy has also evolved. On review of current literature, no single or worldwide definition of literacy can be found. Traditionally, literacy was simply defined as the ability to decode written information. In the 1950s UNESCO believed a person to be functionally literate when he/she acquired the basic knowledge and skills in reading and writing (Baker & Street, 1994). By 2003 the United Nations (UN) had broadened the definition by recognizing and coining the term "multiple literacies." Sheldon Schaeffer described the term during the official launch of literacy in Thailand, as diverse, with many dimensions and learnt in many different ways (Lonsdale & McCurry, 2004, p. 5). The UN acknowledged at this time that the uses of literacy were changing rapidly in contemporary societies in response to broad social, economic and technological changes, recognizing that there were many practices of literacy embedded in different cultural processes, personal circumstances and collective structures (Lonsdale & McCurry, 2004).

In 1996 the term "multiliteracies" was developed by a small group of academics, now referred to as the New London Group. Brought together in New Hampshire, New London the team considered the future of literacy teaching and made predictions on how and what should be taught in a rapidly changing world. The team believed the term "multiliteracies" best described the emerging cultural and institutional order of the day. They believed it encapsulated the "multiplicity of communication channels and media" available to learners, while recognizing the increasing "salience of cultural and linguistic diversity" between and amongst the learners (Cope & Kalantzis, 2000). The New London Group proposed that multiliteracies "supplements traditional literacy pedagogy." According to the group, "A pedagogy of multiliteracies, by contrast, focuses on modes of representation much broader than language alone" (p. 5) The pedagogy may differ according to the culture or the context. For example, some cultures may rely more heavily on visual representation to make meaning, while others rely on language.

As societies become increasingly globalized, complex new literacies are required for learners to transform, create and deal with new knowledge. Tyner (1998) advocates that when literacy, technology and pedagogy align, learning is most effective. According to Tyner, critical literacy, experiential education and critical pedagogy combine to improve the learning of children through a democratic education.

The Australian National Centre for Vocational Education Research (NCVER) paper, *Literacy in the New Millennium*, proposes a number of external factors that have shaped current thinking about literacy. New literacies must be understood against a background of economic, social, political, economic and cultural change. Lonsdale and McCurry (2004) suggest that factors that have shaped and changed the traditional conception of literacy include the developments of technology, globalization of national economies, the proliferation of information, lifelong educational experiences, the diversity of cultural perspectives, the broadening of interdisciplinary studies, new teaching and learning practices, flexible modes of delivery and the critical dimension of questioning traditional practices. According to Lonsdale and McCurry, literacy is multiple with multiple purposes (2004, p. 10).

Learners are presented with a range of ways to make meaning of their world. Increasingly, there is a move from the written word to a broader, more complex multimodal suite of designs, which may include the visual, audio or spatial. Included in the broader view of literacy is a range of disciplines or subject areas such as information literacy (Farmer & Mech, 1992; Senn Breivik, 1998; Grassian & Kaplowitz, 2001, 2005; Bruce, 2003), technology literacy (Leu, 2000; Knezek, Taylor & Thomas, 1993; Knezek & Christensen, 2006), media literacy (Hobbs, 2004; Kress & van Leeuwen, 2001), critical literacy (Frye, 1997) and digital literacy (Tyner, 1998; Selber, 2005).

Students should actively be involved in the construction of meaning through a collaborative, problem-solving approach (Kellner, 2000, 2004). Students need to be literate in multiple modes where a combination of literacies is necessary to develop multiple literacy skills. New skills and new knowledge is required to cope with the demands of everyday life and the demands of work, which often differs greatly from current literacy curriculums (Johnson & Kress, 2003).

Literacy today must include the ability to read and interpret media (text, sound, images), to reproduce data and images through digital manipulation, and to evaluate and apply new knowledge gained from digital environments (Jones-Kavalier & Flannigan, 2006). Multimodal learning today combines, utilizes and exploits a range of literacies, allowing students to access and use information, gain a deep understanding and effective use of technology, critically discern meaning from the visual, as well as multimedia environments, while acquiring the ability to communicate in all media forms.

From a decade or so ago, when the New London Group met to predict the future literacy needs of the world, many things have changed at a very rapid rate. A new technology for literacy (Coiro, Knobel, Lankshear & Leu, 2008), the Internet, has brought with it a whole new way of looking when referring to multiliteracies or multimodal learning. With increased use and rapid speed, this new technology cannot be dismissed merely as another phase within education designs: "The Internet, possessing the potential to contribute to the continuous redefinement of literacy, has been a major factor in making literacy deictic" (Coiro et al., 2008, p. 5).

Background: The Changing Nature of Assessment—A Case for Assessment Renewal

Recently in Australian schools, like many countries, there has been curriculum renewal and a revisit of the associated pedagogy. One such example is the Productive Pedagogies Project (referred to as the New Basics Project) implemented recently by the Queensland government (Education Queensland). Stemming from the Queensland School Reform Longitudinal Study (QSRLS), the project heralded a strategy for renewal and reform for both teaching and learning. Concentrating on classroom environments, effective pedagogy and quality teaching, the New Basics Project allows teachers to consider students' preferred learning styles, identify repertoires of practice and evaluate appropriate teaching strategies (Queensland State Government, 2004). In keeping with progressive thinking in the area of multiliteracies, Education Queensland claims that the New Basics Project deals with "new student identities, new economies and workplaces, new technologies, diverse communities and complex cultures" (http://education.qld.gov.au/corporate/newbasics/index.html).

This new form of pedagogy encourages teachers to engage students through a series of "rich tasks." According to Education Queensland, a rich task is a "reconceptualization of the notion of outcome as demonstration or display of mastery; that is, students display their understandings, knowledges and skills through performance on transdisciplinary activities that have an obvious connection to the wide world." Transdisciplinary activities are not necessarily totally integrated nor related to holistic teaching, but instead a series of real problems that learners engage in and solve. These rich tasks provide students with opportunities to analyze, theorize and engage intellectually. As in multimodal learning, "transdisciplinary learnings" draw upon practices and skills across disciplines, while retaining the integrity of each individual discipline (Queensland State Education, 2004, p. 5). In relation to assessment of transdisciplinary activities, teachers use shared understandings to set standards for what is required from students. Standards are set for student performance on each of the rich tasks developed. This process requires teachers to match student work to the standard descriptors developed, and make judgments as to the quality of the work. The new elements of assessment allow teachers to make decisions about the quality of student work using task-specific criteria and standards. Drawing on a range of core learning outcomes from a range of disciplines, the assessment, which includes social moderation (the student work, standard descriptors and consensus by a group of teachers) allows for quality assurance and reporting processes (Education Queensland, 2004).

The New South Wales Department of Education and Training (NSWDET) has recently developed a planning framework for Kindergarten to Year Six, called "Connected Outcomes Groups (COGs)." The framework enables learning outcomes derived from a number of subject disciplines, managed by connecting similar content, processes and skills taught in an integrated approach. According to the NSWDET (2008), working in this multidisciplinary model requires assessment that investigates and reveals individuals' understandings and concepts, while drawing on different and more sophisticated assessment tasks. Similar to Queensland, a standards framework is recommended as it allows teachers to compare student achievement against syllabus standards. In relation to COGs, the NSWDET recommends a five-step process for assessment: defining the domain; selecting the assessment method; developing tasks; judging the evidence; and inferring a level of achievement (NSWDET, 2008). Teachers are encouraged to use a variety of assessment evidence, including performances, projects, products, work samples and rubrics. The standards framework includes both content standards as well as performance standards.

While progressive and open teachers develop well-rounded, challenging learning experiences, the nature of appropriate assessment has not kept pace. It is important for teachers to develop assessment practices which explore and understand the multimodal learning taking place within and outside the classroom. It is important for teachers to understand how assessment practices impact on teacher engagement; what structures within the education system impede or facilitate multimodal practice; and the changing literacy demands on students. New theories concerning pedagogies in relation to multiliteracies will inform classroom practice. Learning must form the basis of our assessment practice as assessment is representational and interpretative (Johnston & Costello, 2005).

Johnson & Kress (2003) confirm that the conceptualization, teaching and assessment of literacy need to be re-evaluated. They acknowledge the rapid shift globally toward electronic communication and the need for educators to focus on the literacy aspects of assessments. They make an interesting observation that most major countries' definition of literacy practice has actually narrowed rather than broadened. They argue that assessment of literacy needs to take account of the social contexts in which literacy practice is now developed, through linguistic and cultural pluralism. Current assessment practices are geared toward measuring the "basics," that is, factual knowledge. Johnson and Kress demand a broader re-conceptualization of literacy, which takes into account assessment practices, and encourages open, exploratory forms of pedagogy. It is important that assessment practices need to be more closely aligned with the curriculum, and assessment techniques need to include multimodal forms.

Partnership for 21st Century Skills (2007), a leading US advocacy organization, which includes the business community, education leaders and policy-makers, also confirm the need for a change in the way assessment currently operates. The organization focuses on exploring key dimensions for learning and infusing 21st-century skills into education. It acknowledges that while assessments of student achievement have become essential in educational practice, much of this assessment focuses on measuring core knowledge of content areas and that there is a lack of assessment that focuses on 21st-century learning. An area of further concern raised by the Partnership is the inadequacy of current assessment methods to measure students' complex thinking and problem-solving ability. The Partnership's advice is that new assessment tools must be developed. It suggests that assessment for the 21st century should measure mastery of skills, diagnose areas in need of intervention, measure the effectiveness of the system delivering the learning and allow for a demonstration of proficiency.

Kalantzis, Cope and Harvey (2003) suggest that while assessment methods such as standardized basic skills tests are increasing, they do not have the ability to effectively promote and measure the skills required by students in today's society. Unfortunately, the knock-on from standardized basic skills testing is a curriculum model that focuses on the traditional "basics" of numeracy and literacy. Kalantzis et al. (2003) argue that assessment methods need to be altered to reflect the skills and knowledge needed in the 21st century. Many education systems have adopted the term "new basics" to explain the paradigm shift in practice. Kalantzis et al. (2003) suggest that the broad range of skills and competencies cannot be measured on assessments focused on the "old basics" of literacy and numeracy, which aim to measure knowledge in terms of right or wrong answers. The authors argue that it may be more appropriate to explain this new content in terms of "multiliteracies." The authors suggest that what is considered the basics of learning needs to be reconsidered in light of developments in cultural and linguistic diversity, as well as the increase in variations of English; the increasingly multimodal nature of meaning-making; and the need for metalanguages as a result of digital technologies.

Kalantzis et al. (2003) argue that existing standardized testing is inadequate in measuring new learning as it is inherently individualized, relies heavily on memory and only measures limited kinds of intelligence. Today, learning is increasingly collaborative and relies much more heavily on "props" such as books or scaffolds such as learning objects. Kalantzis et al. (2003) suggest that—in developing new assessment techniques to assess competence, ability and capacity—intelligence may need to be redefined.

Leu and Coiro (2004) believe that the central reason for the failure to increase the use or inclusion of new literacies in the curriculum is the "paralysis of state assessment practices that only test foundational literacy skills." They suggested at that time, that in the United States, the increased testing required by the No Child Left Behind Act of 2001 compounded the problem. Literacy teachers were forced to teach increasingly to the test, which did not measure the new literacies. Leu and Coiro (2004) believe the Internet and other forms of ICT are central technologies for literacy within a global community in an information age, and developing these new literacies requires educational systemic reform, including changes to assessment.

Implications for Assessment Alternatives

Any consideration of multiliteracies and their assessment is necessarily underpinned by a discussion of validity. Test scores and assessment do not sit in isolation. They are (usually) used to make inferences about the examinee. Traditionally, validity is defined as the extent to which a construct measures what it is intended to measure (Anastasi & Urbina, 1997). This definition highlights the importance of measuring or assessing the construct of interest, but it also highlights the importance of understanding the construct theoretically. Three related concepts—content, construct and criterion validity—are used with a traditional framework for validation (Cronbach, 1971). Content validation refers to the ability to generalize inferences about assessment to the larger domain (Crocker & Algina, 1986). In situations where "no criterion or universe of content is accepted as entirely adequate to define the quality to be measured" (Cronbach & Meehl, 1955, cited in Crocker & Algina, 1986, p. 218), yet it is still possible to relate test scores to performance under the umbrella of a "psychological construct," construct validation is relevant. Criterion-related validation refers to decisions and inferences based on the relationship between test scores and some behavioral, real-world criteria (Crocker & Algina, 1986, p. 218). The process of validation, then, refers to what Murphy and Davidshofer (2001) call the validation of measurement ("Are test scores valid?") and validation of decision-making ("Are the decisions and inferences made on the basis of test scores valid?").

The traditional view of validity has met with some criticism. Messick (1989) argued that the notion of having separate and different aspects of validity was limited. Indeed, Sireci (2007) noted that Messick and others have argued that demonstrating that a *test* is valid is quite difficult. Messick (1989) argued for an integrated and unified approach to validity, with construct validity at the core of this unification, subsuming other components of validity. Moreover, Messick argued that the social consequences of test score use are a key feature of validation. That is, what is the value of the test scores, and what are the consequences of using and interpreting those test scores? Validation does not stop with an examination of test scores, but we also need to examine how we use those test scores and the consequences of using those scores. However, Messick (1989) also noted that there are threats to the validation process. For example, Messick pointed out that validation was affected or threatened by under-representing the construct of interest or, conversely, assessing something that is not part of the construct of interest. In other words, validation is threatened if the measure of the construct is not faithful to how the construct has been defined. This last point has implications for the assessment of complex constructs such as multiliteracies.

A consideration of some of the issues relating to validity has implications for how we assess multiliteracies, and if necessary, what we should consider when seeking alternative forms of assessment. These implications closely mirror conclusions arrived at by Sireci (2007, p. 477) regarding key aspects of validation. First, we validate the use of a test for a specific purpose rather than validate the test. Although we do not dismiss the importance of good test construction, it is imperative that we are also aware of the consequences and implications of test use. Second, a theory of the construct is imperative not only for clarifying the construct, but also for designing good validation studies. Third, justifiable and sound evidence of test use must come from a variety of sources. Finally, Sireci recognizes that validation is an ongoing, continuous process, and not necessarily established at a single testing. It follows that the complex, multi-layered nature of multiliteracies raises challenges if appropriate assessment tools of multiliteracies are to be developed. The four challenges raised by Sireci (2007) resonate when considering the development and subsequent validation of measures of multiliteracies. It is imperative that the complexities of this construct be captured as completely as possible so that use of any assessment based on a measure of multiliteracies is valid, and the implication of the consequences of its use justified.

Of relevance to the current discussion is the distinction between criterion-referenced and norm-referenced assessment. It is not the intention of this brief discussion to debate merits of either approach. Rather, we wish to highlight the difference in approaches and highlight some of the advantages of using criterion-referenced assessment of multiliteracies. Criterion-referenced tests differ from norm-referenced tests in terms of "the standard to which the test performance is referenced" (Crocker & Algina, 1986, p. 192). With criterion-referenced assessment, an individual's performance is compared to a set of pre-determined criteria (these criteria can be pre-specified goals, outcomes or behaviors). In contrast, norm-referenced assessment compares a person's performance to normative data based on his or her peers (Crocker & Algina, 1986).

Criterion referencing may be difficult to implement in certain situations (Dunn, Parry & Morgan, 2002). The development of criterion-referenced assessment should begin with a clear definition of the construct being assessed, and the tasks that mirror that construct. At times (in certain disciplines) the articulation of these tasks or learning outcomes may be difficult (Dunn et al., 2002). However, if these objectives are achievable, then there are clear benefits to the examinees. If achievable, criterion referencing, by definition, requires clear articulation of what is required to meet the objectives of the tasks (Dunn et al., 2002). This requirement also meets a key aspect of validation, namely, clear construct definition.

Support for criterion-referenced approaches have led to a recent variation in the move to standards-based assessment (FairTest, n.d.). As indicated by Young and Zucker (2004), "the current era of standards-based education reform has contributed to the emergence of the standards-referenced interpretive frameworks" within a number of educational systems worldwide. In Australia, student learning in New South Wales schools relates to an outcomes-based staged syllabus (Board of Studies NSW, 2001). Assessment is linked to standards, with the learning experiences focusing on outcomes. Stage 5 (14–16 year olds) students are externally tested in their final year of secondary education using a standards-referenced approach. In a standards-referenced approach, marks awarded to a response given by a student reflect the extent to which the response addresses the question asked and the criteria developed by the marker.

Assessing Differently

Internationally, attempts have been made to re-think multiliteracy assessment. This has involved researchers and practitioners from a range of disciplines. Such examples provide insight into how we might engage in alternative assessment practices.

Quellmalz and Haertel (2008) adopt the term "new literacies" in relation to expertise in digital media and ICT. While acknowledging that technologies are changing and improving learning in schools, Quellmalz and Haertel recognize that neither traditional large-scale assessment methods nor curriculum-embedded formative methods are successful in measuring the impacts of technology on learning. In addition, Quellmalz and Haertel contend that the development of assessments of new literaciaes is in its early stages (p. 967). Problems associated with assessment of technology include the dilemma of whether technology should be assessed as a distinct domain (Quellmalz & Haertel, 2008) and which knowledge or skills should be assessed. Quellmalz and Haertel advocate that the design of assessments of new literacies follow a systematic, evidence-centered approach (p. 968).

Quellmalz and Haertel highlight three issues as complicating the aim of assessing the impact of technologies on learning and of new learning enabled by technology:

1. multiple definitions of new literacies;
2. overlapping frameworks of assessment of technology;
3. multitudes of assessment designs.

The ICT assessment framework developed follows evidence-centered assessment design principles which, as outlined by the authors, relate learning to be assessed (student model) to the features of a task, and questions eliciting observable evidence of learning (task model) to the quality of responses and scores indicating high levels of proficiency (evidence model). Applied to assessing new literacies, it would look like:

- Student model—define constructs to be measured based on ICT domain knowledge and processes and define strategies students would draw on to make use of technologies. Must specify ICT and domain knowledge and skills.
- Task model—specify items that would elicit observations of achievement in ICT and the domain of interest.
- Evidence model—evidence of learning that needs to be extracted, how scoring will occur and statistical models to be used.

The model for the Coordinated ICT Assessment Framework comprises a subject-matter domain—content and processes of the specific discipline (declarative knowledge and a process dimension); ICT strategies used by learners to integrate technologies into problem-solving activities; and technology tools used to accomplish ICT strategies. The Framework itself is presented in a table, which includes general cognitive demands, ICT knowledge and strategies, and sample component strategies (derived from analyses of technology use in research and practice). The authors suggest that despite the ICT framework being developed for new literacy assessment in maths and science, it also addresses outcomes in frameworks in other academic areas.

Newfield, Andrew, Stein and Maungedzo (2003) considered various assessment perspectives within the context of their study of the implementation of multimodal pedagogies within a new South African outcomes-based curriculum framework. The study involved students' engagement in a multimodal poetry-and-cloth project representing their origins and culture through cloth maps, poems, 3D objects and photos, which necessitated new assessment considerations. Reflections on the project from the perspectives of the teachers involved lead to a set of conclusions and recommendations:

1. Multimodal assessment should not assess each mode individually, but should involve recognition of the way in which the modes have been

used. Assessment is a process that engages with the student's thinking about the value of the object and process in relation to the context.

2. The authors draw on the idea of process at the core of their discussion. Reflection is a key factor in the kinds of processes that occur and in the nature of the assessment of multimodal products. The authors suggest that the comments on the process from the learners indicate that they have been involved in reflection throughout the project.
3. Assessment should move away from the concept of a numerical mark being assigned to a piece of work. While the learners in the project presented suggestions for assessment that focused on technical or formal aspects of assessment, new ways need to be explored to incorporate these with more open methods.
4. The authors also recommend that assessment be integrated, drawing the formal/technical and the process/collaborative aspects together in an attempt to provide a more comprehensive account of achievement.
5. Another aspect discussed focuses on the assessment of the voice. The authors suggest that voice should be seen as an important criterion in the design of assessment.
6. Assessment of multimodal processes and products seem "to demand the presence of the 'creator of meaning'" and assessment should take place in conjunction with the learners.
7. For multimodality to be successful in an outcomes-based education system the outcomes need to be flexible and open to individual and collaborative shaping.
8. Resourcefulness—the use of suitable resources to represent meaning—should be a criterion in the development of an assessment for the multimodal classroom.

The following case study addresses such new perspectives and recommendations about multiliteracy assessment.

Case Study: Multiliteracy Assessment in a News Media Context

Based at the University of Wollongong, the *Making News Today* project investigated middle high-school students' multiliteracy development through engagement in a news media analysis, construction and deconstruction education program of work (Lockyer, Brown & Blackall, 2003). This research involved more than 200 students within eight English classes across seven high schools located in New South Wales, Australia. The *Making News Today* education program was implemented with each class and facilitated by the classroom teacher. The eight-week program involved a range of learning activities including students analyzing stories found via a range of new sources (Internet, radio, television, newspaper); constructing a news story related to their community; and deconstructing the meaning of their story and those of their peers.

Qualitative analysis of classroom observations, the participants written-work samples and digital video news stories, as well as perspectives that were gathered via interview, allowed for an in-depth understanding of multiliteracy outcomes for students (Lockyer, Brown, Blackall, Harper & McKerrow, 2007). An attempt was also made to investigate alternatives to literacy assessment (Brown & Lockyer, 2007). A measurement tool was constructed and trialed with each implementation of the program. For this project, the concept of multiliteracies was defined to encompass visual, technology, information and media literacies.

The test structure and marking guidelines were based on the standards-referenced approach used by the NSW Board of Studies for state-wide high-school certificate examinations. The test focused on a number of broad areas that the researchers had included as learning outcomes in the development of the educational program. These skills and understandings were drawn from the NSW syllabus (NSW Board of Studies, 2001) outcomes required by Stage 5 students. Critical skills included the ability to analyze, infer, describe, interpret, explain, justify, recognize, discern, identify, provide opinions, predict, construct, deconstruct, contrast, respond, visualize, encode and decode.

In keeping with a multimodal approach, images, headlines and text from local, national and international news and popular media were used as stimulus material for test items. The questions, some with sub-questions, were open-ended in nature and students were asked to provide text-based responses. The test was administered through a website—all participants were given unique identification codes and passwords. Participants were asked to complete the test prior to, and at the conclusion of, the implementation of the *Making News Today* educational program. Thus, these pre- and post-test measures were expected to provide an indicator of student achievement in these areas.

A team of expert assessors (i.e., teachers with a background and experience in standards-based testing) developed assessment criteria for each item of the test. Marks would be awarded to a response based on the extent to which the response addressed the criteria. Responses that demonstrated more complex development and higher-order achievement would receive greater marks than a more basic level of achievement.

Once pre- and post-test data were collected from participants, the assessment team, comprised of five members, was asked to mark responses. The assessors were asked to concurrently reflect on the test items, marking criteria, marking process and responses, in order to gain a qualitative perspective on the assessment tools. In keeping with the standard approach undertaken for criteria-referenced tests, the marking team was provided with detailed marking guidelines and criteria sheets, the outcomes being assessed as well as the assessment criteria. As was hoped for by the researchers, the marking team—after a process of rigorous educational debate and marking—provided a number of recommendations and modifications for both the test and the marking criteria.

Initially, the marking criteria allowed for numerical grades to be applied to the test. These marks ranged from two to five marks for each question or subquestion. The expert panel recommended that a rating scale of high (3), medium (2) or low (1) would be more appropriate. It was agreed that the marking guidelines were beneficial and provided support to the markers. These guidelines provided necessary indicators for the marker to identify lower, mid-range and better responses.

Characteristics of the low, middle and high range responses were identified. Low range responses: only listed; included no exploration; provided little or no reference; were descriptive only; neglected to compare if required; simplistic response; clichéd answers; clumsy language; little attempt at an answer. Middle range responses: limited exploration of topic; able to identify; limited reference; more literal approach; employed more description than interpretation. High range responses: included high level of evaluation; offered analysis; were able to discuss; supported claims; articulated ideas well; able to discern; acknowledges; contrasts; demonstrates; provided information understandings; contextualized; conceptualized; gave holistic account; explained connections.

In the context of this project, the assessment was delivered pre- and post-intervention with a view to determining if the educational program—which was designed based on multiliteracies pedagogy—led to some change in multiliteracy development for students. The assessment was run as an introductory and concluding activity in the series of activities in the program. For students, the concept and relevance of the repeat assessment was difficult to come to terms with. As such, the extent to which they took the post-test seriously and provided appropriate responses to the items could be called into question.

Discussion and Conclusions

There is a continued discussion focused on the relationship between classroom (or online) learning activities and assessment. Buhagiar (2007) contends that the move toward learning as meaning-making relates to a theoretical shift away from "measuring" learning, toward assessment practices that are explicitly designed to promote learning. He argues that the traditional assessment models that focus on selection, certification and accreditation, hinder learning in multiple ways. Yet, examples (such as that presented within the *Making News Today* program) suggest there is opportunity for what Gipps (1994) described as the "dynamic interaction" between teaching, learning and assessment (p. 15).

This theoretical discussion of the need for alignment between instruction and assessment has been taken up at the advocacy level by the US-based Partnership for 21st Century Skills (2007). However, based on their survey of current assessment practice (Honey, Fasca, Gersick, Mandinach & Sinha, 2005), they are also aware of the barriers to such a suggestion and note the need for professional development of teachers in terms of their skills in designing and implementing teaching, learning and assessment strategies that incorporate these new literacies.

While educators recognize the transformative nature of education in the 21st century and the increased use of new technologies, the how and why of assessment still eludes many. The literature, and the experience from the news media project presented in this chapter as a case study, suggests that teachers struggle with both the implementation of multiliteracies pedagogies and assessment. Thus, we need to explore the professional development issues necessary to move practice toward these concepts.

"New basics" need new assessment practices. These assessment practices need to promote new learning, new skills and new competencies while understanding learning to improve student outcomes (Kalantzis et al., 2003).

While accepting the underlying concept of multiliteracies and the need to structure learning experiences to address these needs, there remain difficulties in the way we assess both in the classroom and through large-scale high-stakes testing. While attempts have been made to investigate assessment alternatives, the main current practices do not cater for the interdisciplinary nature of multiliteracy learning. The focus is often on individual disciplines, which negates the exploitation of the multimodal nature of the learning experience.

Further, there is a tension between what is possible through teacher-developed, classroom-based assessment practices, which might better cater for multimodal learning, and state-wide testing, which may be more focused on performance. Castek, Leu, Coiro, Gort, Henry and Lima (2007) contend that state-wide assessments will need to change to include new literacies, but are not optimistic that this will occur in the near future.

As learners create and deal with new multiliterate learning environments, the nature of assessment practices also becomes increasingly more complex. Emerging policies and research investigations explored in this chapter tend to point to the application of criteria-referenced or standards-based approaches to assessment as a possible solution to support this new form of learning. While the argument for the inclusion of multiliteracies in learning today is becoming increasingly stronger, the argument must also be made for reliable and supportive assessment practices which complement and support this unique style of learning.

References

Anastasi, A., & Urbina, S. (1997). *Psychological testing* (7th ed.). New Jersey: Prentice-Hall.

Baker, D., & Street, B. (1994). Literacy and numeracy: Concepts and definitions. In T. Husén & T. Postlethwaite (Eds.), *The international encyclopedia of education* (Vol. 6, pp. 3453–3459). London: Pergamon.

Board of Studies NSW. (2001). English years 7–10 syllabus. Retrieved October 21, 2003 from: www.boardofstudies.nsw.edu.au/writing_briefs/english/english_710_syllabus.pdf.

Brown, I., & Lockyer, L. (2007). Don't mention the "T" word: Value and validity in testing visual literacy. In R. E. Griffin, M. Avgerinou & J. Giesen (Eds.), *History, community, & culture: Celebrating tradition & transforming our future, selected readings of the International Visual Literacy Association* (pp. 7–13). Loretto: International Visual Literacy Association.

Bruce, C. (2003). *Seven faces of information literacy: Towards inviting students into new experiences.* Retrieved November 1, 2008 from: http://crm.hct.ac.ae/events/archive/2003/speakers/bruce.pdf.

Buhagiar, M. A. (2007). Classroom assessment within the alternative assessment paradigm: revisiting the territory. *Curriculum Journal,* 18(1), 39–56.

Castek, J., Leu, D. J., Coiro, J., Gort, M., Henry, L. A., & Lima, C. O. (2007). Developing new literacies among multilingual learners in elementary grades. In L. L. Parker (Ed.), *Technology mediated learning environments for young English learners* (pp. 111–153). Mahwah: Lawrence Erlbaum Associates.

Coiro, J., Knobel, M., Lankshear, C., & Leu, D. J. (Eds.). (2008). *Handbook of research on new literacies.* New York: Routledge.

Cope, B., & Kalantzis, M. (Eds.). (2000). *Multiliteracies: Learning and the design of social futures.* London: Routledge.

Crocker, L., & Algina, J. (1986). *Introduction to classical and modern test theory.* New York: Holt, Rinehart & Winston.

Cronbach, L. J. (1971). Test validation. In R. L. Thorndike (Ed.), *Educational measurement* (pp. 150–165) (2nd ed.). Washington: American Council on Education.

Dunn, L. Parry, S., & Morgan, C. (2002). Seeking quality in criterion referenced assessment. Paper presented at the Learning Communities and Assessment Cultures Conference organized by the EARLI Special Interest Group on Assessment and Evaluation, University of Northumbria. Retrieved August 28, 2002 from: www.leeds.ac.uk/educol/documents/00002257.doc.

Education Queensland. (2004). Growing assessment culture. Retrieved November 2008 from: http://education.qld.gov.au/curriculum/assessment/pdfs/gac3.pdf.

FairTest—National Centre for Fair & Open Testing. (n.d.). Criterion- and standards-referenced tests. Cambridge, MA: National Centre for Fair & Open Testing. Retrieved February 2, 2009 from: www.fairtest.org/criterion-and-standards-referenced-tests-pdf.

Farmer, D. W., & Mech, T. F. (Eds.). (1992). *Information literacy: Developing students as independent learners.* San Francisco: Jossey-Bass.

Frye, P. (1997). Critical literacy: Using "Frontline." *The Journal of the Australian Association for the Teaching of English,* October, 119–120.

Gipps, C. V. (1994). *Beyond testing: Towards a theory of educational assessment.* London: Routledge Falmer.

Grassian, E. S., & Kaplowitz, J. R. (2001). *Information literacy instruction: Theory and practice.* New York: Neal-Schuman.

Grassian, E. S., & Kaplowitz, J. R. (2005). *Learning to lead and manage information literacy instruction.* New York: Neal-Schuman.

Hobbs, R. (2004). A review of school-based initiatives in media literacy education. *American Behavioral Scientist,* 48(1), 42–59.

Honey, M., Fasca, C., Gersick, A., Mandinach, E., & Sinha, S. (2005). *Assessment of 21st Century Skills: The Current Landscape* [Electronic Version]. Retrieved January 9, 2009 from: www.21stcenturyskills.org/index.php?option=com_content&task=view&id=27&Itemid=120.

Johnson, D., & Kress, G. (2003). Globalization, literacy and society: Redesigning pedagogy and assessment. *Assessment in Education: Principles, Policy & Practice*, 10(1), 5–14.

Johnston, P., & Costello, P. (2005). Principles for literacy assessment. *Reading Research Quarterly*, 40, 256–267.

Jones-Kavalier, B. R., & Flannigan, S. L. (2006). Connecting the digital dots: Literacy of the 21st century. *EDUCAUSE Quarterly*, 29(2), 8–10.

Kalantzis, M., Cope, B., & Harvey, A. (2003). Assessing multiliteracies and the new basics. *Assessment in Education*, 10(1), 15–26.

Kellner, D. (2000). New technologies/new literacies: reconstructing education for the new millennium. *Teaching Education*, 11(3), 245–265.

Kellner, D. (2004). Technological transformation, multiple literacies, and the re-visioning of education. *E-Learning*, 1(1), 9–37.

Knezek, G., & Christensen, R. (2006). IT competencies and attitudes: A worldwide perspective. In C. Crawford et al. (Eds.), *Proceedings of society for information technology and teacher education international conference 2006* (pp. 1671–1676). Chesapeake: AACE.

Knezek, D. G., Taylor, H. G., & Thomas, L. G. (1993). National accreditation standards impact teacher preparation. *T H E Journal (Technological Horizons In Education)*, 20(11), 62–63.

Kress, G. R., & van Leeuwen, T. (2001). *Multimodal discourse—the modes and media of contemporary communication.* New York: Oxford University Press.

Leu, D. J. (2000). Literacy and technology: Deictic consequences for literacy education in an information age. In M. L. Kamil, P. Mosenthal, P. D. Pearson & R. Barr (Eds.), *Handbook of reading research* (Vol. III, pp. 743–770). Mahwah: Erlbaum.

Leu, D. J., & Coiro, J. (2004). New literacies for new times: Why and how the literacy community needs to rethink its mission. *Wisconsin State Reading Association*, 44(5), 3–7.

Lockyer, L., Brown, I., & Blackall, D. (2003). A learning design to support multi-literacy development in K-12 contexts. In A. Rossett (Ed.), *Proceedings of the 2003 world conference on e-learning in corporate, government, healthcare and higher education* (pp. 1703–1706). Norfolk, VA: Association for the Advancement of Computing in Education.

Lockyer, L., Brown, I., Blackall, D., Harper, B., & McKerrow, P. (2007). Becoming multiliterate: Digital video news construction within a technology-supported learning environment. In T. Bastiaens & S. Carliner (Eds.), *Proceedings of e-learn 2007 world conference on e-learning in corporate, government, healthcare and higher education* (pp. 6247–6254). Norfolk, VA: Association for the Advancement of Computing in Education.

Lonsdale, M., & McCurry, D. (2004). Literacy in the new millennium. Report prepared for National Centre for Vocational Education Research (NCVER), *Australian Council for Educational Research* (pp. 1–50). Adelaide: Department of Education, Science and Training.

Messick, S. (1989). Validity. In R. Linn (Ed.), *Educational measurement* (3rd ed.) (pp. 13–103). Washington: American Council on Education/MacMillian.

Metiri Group. (2008). *Multimodal learning through the media: What research says.* Cisco Systems. Retrieved March 17, 2009 from: www.cisco.com/web/strategy/docs/education/Multimodal-Learning-Through-Media.pdf.

Murphy, K. R., & Davidshofer, C. O. (2001). *Psychological testing: Principles and applications* (5th ed.). New Jersey: Prentice-Hall.

New London Group. (1996). A pedagogy of multiliteracies: Designing social futures. *Harvard Educational Review*, 66(1): 60–92.

New South Wales Department of Education and Training. (2008). *Curriculum, planning, programming, assessing and reporting to parents K-6.* Retrieved November 1, 2008 from: www.curriculumsupport.education.nsw.gov.au/timetoteach/cogs/curricplanframe.htm.

Newfield, D., Andrew, D., Stein, P., & Maungedzo, R. (2003). "No number can describe how good it was": Assessment issues in the multimodal classroom. *Assessment in Education*, 10(1), 61–81.

Partnership for 21st Century Skills (2007). *21st Century Skills Assessment.* Retrieved January 9, 2009 from: www.21stcenturyskills.org/documents/21st_century_skills_assessment.pdf.

Queensland State Education. (2004). New basics: The why, what, how and when of rich tasks. Retrieved November 2, 2008 from: www.education.qld.gov.au/corporate/newbasics.

Quellmalz, E. S., & Haertel, G. D. (2008). Assessing new literacies in science and mathematics. In J. Coiro, M. Knobel, C. Lankshear & D. J. Leu (Eds.), *Handbook of research on new literacies* (pp. 941–972). New York: Routledge.

Selber, S. (2005). *Multiliteracies for a digital age*, Carbondale: Southern Illinois University Press.

Senn Breivik, P. (1998). *Student learning in the information age.* Phoenix: American Council on Education/Oryx Press.

Sireci, S. G. (2007). On validity theory and test validation. *Educational Researcher*, 36(8), 477–481.

Tyner, K. (1998). *Literacy in a digital world: Teaching and learning in the age of information.* New Jersey: Lawrence Erlbaum Associates.

Young, M. J., & Zucker, S. (2004). The standards-referenced interpretive framework: Using assessments for multiple purposes. Pearson Education, Inc. Retrieved February 2, 2009 from: http://pearsonassess.com/NR/rdonlyres/1AD36406-3B2A-491C-A280-D4A47D3121E8/0/InterpretiveFrameworks.pdf.

12 Young Australians Reading in a Digital World

Jennifer Rennie, Monash University, and Annette Patterson, Queensland University of Technology

What We Know about Students' Engagement in Multimodal Communications

We know from recent research and reports from Australia, the United Kingdom and the United States (ABS, 2007; DeBell & Chapman, 2006; Livingstone & Bober, 2005; Marsh, 2006) that young people are highly engaged with multimodal communications through computers, online games, blogs, wikis, email, social networking sites, phone messaging, music, video and other visual media. Not only are they engaging frequently with these reading and writing activities, but they are active creators of online content and they are interactively participating in collaborative production strategies through inventive uses of media technologies.

The fact of the intensive engagement among young people in online activities cannot be disputed and the study we report on here provides further evidence of the high level of activity that is taking place outside the classroom around new media. The continuing, wide distribution of knowledge networks and the rush toward social connectivity via rapidly developing expertise in forming, blending, merging and transforming language, video, still pictures and sounds impacts our everyday lives in ways unimagined even five years ago. Furthermore, this developing expertise appears to be across the generations (Hart, Bober & Pine, 2008). Grandparents make digital stories for their grandchildren's amusement and create electronic photo books, teenagers create and upload videos to YouTube, and parents use Flickr and read newspapers online, while pre-schoolers make electronic, interactive cards for their friends. This is a cross-generational revolution in knowledge creation, and while issues of access remain a concern, there is growing evidence that parents across the economic divide are increasingly prioritizing computer ownership and Internet connections for their children (ABS, 2007; Lenhart, Madden, Macgill & Smith, 2007; UK Statistics, 2008).

The implications for curriculum and classroom practice of the current high rate of engagement with new media among young people are far reaching (Marsh, 2006). The initial advice paper on Australia's proposed national English curriculum (Freebody, Bennett, Arnold, Ewing & Fielding-Barnsley, 2008) notes:

> The subject of English has historically been largely about the reading and writing of printed texts. More recently there has been debate about the growing significance of visual and non-print communication such as speaking and listening, combinations of visual information with language, and the new digital developments. In considering the tasks that young learners face in school, in their further education and training, and in workplaces, the argument has been that the school subject of English should expand its scope to include more focus on these non-print forms. Clearly these forms of communication are expanding in and out of formal education, and so they have an important place in a national English curriculum.
>
> (p. 8)

Just how these multimodal communications will transform learning and teaching, pedagogy and curriculum is yet to be decided. At present we can but observe the transformations that are taking place in everyday life and try to predict the impact they will have on the learning and teaching environments of the future.

When we set out to survey over 600 14-year-old students attending schools in an Australian city we asked ourselves a number of questions, such as: "What types of texts are students reading outside the classroom?" "What connections, if any, can be made between various print-based and new media communication activities?" and "What might be the implications of students' out-of-school literacy practices for curriculum development?" We were particularly interested in the reading practices of young people since these are under question through some sections of the popular media. Adults worry that young people are not exposed by modern schooling to the more traditional print-based texts and they express concern that computers could be displacing "the book" as the preferred technology for disseminating knowledge and providing pleasurable leisure reading activities. On the other hand, researchers highlight different concerns from some sections of the popular media. Several writers have noted the lack of current evidence about the extent to which schools are making connections between the out-of-school literacy practices of young people and the curriculum and pedagogy of classrooms (Ladbrook, 2009; Lankshear & Knobel, 2006) and it is likely that these concerns informed the point made by the writers of the (Australian) National English Curriculum Position Paper (Freebody et al., 2008), that English should broaden its view of what constitutes appropriate engagement with communications technologies. There is little doubt that the students who took part in our survey were engaging in a broad range of literacy practices outside school. They were almost all connected to the Internet and using a computer on a daily basis; most possessed a cell phone and some form of game technology. In recent years there has been a growing interest in the online experiences of young people and the creativity and knowledge production of a savvy generation of multimodal operatives (Alvermann, 2001; Alvermann, Hinchman, Moore, Phelps & Waff, 2006; Gee, 2003; Knobel & Lankshear, 2004; Ladbrook, 2009; Lankshear & Knobel, 2006; Lewis & Fabos, 2005; Marsh, 2006; Snyder, 2004).

In the remainder of this chapter we contribute to this emerging body of research and discuss aspects of our study where we set out to better understand the current reading experiences and habits of young Australians.

The Social Practice of Reading

It is common now to think about reading as a socially, culturally and historically located practice, and these aspects of reading have been explored extensively by scholars such as Manguel (1996), who observed, for instance, that silent reading was "sufficiently strange" in the 4th century to be noted by St. Augustine in his *Confessions* (p. 38). As Manguel relates, the Bishop Ambrose's silent reading practice was unusual for that time when the common form of reading practice was to read aloud, even when alone with a book (Manguel, 1996, p. 38). Silent reading became a revolution in reading practice that is so taken-for-granted today that we generally reserve reading aloud for particular pedagogical purposes in beginning reading classrooms, where teachers can check the accuracy of a child's pronunciation and decoding skills, or for entertaining (usually children) by reading stories aloud to them. The shift in reading practices from spoken to silent reading took place from around the 4th century and was slow to develop in comparison to the revolution in reading practices that is currently taking place in response to developments in communication technologies. The computer, the Internet, the cell (mobile) phone and other electronic reading devices are providing readers with opportunities to access the written word in new and exciting ways, but does the fact that we can read Shakespeare on our iPhone on the bus on the way home from work mean that reading practices are different from those of our ancestors? The answer probably is "yes," but what does this mean for 21st-century readers? The questions most commonly posed are those in relation to "reading for pleasure." Whether we read in the classroom or out of it, reading for pleasure or enjoyment is an aspect of reading that is considered important to modern readers (Patterson, 2002). This form of reading practice, however, also has a history. Pleasure was not considered a part of reading in the classrooms of scholastic teachers, or in the homes of early Christians. Therefore, it is possible to think about reading for enjoyment or pleasure as a learned practice (Mellor & Patterson, 2004). This practice was named in the 17th century when the first mention of reading for pleasure emerged in the texts written for home tutors and mothers of young children (Patterson, 1997). The idea gained in popularity until the 20th century, when we could claim that reading for pleasure and enjoyment was not only accepted as a natural part of the activity of reading, but it was a *requirement*. Evidence of this requirement is not difficult to locate in most Australian school syllabi (Patterson, 2008) or in general discussions about reading. Publishers use it as a marketing tool, readers expect to find it and syllabus writers include it as an aim of English teaching. Reading for pleasure is but one example of the cultural, social and historical dimensions of modern reading practices.

Another powerful, although somewhat fraught, aspect of modern reading practices is the rapid uptake, particularly by young people, of digital technologies that support a range of reading practices hitherto unknown. These reading engagements have prompted a number of researchers to investigate the impact on reader identities of modern communication technologies (Alvermann et al., 2006) and to examine students' level of engagement with traditional paper-based texts and online reading (Lankshear & Knobel, 2006). We know too that there is evidence of a mismatch between the in-school reading activities of children and their out-of-school reading experiences (Ladbrook, 2009) and that students are increasingly challenging their teachers to find ways to engage them in meaningful reading activities in the classroom (Honan, 2008). It is perhaps too soon to fully understand the intersection of new media and modern reading practices. However, it is useful to track the changes in reading habits that are currently taking place in order to better understand how these practices are shaping societies and impacting the everyday lives of individuals.

In considering the impact of digital texts on students' reading habits we asked ourselves questions such as: "How varied are the reading activities engaged in by adolescents? How might these practices be described? Is there a difference between the reading practices of different groups: females and males, those who describe themselves as avid readers and those who do not?"

In framing these questions we approached the issue of reading from a particular socio-cultural theoretical perspective on reading and literacy, informed by the work of a group of critical social theorists (Barton & Hamilton, 1998; Cairney & Ruge, 1997; Gee, 1996; Heath, 1986; Luke & Freebody, 1997; Street, 1993; Welch & Freebody, 1993) who collectively argue that reading is a social practice and that readers draw on a repertoire of resources—including cultural, social and cognitive practices—to construct and reconstruct meanings from texts (Mellor & Patterson, 2000; Mellor, Patterson, & O'Neill, 1991). The enactment of reading events, these theorists argue, varies according to the purpose and context in which they occur. This broad, socio-cultural view of reading recognizes that student readers engage in a range of different kinds of reading practices in and out of the classroom and in different knowledge contexts. In Australia, the wide range of reading practices engaged in by students is referred to as "multiliteracies" (Healy, 2007; New London Group, 1996) and includes reading practices associated with mobile phones and other less traditional, web-based texts such as reading reputation systems on eBay and "blogging" (Knobel & Lankshear, 2004). This study recognizes that engaging in these kinds of activities involves different kinds of reading practices across a range of multimodal reading sites.

Background to the Study

The study built on and refined a previous pilot study where a small sample of regional and urban youth was surveyed in the North of Australia (Rennie & Patterson, 2005). Recommendations from recent reviews into education, the changing view of what "reading" is, work being conducted around a national curriculum and the limited number of studies concerning the reading and viewing choices of adolescents, fueled our interest in this work. Adolescents are rarely the focus of studies of reading. However, knowing what, how and why adolescents read in the digital era provides an important evidence base for English curriculum development and classroom practice and for school infrastructure planning. Most studies nationally and internationally have tended to connect out-of-school reading practices with students' leisure activities and with paper-based texts (Manuel & Robinson, 2002; Mullis, Martin, Gonzalez & Kennedy, 2003; Nieuwenhuizen, 2000; Ryan, 2005; Thomson, 1987) rather than focus on the broader context of "new literacies" (Cope & Kalantzis, 2000; Gee, 2003; Knobel & Lankshear, 2004; Snyder, 2004) and on the purpose of reading beyond leisure. Studies of reading habits that have included information related to the reading of digital texts have tended to limit their investigation to the time spent engaging with technology. Furthermore, questions concerning what texts are read, the purpose of the reading and how they are read have not featured in these studies. For example, recently the Progress in International Reading Literacy Study, which was a comparative study of the reading achievement and habits of Year 4 students from 40 different countries, not including Australia, limited their questions related to digital texts to the time spent playing computer games and the time spent watching television or videos (Mullis, Martin, Kennedy, & Foy, 2007). Large-scale Australian studies also have tended to fall within the literature/leisure framework (Nieuwenhuizen, 2000; Thomson, 1987). They have not considered reading beyond pleasure, reading associated with anything other than print-based texts or viewing. Other studies have examined single aspects of students' engagement with specific texts, such as email or video games (Gee, 2003; Unsworth, 2001). These researchers have acknowledged that students inhabit a rapidly changing cultural, political, social, economic and technological climate where reading now encompasses multimodal texts and complex reading practices.

Reading habits considered in this project included the students' engagement with text through computers, mobile phones and console games, magazines, newspapers and junk mail, as well as fiction and non-fiction books. Students were required to complete a survey which asked a number of questions related to the types of texts read, the purpose of the reading, how the reading occurred, the amount of time spent reading and where the reading occurred.

In total, 606 students completed the survey. The sample included 239 male students and 367 female students. The students were from five different schools in the Brisbane metropolitan area in South-east Queensland, Australia. Of the schools, four were single-sex schools (three female and one male), and one school was co-educational.

The Text Pleasures of Our Youth

All of the participants reported experiences of reading digital, visual and print-based texts in varying degrees. Not surprisingly, only eight of the 606 students surveyed reported not having access to a home computer, with only three students stating that they did not use a computer out of school. Sixty percent of the participants claimed to use computers on a daily basis, and over 80% claimed to use it either daily or every few days. The most frequently reported digital reading practices included reading websites, social networking sites, using search engines, engaging in chat forums on MSN and downloading music. Less frequently reported digital reading practices included email, eBay and online shopping catalogues. Although participants stated they rarely used email and preferred to use sites such as MSN to communicate with their peers, 86.5% reported having an email address. This is consistent with the findings of a recent study by Thorne (2003) who found email to be a very unpopular communication tool amongst young adults enrolled in a tertiary French course (Knobel & Lankshear, 2004).

Cell phones also feature in the social networking lives of the young people surveyed. In total, 92.4% of participants reported owning a cell phone, with 72.3% stating they used their phone daily. The participants reported high use of sending and receiving calls, sending and receiving text messages and taking photos and videos. Again, email did not feature predominantly in their cell phone practices.

Similarly, the ownership and engagement with various gaming consoles was high. More than 77% of students reported owning some form of console game, and that they played games that required them to read instructions.

Print-based texts also featured highly in the out-of-school reading experiences of the young people surveyed. Over 40% of the students surveyed indicated that they read both magazines and newspapers sometimes. The reading of magazines was often connected to the student's interests and the entertainment, sport and TV guide were the most frequently read sections of the newspaper.

Similarly, approximately 40% of the students surveyed reported reading novels frequently out-of-school and approximately 30% reported reading novels sometimes. Only 30% reported limited engagement with these texts.

While it was clear from the data that the reading of both digital and print-based texts was a frequent activity in the out-of-school experiences of these students, a closer examination of the data revealed some interesting findings in relation to gender and the ways in which individual participants described themselves as readers.

Is it a Girl or a Boy Thing?

Analysis was conducted on each question of the survey that students completed according to gender. Overall responses by both genders typified a similar pattern, particularly in terms of time spent engaging with all forms of literacies. Variances occurred in terms of content and purpose. Figure 12.1 provides a summary of various uses of computers by the participants surveyed.

There were no significant difference between males and females with regard to having a computer at home. Over 97% of both male and female students stated that they had a computer at home, with only three male students stating that they did not use a computer outside of school. The results for the frequency of the use of computers outside of school were similar for male and female students, with over 88% in both groups using a computer daily or at least every few days. A high percentage of both male and female students accessed websites (more than 96%), MSN (more than 83%) and music sites (more than 77%). Although a high percentage of both male and female students were not accessing chat rooms, the difference between males who stated they did not use chat rooms (87%) and females who stated they did not use chat rooms (93.7%) could be an area of interest for future investigation. A high percentage of male (77%) and female (90%) students used email, with females showing a much higher level of engagement than males. While some surveys indicate that slightly more males than females report using email on a daily basis (Hart, Bober & Pine, 2008, p. 19), these surveys tend to canvass the views of a younger age group than the survey reported on here. The widening gap between males and females in their reported use of email could be an indication that older females continue to increase their email usage while

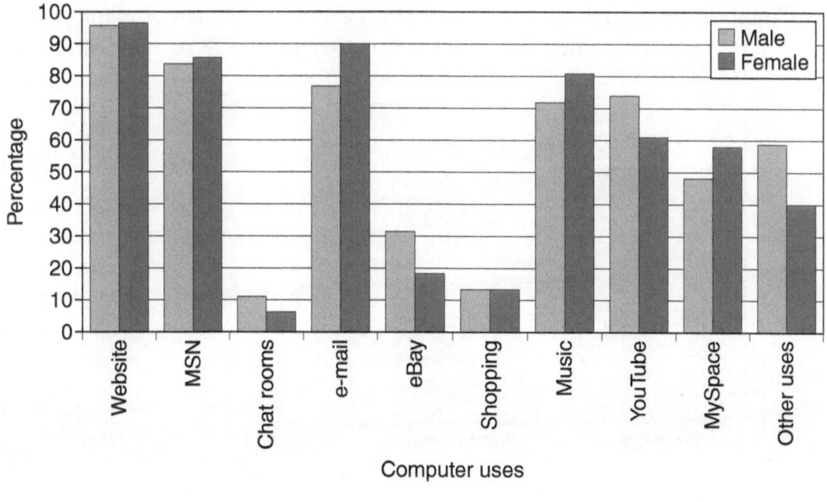

Figure 12.1 Computer Uses.

males take less interest in this form of communication. While the majority of male (67.8%) and female (80.9%) students did not use eBay, the difference between the male and female figures was again noteworthy. Furthermore, of the students who did access eBay, their rate of usage was infrequent, and of those who were using eBay it was more likely that the male students would be buying and selling online than the female students. There was no significant difference between male and female students recorded for students using online shopping, with the majority not using this service (86% of males and 87% of females did not use online shopping). While a high percentage of male and female students accessed YouTube, the difference between males (75%) and females (61%) again was worth noting. Although the percentages were quite similar for students accessing or not accessing MySpace, the results indicated a slightly greater percentage of females (58%) than males (51%) did access the site. High percentages of both female and male students accessed MSN, although more female students used the site as a means to socialize with their peers. There were similar differences between males and females in relation to having an email address, with 77% of males and 92% of females. However email was not often used by either group.

A slightly larger percentage of males (59%) than females (40%) also stated they used the computer for other reasons than those already discussed. Online gaming was frequently reported in this category.

There were no significant differences between male and female use and ownership of mobile phones. There were, however, significant differences in the ownership of gaming consoles. Overall, 91.6% of males reported owning a game console compared to 74.9% of females.

Gender differences in relation to engagement with texts were more significant in students' engagement with print-based texts. Both male students (45.2%) and female students (44.4%) stated that they sometimes read magazines.

Significantly though, as Figure 12.2 shows, 40.1% of female students stated that they read magazines frequently compared to 15.9% of male students,

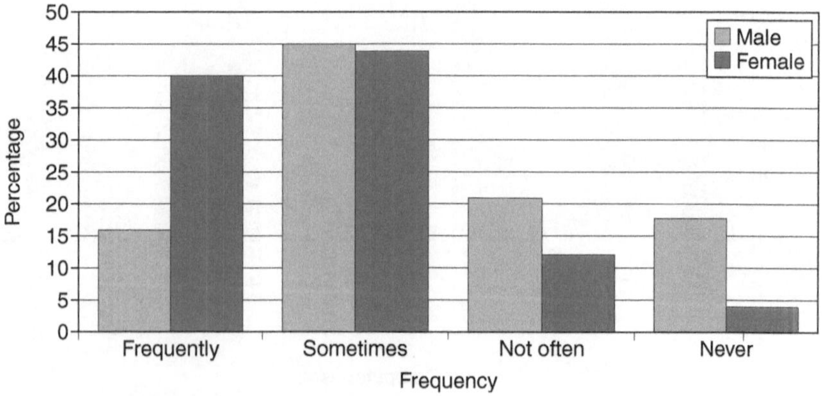

Figure 12.2 Frequency of Reading Magazines.

with 18% of male students stating that they never read magazines, compared to 4.1% of female students. Furthermore, a higher percentage of female students (56.4%) stated that they frequently read magazines connected to their interests compared to the male students (27.6%), who stated that they sometimes read magazines connected to their interests. Although neither group often read magazines not connected to their interests there was a higher percentage of female students (23.7%) who stated that they sometimes would in comparison to the male students (13.4%).

The data indicated that neither male students nor female students read much of the newspaper. Of the sections that they did read, a slightly greater percentage of female students were more likely to read the local, national and international stories and the entertainment section than male students. A significant percentage of male students (54.4%) were more likely to read the sports section than the female students (24.3%), while over half of both groups of students read the TV guide.

As Figure 12.3 shows, the data indicated a trend for female students to be more likely to read novels outside of school than male students, with 47.1% of female students stating they frequently read novels, compared to 31% of male students, and 30.2% of female students stating they sometimes read novels outside of school, compared to 35.1% of male students.

A greater percentage of females stated that they liked to read drama (57.2%) and romance (49.6%), while greater percentages of male students stated that they did not like to read these genres. Both groups enjoyed reading comedy and mystery, while neither group stated a preference for reading historical fiction, science fiction, horror or biographies. The female students stated that they were more likely to read novels when they were bored, found it hard to stop reading a good book, read on long journeys and borrowed books to read. Both groups stated that they sometimes borrowed books from the library. Over 70% of male and female students could list their favorite authors, over 79% of students could name recently read books, and over 80%

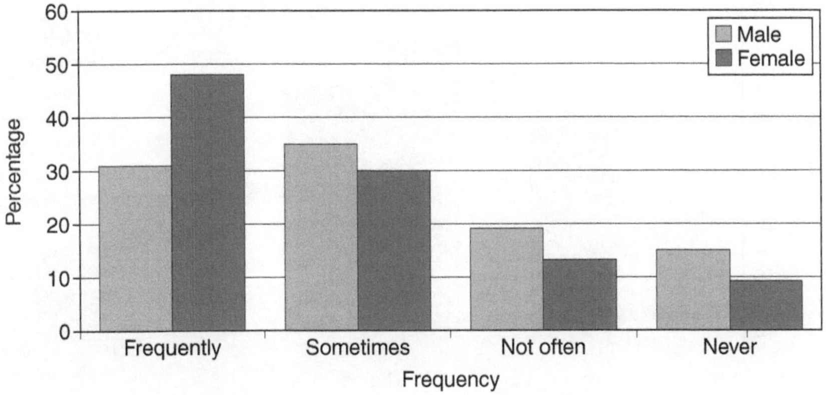

Figure 12.3 Frequency of Reading Novels Outside of School (Gender-based).

could list the author or title of the book most recently read. In total, 227 authors were cited by the participants. Not surprisingly, the most frequently cited author was J. K. Rowling, with 166 females and 73 males indicating they had read her work. The male students stated that they were more likely than the female students to read short stories and factual texts, and in particular those factual texts related to their interests.

The data indicated that there were minimal gender differences in terms of students' rate of use of literacies outside of school hours. When differences were apparent this was usually related to the content of the reading material chosen. However, there was an overall trend for female students to engage with all forms of text outside of school to a greater degree than the male students.

I'm an Avid Reader!

The data from this study suggest these students spent a great deal of time engaging in different kinds of reading practices outside of school. Further, interest and pleasure clearly informed this reading. As part of the questionnaire, students rated themselves as a reader on a scale of 1–10. These ratings were transformed into categories where ratings from 1–3 were considered in the low range, 4–7 as medium range, and 8–10 as high range. Figure 12.4 provides a summary of the reported ratings.

Overall, 33.2% of students placed themselves in the high category, 49.2% of students placed themselves in the medium category, and 17.5% of students placed themselves in the low category.

A high percentage of students in all of the reading scale categories indicated that they had a computer at home. Interestingly, the highest percentage stating that they did not have a computer at home came from the students who rated themselves in the highest reading scale. However, this only

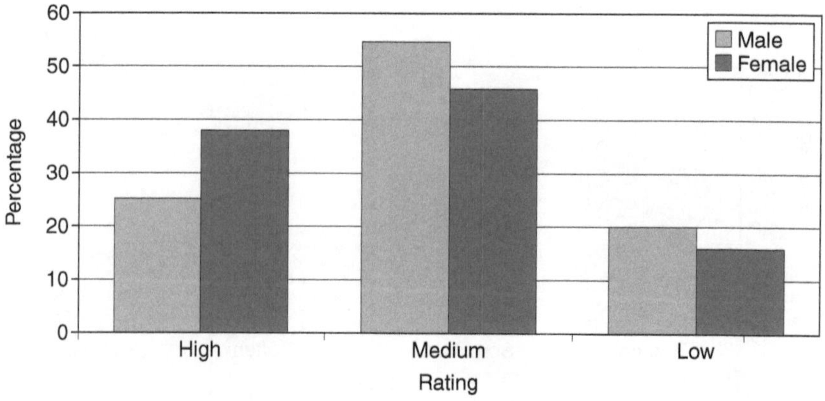

Figure 12.4 Gender Reading Scale.

amounted to eight students out of the 606 surveyed. Again, this result was repeated with computer use outside of school, where only three students stated that they did not use a computer outside of school hours. All three students rated themselves in the high range of reading ability. Frequency of computer use outside of school was high for all groups, with over 60% claiming daily use of the computer and over 80% claiming to use a computer either daily or every few days. However, of the students in the low reading range, over 80% stated that they used a computer daily.

Over 88% of students in the low and medium range stated that they used MSN compared to 79% of students in the high range, with a greater percentage of low-range students accessing MSN daily (approximately 30% more). Students from all reading categories were accessing MSN for similar purposes—for example, to chat to friends and not to strangers. However, a higher percentage (12.3% compared to 4.5%) of students in the low category were using MSN to chat to strangers. A higher percentage of students in the low category also used MSN to socialize (to find out what others were doing and to tell others what they had been doing). MSN was used to communicate more frequently by all categories of students than email, with students stating that they did not often use email.

Help menus and/or manuals were more likely to be accessed by high-range readers to troubleshoot computer problems, though only a small percentage within all groups stated that they would always use these. This also applied to manuals associated with cell phones and gaming consoles.

While engagement with computers was high for all reading categories, reading the information provided on the website differed. High category readers were more likely to read the information on a website whether it interested them or not, whereas low category readers tended to read the information only when it interested them.

While both high category and low category readers were frequent users of computers outside of school, the high category readers generally spent more time online than those who categorized themselves as low readers.

No differences were recorded with students' engagement with magazines, with similar percentages of students from all categories sometimes reading magazines. However, students from the high category were more likely to read magazines not connected to their interests than those who were in the low category.

Students in the high category were more likely to read some of the newspaper than students in the other categories. Of the students who did read the newspaper, high category students were more likely to be reading the local, national and international news items than low and medium category students. While none of the students in any category frequently read the sports section, a higher percentage of low and medium category students read this section than students in the high category. All students read the TV guide. The higher percentage of students stated that if they did read a newspaper it was more likely to be the state daily or state weekend newspaper.

As Figure 12.5 shows, there were statistically significant differences between the categories of students in their reading of novels and other print-based material. For example, approximately 85% of students in the high category stated that they frequently read novels outside of school, compared to 1% of students in the low category. There was a direct correlation between the reading scale and whether novels were read outside of school, in that the majority of students who rated themselves as high on the reading scale also stated that they read novels outside of school frequently; the students who rated themselves in the medium range stated that they read novels outside of school sometimes; and the students who rated themselves in the low range stated that they either read not often or never outside of school. Within reading genres, mystery was stated as a genre that students in the high (72%) and medium (54%) categories enjoyed. High category students (55%) were more likely to read drama and other books from genres not included in this survey than students in the other two categories. The majority of students in all categories stated they liked to read comedy, while they did not like to read historical fiction, science fiction, horror, romance or biographies.

A higher percentage of students from the high and medium categories stated that they read novels when they were bored, did not find it difficult to read a good book, and found it hard to stop reading a good book. Also the higher percentage of students in the high category stated that they read on long journeys, purchased or borrowed the books they read, and read to pass the time. While approximately 80% of students in the high category borrowed books from the library frequently or sometimes, 60% of the students in the medium category stated they did, and 31% in the low category stated they sometimes or never borrowed books from the library.

While approximately 92% of students in the high category could name some of their favorite authors, only 30% of students in the low category could do this. The majority of students in all categories could list some books they had recently read, but the difference between the high category (96%) to the

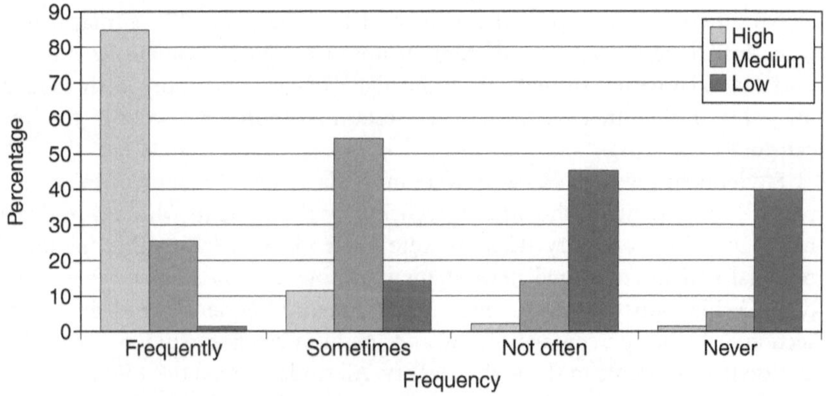

Figure 12.5 Frequency of Reading Novels Outside of School (Reading Scale-based).

low category (50%) is significant. A similar finding resulted when the students were asked to list the author and/or the title of their most recently read book outside of school. Again it is evident that the high category students are engaging with novels more frequently, as 91% stated they had read their most recent novel less than one month ago, compared to 71% of medium category and 33% of low category students, with no student in the high category stating it had been more than six months since they had read this book. While students from the high category were more likely to engage with all forms of text, students from the low category were more likely to read texts if they were related to their interests or hobbies.

Data indicate that all students are engaging with information and computer technologies at a high rate. However, the general trend indicated that students from the lower reading category were spending more time with these technologies, particularly for the purpose of socializing. Differences between students in the different categories were found for their engagement with text used for informative purposes—for example, students from the high reading category were more likely to access information manuals. A significant difference was found for students' engagement with print text in the form of newspapers and novels, with students from the high category engaging with this text more frequently and accessing a wider range of text types. In particular, reading novels outside of school directly correlated with the student's perception of himself or herself as a reader.

This could suggest that most students did not recognize reading associated with computers, cell phones or magazines and newspapers as "reading." A recent study which examined "oral reading" practices in primary schools also found that students often equated "good" readers with those students who read "lots" of "thick" novel-type reading material (Rennie, 2004).

Reading tends to be viewed by teachers and parents as an activity involving books. This view of reading appears to be adopted also by the students in this study. Students' in-school reading practices tend to be defined in terms of paper-based, print texts, although curricula also call for the inclusion and assessment of "viewing texts," and the latter are definitely a part of the English curricula guiding the studies undertaken by these students. Nevertheless, students had trouble viewing their prodigious engagement with non-paper-based texts with their own assessment of themselves as either "reluctant" or "avid" readers. Rennie's earlier studies (Rennie, 1994, 2000, 2003) also indicated that student assessments of other children as "good readers" tended to depend on definitions of reading premised on the activity of reading books.

This important aspect of students' understanding of themselves as readers is based on their experience of what counts as reading in school. Although reading practices are being dramatically re-shaped by information communication technologies, students' and adults' concept of reading appears to remain fixed in terms of traditional views of what constitutes reading as a book-based activity.

We believe this is a very important finding from our study. We know from the work of Gallik (1999) that there is a connection between reading for pleasure and students' academic achievement at the tertiary level, and a connection between reading for pleasure and age range. Children tend to report less pleasure in reading during the teenage years than during their primary schooling years (Clark & Rumbold, 2006, p. 12). While we did not record students' academic achievement, the self-rating scale acted as a guide to how students perceived the level of interest and engagement in reading. Our findings point to a need to ensure that reading of different text types is incorporated into school curriculum as suggested in the recent National English Curriculum Initial Advice Paper (Freebody et al., 2008). This also necessitates more intensive work related to "how" students are engaging with these "new" texts so that teachers are more prepared to use them as legitimate reading resources in their classrooms.

Where To From Here

This study, unlike previous studies of students' reading habits (Manuel & Robinson, 2002; Mullis et al., 2003; Nieuwenhuizen, 2000; Ryan, 2005; Thomson, 1987) tried to get a sense of the extent and nature of students' reading experiences with both traditional print and digital texts. The study allowed us to get a sense of what these young people's reading practices look like in the 21st century.

We found some interesting differences in relation to gender, particularly in relation to the content and purpose of the reading. We also found some interesting data in relation to the ways in which these young people described themselves as readers, which suggested that online reading experiences are not necessarily perceived to be reading. We suggest that more research needs to be conducted around what these 21st-century reading practices look like.

The students surveyed were undoubtedly engaging in a wide range of reading activities for specific purposes, including communicating with friends, obtaining information about hobbies and interests, finding out about shopping opportunities or specific products and keeping up with current events. Digital communications technologies—such as cell phones, computers and games—play a significant role in the everyday reading practices of students.

However, we also found that with the advent of these new texts, students are not necessarily engaging in print texts less, but are possibly reading more. In addition to their frequent online reading, most students also indicated a high interest in reading print-based material such as magazines and, to a lesser extent, newspapers, but engagement with books was high on their list of out-of-school reading activities. Our study suggests that students who enjoy reading, read everything. They have not given up traditional print material in order to engage with new media, but rather they have added new dimensions to their reading interests by engaging with computer-supported multimodal materials in addition to the more traditional activities.

References

ABS. (2007). Household use of information technology, Australia, 2006–07. Retrieved December 12, 2008 from www.abs.gov.au/Ausstats/abs@.nsf/mf/8146.0.

Alvermann, D. E. (2001). Reading adolescents' reading identities: Looking back to see ahead. *Journal of Adolescent and Adult Literacy*, 44(8), 676–691.

Alvermann, D. E., Hinchman, K. A., Moore, D. W., Phelps, S. F., & Waff, D. R. (Eds.). (2006). *Reconceptualising the literacies in adolescents' lives* (2nd ed.). Mahwah, NJ: Erlbaum.

Barton, D., & Hamilton, M. (1998). *Local literacies: Reading and writing in one community*. London: Routledge.

Cairney, T. H., & Ruge, J. (1997). *Community literacy practices and schooling: Towards effective support for students*. Canberra: Department of Employment, Education, Training and Youth Affairs.

Clark, C., & Rumbold, K. (2006). *Reading for pleasure: A research overview*. London: National Literacy Trust.

Cope, B., & Kalantzis, M. (Eds.). (2000). *Multiliteracies: Literacy learning and the design of social futures*. South Yarra, Victoria: Macmillan.

DeBell, M., & Chapman, C. (2006). Computer and Internet use by students in 2003. Retrieved December 12, 2008 from http://nces.ed.gov/pubs2006/2006065.pdf.

Freebody, P., Bennett, B., Arnold, R., Ewing, R., & Fielding-Barnsley, R. (2008). National English Curriculum: Initial advice. Retrieved December 12, 2008 from www.ncb.org.au/verve/_resources/English_Initial_Advice_Paper.pdf.

Gallik, J. D. (1999). Do they read for pleasure? Recreational reading habits of college students. *Journal of Adolescent and Adult Literacy*, 42(6), 480–488.

Gee, J. (1996). *Social linguistics and literacies: Ideology in discourses*. London: Taylor and Francis.

Gee, J. (2003). *What video games have to teach us about learning and literacy*. New York: Palgrave/Macmillan.

Hart, R., Bober, M., & Pine, K. (2008). Learning in the family: Parental engagement in children's learning with technology. Report of the Intuitive Media Research Services, University of Hertfordshire. Retrieved December 11, 2008 from www.intuitive-media.com/np.html.

Healy, A. (Ed.). (2007). *Multiliteracies and diversity in education: New pedagogies for expanding landscapes*. South Melbourne, Victoria: Oxford University Press.

Heath, S. (1986). What no bedtime story means: Narrative skills at home and school. In B. Scheifflin & E. Ohs (Eds.), *Language socialisation across cultures* (pp. 97–124). Boston, MA: Cambridge University Press.

Honan, E. (2008). Barriers to teachers using digital texts in literacy classrooms. *Literacy*, 42(1), 36–43.

Knobel, M., & Lankshear, C. (2004). Planning pedagogy for i-mode: From flogging to blogging via wi-fi. *English in Australia*, 12(1), 88–94.

Ladbrook, J. (2009). Teachers of digikids: Do they navigate the divide? *Australian Journal of Language and Literacy*, 32(1), 67–80.

Lankshear, C., & Knobel, M. (2006). *New literacies: Everyday practices and classroom learning*. New York: Open University Press.

Lenhart, A., Madden, M., Macgill, A. R., & Smith, A. (2007). Teens and social media. PEW Internet & American Life Project. Retrieved December 13, 2008 from www.pewinternet.org/PPF/r/230/report_display.asp.

Lewis, C., & Fabos, F. (2005). Instant messaging, literacies, and social identities. *Reading Research Quarterly*, 40(4), 470–501.

Livingstone, S., & Bober, M. (2005). UK children go online: final report of key project findings. Retrieved December 12, 2008 from http://eprints.lse.ac.uk/399/1/UKCGO_Final_report.pdf.

Luke, A., & Freebody, P. (1997). Shaping the social practices of reading. In S. Muspratt, A. Luke & P. Freebody (Eds.), *Constructing critical literacies: Teaching and learning textual practice* (Vol. 6, pp. 460–475) (1st ed.). St Leonards: Allen & Unwin.

Manguel, A. (1996). *A history of reading*. New York: Viking.

Manuel, J., & Robinson, D. (2002). What are teenagers reading? *English in Australia*, December, 69–78.

Marsh, J. (2006). Popular culture and literacy: A Bourdieuan analysis. *Reading Research Quarterly*, 41(2), 160–174.

Mellor, B., & Patterson, A. (2000). Critical practice: Teaching "Shakespeare." *Journal of Adolescent and Adult Literacy*, 43(6), 508–518.

Mellor, B., & Patterson, A. (2004). Poststructuralism in English classrooms: Critical literacy and after. *International Journal of Qualitative Research*, 17(1), 83–98.

Mellor, B., Patterson, A., & O'Neill, M. (1991). *Reading fictions*. Scarborough, WA: Chalkface Press.

Mullis, I. V. S., Martin, M. O., Gonzalez, E. J., & Kennedy, A. M. (2003). *IEA's study of reading literacy achievement in primary school in 35 countries*. Boston, MA: International Study Center Boston College.

Mullis, I. V. S., Martin, M. O., Kennedy, A. M., & Foy, P. (2007). PIRLS 2006 international report: IEA's progress in international reading literacy study in primary schools in 40 Countries. Retrieved December 12, 2008 from http://timss.bc.edu/pirls2006/intl_rpt.html.

New London Group. (1996). A pedagogy of multiliteracies: Designing social futures. *Harvard Educational Review*, 66(1): 60–92.

Nieuwenhuizen, A. (2000). Young Australians reading, 2005. Retrieved December 12, 2008 from www.slv.vic.gov.au/pdfs/yar_report.pdf.

Patterson, A. (1997). A technique for living: Some thoughts on beginning reading pedagogy in sixteenth century England. *The UTS Review*, 3(2), 67–89.

Patterson, A. (2002). Installing English at the "hub" of early twentieth century school curriculum in Australia. *History of Education Review*, 31(2), 45–57.

Patterson, A. (2008). Teaching literature in Australia: Examining and reviewing senior English. *Changing English: Studies in culture and education*, 15(3), 311–322.

Rennie, J. (1994). *School reading: Nine middle primary children define the activity of reading in the classroom*. (Unpublished thesis). Murdoch University, Perth.

Rennie, J. (2000). Teaching reading: Oral reading practices as a pedagogical tool in the primary school. *The Australian Journal of Language and Literacy*, 23(3), 197–211.

Rennie, J. (2003). *Oral reading: The silent debate*. Townsville: North Queensland University Press.

Rennie, J. (2004). Oral reading: Constructing school readers. *Learning Communities: International Journal of Learning in Social Contexts*, 1(February), 35–44.

Rennie, J., & Patterson, A. (2005). The "out of school" reading habits of high school students in regional Australia. *International Journal of Learning*, 12(3), 283–290.

Ryan, J. (2005). Young people choose: Adolescents' text pleasures. *Australian Journal of Language and Literacy*, 28(1), 38–47.

Snyder, I. (2004). New media and cultural form. In A. Adams & S. Brindley (Eds.), *Teaching English with ICT.* London: Open University Press.

Street, B. V. (Ed.). (1993). *Cross-cultural approaches to literacy.* Cambridge: Cambridge University Press.

Thomson, J. (1987). *Understanding teenagers' reading.* Norwood: AATE.

Thorne, S. L. (2003). Artifacts and cultures-of-use in intercultural communication. *Language Learning & Technology,* 7(2), 38–67. Retrieved December 11, 2008 from http://llt.msu.edu/vol. 7num2/pdf/thorne.pdf.

UK Statistics. (2008). Society: Internet access. Retrieved December 13, 2008 from www.statistics.gov.uk.

Unsworth, L. (2001). *Teaching multiliteracies across the curriculum: Changing contexts of text and image in classroom.* Philadelphia: Open University Press.

Welch, A. R., & Freebody, P. (1993). Introduction: Explanations of the current international "literacy crises." In A. R. Welch & P. Freebody (Eds.), *Knowledge, culture and power: International perspectives on literacy as policy and practice* (pp. 6–22). London: Falmer Press.

13 Multiliteracies

Resources for Meaning-making in the Secondary English Classroom

Douglas McClenaghan and Brenton Doecke, DEECD and Monash University

Introduction

This chapter draws on practitioner research with classes in a suburban secondary college in Melbourne, Australia to examine some of the complex interactions between school literacy practices and the literacy practices students engage in within school and outside of school. In particular, it focuses on student texts as instances of successful experiences of using multiliteracies for reading, writing and speaking in English classrooms.

Interfaces

Perhaps nothing shows the incapacity of school systems around the world to meet the challenges of the 21st century more than the way they continue to privilege traditional print-based versions of reading and writing, reifying specific literary skills in the form a developmental sequence through which students "typically" progress (Australian Education Council, 1994), and then testing them to show whether they have reached the required benchmarks. This opening sentence roughly captures bi-partisan educational policy in Australia over the past decade or more. Such constructions of literacy do powerful ideological work, enabling schools to classify students according to their performance on standardized tests, and thus ultimately to consign them to a place in the social order. Schools can thereby be held accountable for educational "outcomes" mapped against mandated learning continua, including comparison with the performances of "like" schools, i.e., schools with a similar demographic, and calculation of the "value add" that has been achieved over a school year.

A key way to confront this psychometric mindset is by highlighting the contrast between the traditional literacy practices that young people are obliged to perform at school and the multimodal forms of communication available to them in their out-of-school lives. At the very least, these forms of communication expose a gap in the curriculum and a failure to use the experiences of young people as a basis for meaningful communication and engagement in school settings. Multimodal texts that use visual images and sound, as well as the printed word, challenge the idea that literacy refers only to print, and provide a strong rationale for enabling students to explore a wider range of semiotic resources than those which have traditionally been used in schools. For Alvermann, "the performative, visual, aural and semiotic understandings necessary for constructing and reconstructing print and non-print based text" should be at the heart of any school curriculum (Alvermann, 2002b, p. viii; cf. Bruce, 2002, p. 15).

"Multiliteracies," "new literacies," "multimodal communication"—these terms are frequently used to refer to the meaning-making practices in which children and adolescents engage outside school. New multimedia technologies provide young people with ways to negotiate the social relationships and situations presented to them in their everyday lives, though it is important to recognize that they have differential access to these semiotic resources (cf. Sefton-Green, 2000). We wish to resist sweeping claims about a cyber generation or "aliens" in the classroom that somehow belong to another space and time (Bigum & Green, 1993; Doecke & McClenaghan, 1998), or who evince a sensibility that is the result of properties that supposedly inhere within new technologies. In the following discussion we use words like "multiliteracies" and "multimodality" interchangeably to invoke meaning-making practices that often involve new technologies without supposing that they are simply the product of technological innovation.

This is to say that the social relationships in which those technologies are embedded remain primary for any understanding of the cultural practices in which young people engage. Words like "multiliteracies" do more than name a new set of skills or practices to be added to the skills and knowledge formalized by the existing curriculum. The fact that multiliteracies play a vital part within the social practices and networks in which students are involved outside school (Nixon, 2003) raises important issues about the links between schools and the communities they supposedly serve, and ultimately the role that schooling should play in contemporary society. Buckingham uses terms like "literacy events" to emphasize that the literacy practices in which adolescents and children engage in their out-of-school lives are purposeful, and take on different functions according to the situations and relationships in which they are enacted (Buckingham, 2003, p. 38). Such meaning-making practices are manifestly social activities, and as such they challenge the ways schools construct literacy as an individual cognitive activity and a window on a student's "ability." The literacy practices which students pursue in their everyday lives are more richly varied and formally complex than those that have come to typify schooling. Mackey (2002) shows how adolescents use popular cultural texts as a means to create and affirm their identities, "as part of developing a sense of self," both in terms of where they belong in the world and in order to cultivate the emotional resilience to cope with the situations they face (p. 66). Such activities contrast with the drilling and skilling for no immediate communicative purpose that have begun to dominate classrooms in the Western world (institutionalized in rituals like phonics instruction, "literacy hours," lesson scripts designed to produce pre-defined learning outcomes, and standardized testing, including lessons devoted to teaching students how to "do" the test). Educators need to consider how the semiotic practices in which adolescents engage outside of school might become a focus for investigation within school—a legitimate object of inquiry for students and teachers alike—displacing the sterile formalism that has come to typify much "English" or "literacy" instruction.

Yet it is perhaps necessary to draw a line under the foregoing reflections in order to avoid appearing to idealize the literacy practices in which students engage, as though schools and other formal educational settings have no role to play in their students' lives. This reservation applies to some of the rhetoric of prominent advocates of multiliteracies. Gee (2003), for example, is an ardent exponent of what children can learn by engaging in leisure-time activities like computer games. However, for all his emphasis on the situated nature of literacy practices, the learning he describes has a curiously unanchored quality. When he discusses the way people engage in "perspective taking" and "affinity spaces," he constructs them as individuals who exist outside the world of discourses in which they operate. They "relate to each other primarily in terms of common interests, endeavours, goals, or practices, not primarily in terms of race, gender, age, disability, or social class. Indeed, in an 'affinity space,' these latter variables 'are backgrounded'" (Gee, 2006, p. 85). By contrast, our work with students is based on acknowledgment of and sensitivity to the ways their views continue to be shaped by their social positioning.

Paradoxically, Gee almost echoes the views of neoliberal ideologues who maintain that educational inequality can be addressed by a change in instructional techniques without consideration of the socio-economic factors that might affect young people's engagement in schooling (see, for example, Rowe, 2003). The only difference is that neoliberals advocate measures like sustained phonics instruction, whereas Gee touts games like Pokémon as facilitating children's learning, "regardless of their economic and cultural differences" (Gee, 2003, p. 10). To make such a claim about the value of gameplay is to ignore the ways that these activities are mediated by the social structures in which they are located, the network of relationships that stretches beyond the immediate pleasure of the activity, and indeed the immediate situation as it might be perceived by the players as they engage in the activity and draw meaning from it (cf. Buckingham, 2007).

For all the force of the critique of traditional literacy practices and the ideological apparatuses (cf. Althusser, 1971) that have been developed to implement and monitor them, those practices continue to impinge on the work of teachers and students. This is so, even when teachers might be deeply at odds with the ideological work they are performing. At the level of the everyday life of classroom teachers, a hard-and-fast binary between school literacy practices and the multimedia activities which students enjoy outside of school does not really provide a means by which to handle the situations in which they work. Multiliteracies undoubtedly generate a valuable perspective on schooling, but this perspective must be understood from the teacher's standpoint, as he or she negotiates relationships with students in the classroom. The critique of traditional literacy practices that might be prompted by recognition of the multimodal means of communication in which students engage everyday is directed at the very context in which teachers are obliged to work. Indeed, the notion of "obligation" does not really capture the contradictory nature of the situation of committed educators, for their commitment is primarily focused on the welfare of students with whom they have formed relationships within the institutional setting of the school. Those relationships are inevitably shaped by the traditional expectations of teaching and learning that are being promoted by standards-based reforms (Darling-Hammond, 2004), even when they might give rise to forms of communication and sociability that exceed them. Any attempt to investigate the potential of multiliteracies within classrooms is inevitably mediated by traditional forms of curriculum and pedagogy. Such, at least, is the case with the classroom in which one of the authors (Douglas McClenaghan) has been working, where—as a practitioner researcher—he has been seeking to gain a better understanding of the ways in which his students might draw on the multimedia resources available to them to make meaning.

Standards-based reforms of the kind that have occurred in Australia and other national policy settings are undoubtedly making it increasingly difficult for teachers to sustain their professional commitment to the education of the students in their care. Yet we still wish to argue that schools need not be seen as simply imposing a limitation or barrier which prevents the full realization of the potential of young people and the meaning-making practices in which they engage, as in old-fashioned romantic notions of the struggle by students, with the aid of enlightened teachers, to engage in "authentic" forms of creativity vis-à-vis the prison house of schooling (although such a view is somewhat of a caricature of the work of progressive educators—see Reid, 2003). We hold on to the belief that it is still possible for teachers to engage in a "pragmatic radicalism" (Boomer, 1989) which seeks to facilitate the language and literacy of students within the situation in which they find themselves, including the institutional structures around them. Indeed, schools arguably give students an opportunity to cultivate a reflexive awareness of those practices that might not otherwise be available to them. They can enable students to make their informal knowledge of popular cultural practices explicit in relatively formal ways (cf. McClenaghan & Doecke, 2005, p. 126), to develop a "knowing practice" (cf. Kemmis, 2004), an enhanced awareness of the potential and value of their cultural practices as meaning-making pursuits. This is arguably knowledge which students are only able to construct through school, through interacting with their peers and a knowledgeable and interested adult (Wells, 1999). The following discussion shows how a small group of students go about building this kind of knowledge.

School Writing

The multimedia work which Douglas' students produce shows them using their out-of-school knowledge to meet the conventional expectations of schooling. That they are "doing" "school writing" (Sheeran & Barnes, 1991) is a necessary frame for interpreting the artifacts we are about to consider (MacLachlan & Reid, 1994). The fact is that Douglas and his students are obliged to work together within the institutional setting of the school, and their relationships are mediated by the institutional roles defined for them there (Smith, 2005).

Schooling provides a setting where students encounter various forms of sociability. Like people congregated anywhere, they must learn to get along together. They enter the school gates, moving from one conversation to another, one set of relationships to another. This is so, even though standards-based reforms attempt to construct them as competitive individuals, treating the relationships between them as secondary, and denying them the creativity and understanding that might be achieved by working together. Yet, as we have argued in our introductory remarks, the multimedia work in which young people engage—in this case adolescents of around 15–16 years of age—are manifestly social activities. To fully exploit the potential of multimodal forms of meaning-making in the classroom means affirming the social nature of learning. It requires teachers to seize every opportunity to build on and enhance students' sense of belonging to a community in which they can interact meaningfully, engage in productive talk and other forms of collaborative work, sharing their work and learning from one another.

This sociability is evident from the way the texts which Douglas' students produce speak to other texts, constructing meaning intertextually (MacLachlan & Reid, 1994), by both drawing on the cultural resources of their out-of-school lives and engaging with the texts produced by their peers within the classroom. The writing on which we are focusing was produced by students who were completing Year 10 English in a state secondary school in a middle-class suburb in Melbourne, Victoria. This involves a syllabus that would be recognizable anywhere in the English-speaking world, including a number of set texts (novels, plays, films, poetry), as well as certain writing tasks, all culminating in an examination at the end of the year.

Text Response

Perhaps a distinctive feature of the English curriculum in Victoria is the notion of "text response," which refers to school literacy practices designed to reflect students' engagement with the texts that have been chosen for study. "English" has traditionally comprised "set texts," requiring students to complete tasks which show their "comprehension" of what they have read, typically in the form of answers to comprehension questions and essay writing (Teese, 2000). In the early 1990s, however, Victoria witnessed educational reform with a new senior curriculum that allowed students to produce more "creative" responses to text, which could take any number of forms, including such possibilities as rewriting a section of a novel from the point of view of a minor character, producing a poster for a film that might be based on the novel, rewriting the ending of a story and giving a rationale for the choices made, casting a text in a different style and reflecting on the effects (cf. Reid, 1984; Adams, 1998). Any number of alternatives are available to students, although this freedom is only something that can be exercised during the school year, when they complete work for their teacher. At the end of the year, they are still obliged to sit for a written examination which takes the traditional essay form.

Douglas' students have been able to use the latitude provided by "text response" to produce multimedia texts about the novels, poems and other texts chosen for study. Sometimes this work is done individually, sometimes collaboratively, but always as part of a continuing classroom dialogue involving whole-class presentations. The students are encouraged not to think of themselves as writing solely for their teacher, and they accept that their work is only "complete" when it has been presented to a larger audience who construct their own interpretations of the text created. Thus they learn from and build on what they each accomplish. This sense of openness to experimentation, play and continuing negotiation generates a context where students produce formally innovative work that challenges conventional expectations and values, even while—as we have stressed above—meeting the educational outcomes specified for this year level.

The text that prompted the response which we shall examine here was *The Shark Net*, an autobiographical novel by Robert Drewe, evoking the atmosphere of Perth in the 1950s and 1960s. The text had actually been part of a prescribed text list for more senior classes, but had subsequently been set for study for Year 10 (we have discussed how a Year 11 student used the conventions of a manga comic to respond to this text in another essay (see Doecke & McClenaghan, 2009)). *The Shark Net*, interestingly, takes on a different form from autobiographical reminiscence. Juxtaposed with Drewe's first-person account of his childhood and adolescence is another story, namely that of Eric Edgar Cooke, a serial killer and "the last person hanged in Fremantle Gaol, on 26 October 1964, and the second-last person to be executed in Australia" (p. 345). The text, in short, has a hybrid character, combining the nostalgia of reminiscence with journalistic prose and language more akin to that of detective fiction than that of autobiography. In a number of chapters, the narrative is actually constructed from Cooke's point of view. It is perhaps not then surprising that the students respond to the heterogeneity of the text by producing work that has a similarly heterogeneous quality.

The novel obviously appeals to the students because of the way Cooke killed his victims in an utterly random manner. The students are less interested in Drewe's reminiscences as a baby boomer—indeed, most find this thread within the text, including the proliferation of detail that would only be recognizable to someone brought up in the 1950s and 1960s, somewhat tedious. Yet it is not as though they simply respond to the text at the level of a horror story (as in teen flicks about serial killers). They are disposed to accept the parallel narratives and juxtaposition of scenes as a legitimate story-telling device (perhaps because such devices are now a standard feature of television shows, films and other popular cultural genres), and—what is more—they appear to understand how the contrast between Drewe's own story as a successful journalist and Cooke's story as a misfit and serial killer comment on each other. What follows is what one student did. We shall present the following notes somewhat playfully in order to create an ironic distance from more formulaic notions of text response such as the school essay and other school "genres" (cf. Christie, 1991).

How Do You Compose a Response to The Shark Net*?*

Kate creates a video in the style of a music clip, using "Little Red Riding Hood" by Bowling for Soup. This song conveys a sense of the vulnerability of the young women Cooke murdered. Kate changes the lyrics, putting different words up on the screen while the song is playing, thus making connections between Cooke's story and Drewe's. The song starts with "Who's that I see walking in these woods?" The words up on the screen are: "Who's that I see walkin askew?" "Why, it's Little Red Riding Hood!" (song) "Why it's little Robert Drewe!" (words on screen). Later she presents the point of view of one of the victims with these words: "Little Cottesloe Lass, I don't think that you should continue walking in my wood alone." She enlisted her brother's help to make the video by filming him moving through shadows and darkness. The video consists of camera shots that are oblique and suggestive: dark shadows against a fence, silent feet creeping up the barely lit steps leading up to a house. Figure 13.1 shows a shadow, which could be Cooke or Drewe. Figure 13.2 portrays a similarly shadowy, ambiguous figure, surrounded by darkness. Later in the song she swings the focus back to Drewe: "What's wrong with being everything that a journalist should be?"

How did Kate Evaluate Her Work? (Notes Taken in a Conversation with Douglas after the Class Presentation)

> The inspiration for the movie came from hearing a song by Bowling for Soup. It popped back in my mind that this would be a good way to demonstrate Eric Cooke's story when we were told that we were doing a text response. From that I launched into doing a video. The inspiration came together bit by bit. With the scenes I created, I wanted to show that Eric Cooke was sort of a predator. He thought that Perth was his ground at night and that he was in control. The whole video shows him prowling around. I showed footsteps because no one would have seen these murders. You just see his feet. The flashing effects of the camera and the

Figure 13.1 Screenshot from Kate's video.

Figure 13.2 Screenshot from Kate's video.

> darkness I took from *Psycho*. *Psycho* is mentioned in the book. No one ever witnesses his murders apart from the victims themselves. I was trying to give the impression that it could happen anywhere. You only see Eric Cooke's face—my brother's—towards the end. I was modernizing the story. The story is all written. Watching it, it becomes scarier. I wanted to convey a sense of Cooke as predatorial. I was using local scenes, and showing my video clip to a local audience, they would recognize the places, and so feel more threatened by Eric Cooke's story. People like Cooke could be anywhere. The main expertise I needed was patience because the program crashes a lot! I originally thought that I would do a poster, but I then felt I couldn't put any of my emotions into it, and in a video I could channel my emotions much more effectively.

As a form of text response, this artifact reconstructs the imaginative world of *The Shark Net* using the popular cultural resources available (most notably the genre of the music video clip) to convey a vivid impression of how Kate has interacted with this text. The meaning of *The Shark Net* can be seen to emerge out of this interaction—it is not something that is "in" the text (cf. Frow, 2006, pp. 102–103). The writerly quality of many music clips (Barthes, 1978), involving a juxtaposition of imagery and lyrics, arguably enhances students' awareness of the active role they play as readers when engaging with imaginative texts of this kind. The essay has long been privileged as the form best suited to interpreting texts, and there is no doubt that some students become supremely adept at handling this genre (we shall leave aside the question of the culturally loaded nature of this form, and how its privileged status matches the privilege of those who are habituated to the empty fluency that it requires (cf. Teese, 2000)). Yet to our minds, by employing popular cultural conventions, artifacts like the one that Kate has created open up far more interesting insights into students' engagement with texts than might be possible through an essay.

Creative Writing

The playfulness evident in Kate's text is also a function of the interpretive community in which she presented her work. We have already mentioned that Douglas employs a number of strategies in order to encourage students to think of themselves as belonging to an interpretive community, such as asking them to present their work to each other and not simply hand it to him to be marked. This requires dedicated time—whole lessons, in fact—when students view and discuss each other's work. Kate's presentation was the subject of a lively discussion when she presented it, when students remarked on the way her use of local scenes had enhanced the sense of the danger posed by Eric Cooke. A kind of leveling occurs when popular cultural forms are brought into the classroom, partly because students are typically adept at using such media, enabling the teacher to step beyond his or her role as an authority (and the kind of closure that occurs because the teacher's reading of a text is privileged). However, this is not to fall back on clichéd notions of differences between baby boomers, who are supposedly inept at handling new technologies, and Generation X and Y or whatever. Such technologies are a common source of interest for everyone—teacher and pupil alike—with respect to their meaning-making potential.

The text on which we shall now focus was the product of this joint exploration of the possibilities for meaning-making opened up by multimedia texts. It shows how the students not only draw on the semiotic resources provided by the texts they encounter outside school (in Kate's case, the music video clip, *Psycho* and other horror movies) but the texts they themselves create. In this case, the text we are considering is an example of "creative" writing—another familiar school genre that takes on a new life via the use of multimedia. To understand what Bhavini and Olivia are doing, however, it is necessary to know that earlier in the year another girl in the class, Grace, had given a PowerPoint presentation in which she juxtaposed images of war, specifically the conflict in the Middle East, with images of Western affluence. In the background she played the Cranberries' song, "Zombie." The class had been looking at examples of print poetry which use words and images, including some poems which had been recreated in the style of a graphic novel or comic. Douglas had then suggested that they might like to attempt something similar, using photographs or PowerPoint. Grace decided to present a visual interpretation of the Cranberries' song lyric, taking images from the web which she arranged in a PowerPoint display. She was passionate about what was happening in the Middle East, and her aim was to disturb what she saw as the complacency of her audience, choosing graphic images of the human misery created by war. She saw a multimodal text of this kind as a vehicle to confront her audience, a perception that was shared by other students when they saw her text. (For a discussion of Grace's text, see Doecke & McClenaghan, 2009.)

Several weeks later Bhavini and Olivia presented a text that obviously utilized many of the conventions that Grace employed, not in the sense of slavishly imitating what she had done, but in the form of a dialogue with her text. Like Grace's text, their presentation also involved images of war, combined with music, namely "Hide and Seek" by Imogen Heap. Without diminishing Grace's achievement (which has a raw quality that is perfectly appropriate to its confrontational stance), "Ring-a-Ring-a-Rosy" is more self-consciously "literary," as is suggested by the title. By contrast, Grace's piece did not even have a title, but simply began with the thumping pulse of the Cranberries' song, accompanied by a relentless stream of images of war, human mutilation and other acts of inhumanity, involving a crescendo that culminates in five stills showing images of Western affluence, before returning to the parade of scenes of wartime settings.

The content of Grace's text and that of the multimedia text prepared by Bhavini and Olivia is broadly similar, not only because of the proliferation of images of war and violence taken from the Internet, but because they each focus on the situation of the most vulnerable, namely children. This is underlined in Bhavini and Olivia's text by their use of "Ring-a-Ring-a-Rosy," as well as the lyrics of "Hide and Seek." A distinctive feature of their text in comparison with Grace's presentation is the fact that it begins with video footage of young children happily playing "Ring-a-Ring-a-Rosy" in the schoolyard, conveying the pleasures children derive from such games. The presentation then cuts to images of violence, punctuated by stills presenting each line of the nursery rhyme, and further shots of the children as they hold hands, go around in a circle, and then fall down. Figures 13.3 and 13.4 present examples of this juxtaposition. The sounds of the children playing are not heard, only the words of the song, which thus provide an ironic backdrop to the innocence of the children's game. The lines of the nursery rhyme are rendered strange or unfamiliar by being broken up, taken out of their context and presented on the screen as isolated words and phrases that punctuate the text: "Ring-a-ring-a-rosy ... A pocket full of poesies ... A-tishoo, a-tishoo ... We all fall down." The presentation lasts for the duration of the song, and towards the conclusion, the song's opening lyrics displace the lines of the nursery rhyme: "Where are we? What the hell is going on?" Figure 13.3 shows a still from this moment in the video.

A feeling of textual unity is conveyed by the way the song and the written text converge. We have already heard the lines which conclude the presentation ("Where are we? What the hell is going on?") at the beginning, when the presentation and the song started simultaneously. And yet it is not a matter of everything folding neatly into itself. To the contrary, meaning has also been generated by juxtaposition and contrast. Indeed, those who know the origins of "Ring-a-Ring-a-Rosy"—as these girls did—know that this apparently innocent children's rhyme actually describes society during the plague, when people tried to protect themselves from infection by covering their noses and their mouths. "We all fall down" literally refers to the terrible loss of life that occurred in the Middle Ages, when the mortality rate was so great that communities collapsed and people were forced to abandon accepted conventions in an effort to protect themselves. Taken as a whole, the text appears (to an adult reader at least) to present a critique of a society where innocence has been violated, where those in power have abnegated their responsibilities to their children and future generations, and where everyday suburban life is somehow implicated in war and the destruction of human life.

What were Bhavini and Olivia Trying to Achieve by Producing This Text? (Notes Taken in a Conversation with Douglas after the Class Presentation)

BHAVINI: Where we got our ideas from was quite random. Olivia was saying that she wanted to use some kind of multimedia program. I was thinking of poems that sort of had a double meaning to them. And we came up with "Ring-a-Ring-a-Rosy."

Figure 13.3 Screenshot from Bhavini and Olivia's video.

Figure 13.4 Screenshot from Bhavini and Olivia's video.

OLIVIA: We just thought that "Ring-a-Ring-a-Rosy" was one that children use without knowing the true meaning behind it. We wanted it to be a bit different. Images that we found on the Internet showed the other side of the meaning.

BHAVINI: Grace really liked the song "Hide and Seek" at the time. She sent it to me at one time to listen to. Grace listened closely to the lyrics, they really connected with our piece. It was quite lucky that we found that song. Some of the lyrics fitted perfectly with what we were trying to say.

OLIVIA: We really did just "do" the project, and it was only when we finished that we realized how well it worked. We wanted to show how easy we have it as kids, living in a place like Australia. A lot of people our age know the rhyme but they don't know what the plague actually did to people.

Conclusion

What does "Ring-a-Ring-a-Rosy" mean? When teachers direct questions like this about texts to their students, they usually already know the answer. Such questions have been said to typify the discourse patterns that obtain in classrooms (Cazden, 1988; Barnes, 1976). Discourse analysis of this kind often runs the risk of producing reductive accounts of classroom interactions, taking no account, for example, of a teacher's intentions, or how those intentions might conflict with what they feel obliged to say or do in classroom settings. Whatever teachers feel about such practices, they know the pressures that exist to treat a text as though it has only one meaning, as though it forms a single whole or theme into which everything fits. What, after all, is the public ritual of standardized testing about, if not to reduce texts to sameness, to judgments that might be reached by ticking the right box amongst the multiple choices available?

The various levels at which "Ring-a-Ring-a-Rosy" operates resist any attempt to reduce it to a single meaning or statement of intentions on the part of the authors. The authors have drawn on an array of semiotic resources, producing a text in which "a range of meanings blend and clash," to borrow again from Roland Barthes (1978), which is actually richer than their own account of what they set out to accomplish. From the standpoint of a classroom teacher, their text might be read as challenging the learning continua and assessment rubrics that must currently be used when assessing students' work. While the text clearly satisfies the outcomes prescribed for this year level, its semiotic richness prompts a reading on other terms, requiring careful attention to what it offers. Rather than being positioned as a judge of such work, the teacher is invited to assume the role of a knowledgeable and interested reader, drawing on his or her own semiotic resources to make meaning through engaging with this text (cf. Doecke & McClenaghan, 2009; Sawyer, 2005).

Such an interpretive stance is a feature of the standpoint of a practitioner researcher, involving a capacity to treat any framework for reading texts as provisional, always acknowledging the possibility of other meanings and points of view. It is also a stance that we might encourage our students to adopt, as they explore the potential of multimedia texts of the kind we have been examining in this essay. The way the students in Douglas' class learn from each other is instructive. The unspoken rule seems to be that a student can create a similar text, and all the short films they have produced share certain generic features, including the font used for the words that appear on the screen, their use of current but not mainstream pop music, the duration of the song dictating the length of the presentation. At the same time, students cannot copy too closely what has gone before—one student complained privately to Douglas that another student's film was too similar to her own. A film must in some way show its creator has enhanced the collective understanding of what such multimedia texts can do, of the meaning-making potential that they make available to people. Through their formal experiments, the students are developing a sense of what Frow calls "the dynamic nature of textuality," rather than supposing that meaning-making involves slavishly conforming to a model (Frow, 2006, p. 141). Thus their multimedia texts speak back to the regulatory environment around them.

References

Adams, P. (1998). Imaginative re-creation of literature: A critical examination from the perspective of the 90s. In W. Sawyer, K. Watson & E. Gold (Eds.), *Re-viewing English* (pp. 36–50). Rozelle: St Clair Press.

Althusser, L. (1971). *Lenin and philosophy and other essays.* New York: Monthly Review Press.

Alvermann, D. (Ed.). (2002a). *Adolescents and literacies in a digital world.* New York: Peter Lang Publishing.

Alvermann, D. (2002b). Preface. In D. Alvermann (Ed.), *Adolescents and literacies in a digital world* (pp. i–ix). New York: Peter Lang.

Australian Education Council. (1994). *A Statement on English for Australian schools.* Carlton: Curriculum Corporation.

Barnes, D. (1976). *From communication to curriculum.* Harmondsworth: Penguin Books Ltd.

Barthes, R. (1978). *Image—Music—Text.* (S. Heath, Trans.). New York: Hill and Wang.

Bigum, C., & Green, B. (1993). Aliens in the classroom. *Australian Journal of Education,* 37(2), 119–141.

Boomer, G. (1989). Literacy: The epic challenge beyond progressivism. *English in Australia,* 90, 4–17.

Bruce, B. (2002). Diversity and critical social engagement: How changing technologies enable new modes of literacy in changing circumstances. In D. Alvermann (Ed.), *Adolescents and literacies in a digital world* (pp. 1–18). New York: Peter Lang.

Buckingham, D. (2003). *Media education: Literacy, learning and contemporary culture.* Cambridge: Polity Press.

Buckingham, D. (2007). *Beyond technology: Children's learning in the age of digital culture.* Cambridge: Polity Press.

Cazden, C. (1988). *Classroom discourse: The language of teaching and learning*. Portsmouth, NH: Heinemann.

Christie, F. (1991). Pedagogical and content registers in a writing lesson. *Linguistics and Education*, 3, 203–224.

Darling-Hammond, L. (2004). Standards, accountability, and school reform. *Teachers College Record*, 106(6), 1047–1085.

Doecke, B., & McClenaghan, D. (1998). Reconceptualising experience: Growth pedagogy and youth culture. In W. Sawyer, K. Watson & E. Gold (Eds.), *Reviewing English* (pp. 51–59). Sydney: St Clair Press.

Doecke, B., & McClenaghan, D. (2009). The content of students' writing. In R. Beard, D. Myhill, M. Nystrand & J. Riley (Eds.), *Handbook of writing development*. London: Sage.

Frow, J. (2006). *Genre*. Oxford: Routledge.

Gee, J. (2003). *What video games have to teach us about learning and literacy*. New York: Palgrave Macmillan.

Gee, J. (2006). *Situated language and learning: A critique of traditional schooling*. New York and London: Routledge.

Kemmis, S. (2005). Knowing practice: Searching for saliences. *Pedagogy, Culture and Society*, 13(3), 391–426.

McClenaghan, D., & Doecke, B. (2005). Popular culture: A resource for writing in secondary English classrooms. In G. Rijlaarsdam, H. van de Bergh & D. Couzijn (Eds.), *Effective learning and teaching of writing: A handbook of writing in education* (pp. 121–130) (2nd ed.). New York: Kluwer Academic Publishers.

Mackey, M. (2002). *Literacies across media: Playing the text*. London: Routledge Falmer.

MacLachlan, G., & Reid, I. (1994). *Framing and interpretation*. Melbourne: Melbourne University Press.

Nixon, H. (2003). Textual diversity: Who needs it? *English Teaching: Practice and Critique*, 2(2), 22–33.

Reid, I. (1984). *The making of literature: Texts, contexts, and classroom practices*. Adelaide: Australian Association for the Teaching of English.

Reid, I. (2003). The persistent pedagogy of "growth." In B. Doecke, D. Homer & H. Nixon (Eds.), *English teachers at work: Narrative, counter-narratives and arguments* (pp. 97–108). Kent Town: Wakefield Press.

Rowe, K. (2003). The importance of teacher quality as a key determinant of students' experiences and outcomes of schooling. Discussion paper prepared on behalf of interim committee for a NSW Institute of Teaching, February, 2003. Retrieved March 26, 2009 from www.acer.edu.au/research/programs/documents/Rowe_ACER_ResearchConf2003_Paper.pdf.

Sawyer, W. (2005). Becoming a new critic: Assessing students' writing. In B. Doecke & G. Parr (Eds.), *Writing=Learning* (pp. 129–148). Kent Town: Wakefield Press.

Sefton-Green, J. (2000). Beyond school: Futures for English and media education. *English in Australia*, 12(3), 14–23.

Sheeran, Y., & Barnes, D. (1991). *School writing: Discovering the ground rules*. Buckingham: Open University Press.

Smith, D. (2005). *Institutional ethnography: A sociology for people*. Lanham: AltaMira Press.

Teese, R. (2000). *Academic success and social power: Examinations and inequality*. Carlton: Melbourne University Press.

Wells, G. (1999). *Dialogic inquiry: Towards sociological practice and theory of education*. Cambridge: Cambridge University Press.

14 A Virtual School for Rethinking Learning

Julie Faulkner and Gloria Latham, RMIT, Australia

Introduction

This chapter describes how two lecturers in teacher education have been developing a virtual primary school as a digital tool to disrupt some of the norms of teaching and learning. The primary school was created to provide a place of learning not often available to pre-service teachers on their professional practice placements. We will explore how a digitally based scenario approach has been assisting our work at the edge of the traditional and the new, with specific attention to Gee's affinity space and concepts of sustained and disruptive innovation.

Background

Schools need to reinvent themselves and dramatically change to meet the needs of learners in a 21st-century global context. Seymour Papert, in dialogue with Paolo Friere in the late 1980s, signaled these needed changes two decades ago in their talks on the future of schools. Almost one decade ago, Darling-Hammond (1998) stated that "today's schools face enormous challenges ... [they] are being asked to educate the most diverse student body in our history to higher academic standards than ever before" (p. 6). Schools are increasingly populated with students who are shaped by their relationships with information and communication technologies (ICT) in ways that many current teachers could never imagine. These students are adept at multitasking, sophisticated in their use of electronic technologies, and used to a trial-and-error approach to solving problems, contrasting with a more logical, rule-based approach by previous generations (Oblinger, 2003; Oblinger, Martin & Baer, 2004). For anyone under 20 years old, the Internet has always existed, creating a world of digitally aligned communities connected just a "click" away. One journalist comments:

> [It is] no surprise that when we incarcerate teenagers of today in traditional classroom settings, they react with predictable disinterest [...]. They are skilled in making sense not only of a body of content, but of contexts that are continually changing.
>
> (Economist.com, 2008)

Differences in ways that in-school and out-of-school literacies are organized have been commented on by Bernstein (1999). While schooling values vertical, segmentally structured discourses of knowledge, popular culture ways-of-knowing to which everyone has potential or actual access are described as "horizontal." They are "likely to be oral, local, context-dependent and specific, tacit, multi-layered and contradictory across ... contexts" (p. 8). Young people pick up valued knowledge by word of mouth, and there is a rapid turnover of what is required to be a participant across a number of cultural contexts. Students as readers and producers of popular texts thus need to "disembed" themselves from familiar, and increasingly multiliterate ways of thinking, in order to immerse themselves successfully in school knowledge, knowledge which continues to privilege print-based literacies.

The change required of teachers to meet the needs of 21st-century learners is to reconceptualize their roles to fit with the new knowledge economies (Lovat, 2003). Not only has the conceptualization of literacy undergone significant evolution, but so has how we learn and practice multimodal forms of communication. Multiliteracies call for understandings of complex relationships among visuals, space and text, and interpreting a range of symbols in critical and culturally appropriate ways. Arguing that, in the 21st century, we are experiencing a "visual turn," Kress (1995) examines the cognitive shift from print to illustrative text. Syntactic demands on print language have lessened as visual material becomes more complex and abstract. While conservative critics frame this process as "dumbing down," Kress sees the increasingly sophisticated emphasis on visual material as adding force to an expanded approach to literacy.

Given these disparate discursive formations, how is education negotiating "new basics?" In times of rapid transformation, how is the classroom taking up new capacities, forms of knowledge and skills demonstrated in our 21st-century learners? The theory of multiliteracies (New London Group, 1996; Cope & Kalantzis, 2000) takes fresh reconceptions about literacies in a technologized, globalized environment and overlays them on more established notions of situated practice. Through re-visioning the theory, multiliteracies enables forward-looking practices; yet to alter practices, it is necessary to alter teachers' thinking.

Schools have changed over the past two decades to respond to some of the current and emerging demands on learners, yet it is the very nature of these changes that require greater attention. Clay Christensen (1997) argues that the changes that have been undertaken are sustaining innovations; changes that better support the present system and make it more effective. Christensen advocates far more radical change that he terms "disruptive innovations." Innovations of this kind are systemic and dramatically alter the existing culture. Senge, Scharmer, Jaworski and Flowers (2004) support Christensen's views and suggest that the processes most organizations undertake are fundamentally flawed because they seek to impose "old frameworks on new realities" (p. 84).

At RMIT University's School of Education we wondered whether beginning teachers were merely perpetuating an old model of schooling based on the model they had experienced, even when presented with new ideas about learning. Adopting new thinking can be problematic, as novice teachers enter the teaching profession with at least 12 years of being a learner. Pre-service teachers therefore have intimate knowledge and firmly ingrained images of the practices of schooling from direct experience and from the media. Common practices in schools and repeated popular culture narratives tend to reinforce traditional beliefs and assumptions about learning, with beliefs being deeply connected to identity formations around teaching.

Framing Questions within a Multimodal Environment

As our pre-service teachers encounter new kinds of learners in traditional classrooms on their teaching placements, they are presented with difficult teaching challenges. Within the context of needed change and pre-service teacher anxieties over establishing the teacher role, we created a virtual school called Lathner Primary. Unlike many existing digital versions of classrooms, this was not a space designed to replace or simply complement university teaching. Simulations as learning environments are often being used in teacher education (Risco, 1995; Gibson, 2002; Ferry, Kervin, Cambourne, Turbill, Pulisi & Jonassen et al., 2004). Existing simulations seek to replicate school settings in order to have pre-service teachers study them in some detail through roleplays. However, as these simulations are pre-programmed, they often become static representations of schools. Our virtual primary school differs in that it is a dynamic environment that seeks to reflect ideas around what schools might become in response to new learning challenges. Engagement with the school is designed to encourage learner-centered pedagogies, risk taking, problem-solving and creative thinking.

James Gee (2005) offers a useful conceptualization of how we might think about participation within this virtual space. He defines an "affinity space" as a particular kind of social semiotic space. Social semiotic spaces involve people engaging with other people around content, or sets of signs. In our case, the virtual school provides a range of familiar and less familiar signs that are made available on the site for meaning-making. We, as the authors of the site, have generated a physical environment which appears as a brick building typical of a renovated 20th-century Australian primary school. However, the navigational perspective is occasionally (and deliberately) disorienting, with the building and surrounds incorporating "odd" elements such as a hopping dinosaur, Egyptian statues and an outdoor pagoda. Profiles of teachers, a principal and students are included as audio clips and via print text in folders and in filing cabinets, the class blog, and in chapters in a linked book (Latham, Blaise, Dole, Faulkner, Lang & Malone, 2006). These profiles work towards creating virtual actors in the school, but pre-service teachers also become protagonists in the space.

Figure 14.1 Copyright © 2009 RMIT University. Prepared by RMIT Image, Educational Media Group, Educational Technology Advancement Group. Used with permission.

Figure 14.2 Copyright © 2009 RMIT University. Prepared by RMIT Image, Educational Media Group, Educational Technology Advancement Group. Used with permission.

Figure 14.3 Copyright © 2009 RMIT University. Prepared by RMIT Image, Educational Media Group, Educational Technology Advancement Group. Used with permission.

Unexpected Elements in the School Site, such as a Trapdoor, and Old Ideas that Endure, such as an Egyptian Statue and Dinosaurs

Gee further distinguishes between the "external view" of the space (how participants organize their behaviors and interactions within the school), and the "internal view," or design grammar of the space. Discussing design in relation to Internet games, Gee explains:

> The internal design of a game emerges from the work of designers as this work interacts with players' desires, skills, actions and interactions. The external organization of people's thought, deeds and interactions with the signs that compose a game type [. . .] emerges from people's actions and interactions as these begin to take on some (however loose) regularity or patterning.
>
> (2005, p. 219)

Thus, there exists a dynamic between the designers and the users of the virtual space which has a mutually shaping effect. Access to the social semiotic space is provided through a portal, which can also serve as a generator, or something which allows people to add to the sign or change the relationship of the signs.

While the virtual school is not constructed as a game, Gee (2005) links his ideas to the semiotics of a science classroom in ways that, for us, are generative. A textbook, the teacher, lab materials and other things might be generators for people to access the content of a specific area. Questions then arise over how a teacher may rethink curriculum and pedagogy in terms of students' beliefs and actions. How might the choice of a set text or a textbook reflect readers' values, beliefs and practices? Significant for us, as originators of the virtual school, is how the sign system and the way students access the sign system shape thinking and interaction.

The virtual school has some features which link it beyond a semiotic space to Gee's (2005) more specific definition of an "affinity space." "Affinity" here is a common desire to learn how to teach via a simulated environment, through assuming a professional identity in the virtual school. Gee also identifies the ability for participants to generate new signs and relationships among signs as characteristic of these spaces. Information provided on the virtual participants in the school is partial; in other words, pre-service teachers have to build on what they are given in order to construct sound curriculum for the assigned Grade 4/5 students. The pre-service teachers are required, as are most actors in virtual worlds, to make sense of what they find, even when puzzling, and interact in purposeful ways. This process encourages "intensive and extensive knowledge," which Gee claims might be "individual and distributed" (2005, p. 226). To successfully negotiate the design of the virtual school and become a teacher in the classroom, pre-service teachers need to work hard to familiarize themselves with the digital space, as well as print information about the school. They need to map onto their prior understanding of schools, challenging or enhancing what they believe and know. They then need to mobilize their current learning about curriculum design and pedagogical approaches, resituating them in the new environment to complete the complex process. Thus, both broad and specialized knowledge is demanded, and to this end, the "networking" of skills and understanding is encouraged. Online folders containing relevant reading, discussion forums, hands-on classes with ICT, tutorials and lecture sessions are all set up to mediate pre-service teachers' experience with the school. Exchanging knowledge is vital for learners to take on, then "routinize" (Gee, 2003, p. 21) their understandings in the multimodal environment.

These shared social affiliations around the challenges of teaching encourage what Gee (2005) views as "a good effective and modern way to organize [...] deep learning" (p. 232). Positioning the virtual school as an affinity space in Gee's terms enables us to critically reflect on not only how pre-service teachers are negotiating the design grammar of the site, but also how we might continue to expand the learning potential of the technologies.

Change as "Disruptive Innovation"

The virtual environment allows the pre-service teachers to experience a school they could not easily experience in the "real" world. Our novice teachers have a placement in this virtual school in the same classrooms where the school community is attempting to move its thinking and practices to new times. As well as changing thinking, having one school where all pre-service teachers work means we have a shared context from which to dialogue with sedimented, as well as new, beliefs and practices. Over the years, Lathner Primary has become a resident teaching school in our teacher education programs, and it is situated in different year levels of the teacher education program and in different classrooms of the virtual school.

The virtual school was designed to be both a sustained innovation (that of educational reform) and a disruptive innovation (an upheaval from the known to the new). Schlechty (2005) argues that a disruptive change, such as giving students autonomy, may require the role of teachers and the authority of that role to be redefined. It appeared to us that initially both innovative and sustained thinking are needed to take our pre-service teachers from where they are to never before imagined possibilities: "While invention is the first occurrence of an idea for a new product or process, innovation is the first attempt to carry it out into practice" (Fagerberg, 2004, p. 2). It was our intent to use the potential of ICT to play out what new learning looks like, sounds like and feels like in a school context.

We want our pre-service teachers to explore and experience the same school environment where the exterior looks fairly similar to the school they may have attended, yet surprises lie at every turn. Brenda Laurel (1991) believes in the importance of surprise and reversal elements, stating that "the discovery process becomes more interesting when the information found is not what the user might have expected" (p. 90). In the case of reversal or a surprise that reveals the opposite of what might have been expected, a learner's interest might be heightened, or a path might be changed. Laurel suggests that to focus solely on information delivery, we risk missing the opportunity to view web design as engagement and performance. Duffy (2003) asks us to turn surprises into questions. She believes that unexpected occurrences can stimulate unlearning and raise questions that may, in time, alter existing mindsets (Latham, 2007).

Through many hours of consultation, a web graphic designer and a programmer from the Educational Media Group at RMIT built the architecture for the virtual environment over a two-year period. Many of these design concepts were unfamiliar to the designers as well. For instance, there is no site map to guide viewers through the school. We want visitors to get lost and encounter surprises along the way, rather than be directed in their journey. Maxine Green's (1973) concept of "teacher as stranger" was enacted to allow pre-service teachers entry to an experience an anthropologist might encounter in unfamiliar surroundings. We want to allow novice teachers opportunities to become critically conscious of the culture of this virtual school in order to break with "fixed, customary modes of seeing" (Green, 1973, p. 8). We want even the familiar to be viewed differently. The use of Flash-related technologies—Zoomify and Flashpaper—appear over time as the users visit each room. This encourages participants to revisit the places again and again. This act of revisiting lived experience is not possible in the actual classroom, yet returning to the experience virtually and viewing it over time through a range of lenses is essential in promoting reflective practices that might one day transform teaching.

Lathner Primary

We recognized the influence and importance of the wider context for understanding and accepting change. It is often when there is instability or threat that change is sought. The digital innovation allowed us to create carefully orchestrated scenarios to invite pre-service teachers, in that role, into the life of a school educating towards change. One scenario, for instance, plants the seeds for needed change and begins building alternative stories for how schooling can be conceived in this school. The pre-service teachers learn that several converging circumstances prompt the need for some radical rethinking about the direction of Lathner Primary. For the past several years the teachers at the school had been informally annotating changes in students' behavior and general attitudes towards learning. They often spoke about children's shorter attention spans, incessant comments about being bored, tired and unmotivated. The teachers also felt that the students were far less compliant—often refusing to do what they were told. The staff members at the school were finding more students disruptive, while others just tuned out. The rewards and punishments given out were not working. In fact, they were creating even greater divisions between students. The staff generally agreed that the abilities and knowledge base of the students in recent years were greater than ever before, but the students were not performing to their potential and were increasingly difficult to manage. The job of teaching was becoming highly stressful.

We created new stories about Lathner Primary, a school that was under threat of closure. The Principal, Brian Treadwell, was about to retire; he felt tired, worn down by the difficulties the school faced and he was no longer willing to fight to save this school. He describes the passage of change:

> A once middle class predominantly Anglo Saxon population became a far more multicultural community with greater mobility, and quite varied economic levels. There were more rental properties than ever before and more families in financial need. There were also fewer children in the area and the population of Lathner Primary was rapidly declining. So, this once stable and somewhat predictable school community was in the midst of a sizable change.

Along with these two major shifts, five teachers at the school retired or transferred schools. Two of these teachers admitted they had become unable to cope with the daily student demands. One long-standing, highly traditional teacher, Eileen Trigony, remained at Lathner Primary. She would represent the old guard. Mrs. Trigony refuses to adhere to the new pedagogies and holds tightly to her formal teacher-centered approach.

A new group of beginning teachers was hired, along with one more-experienced teacher, each bringing their unique orientations and personalities to teaching and learning, and new challenges to existing staff. These teachers breathed new life and energy into a somewhat tired and troubled school. One of these new teachers was Anna Jones, one of the mentors for our pre-service teachers. At staff meetings Anna, in particular, kept asking questions, important questions about some of the existing and enduring beliefs and practices at the school. From this group of new teachers with current pedagogies and critical questioning came renewed energy for change in Brian Treadwell and several members of staff. Slowly the school started a process of bettering existing conditions. A series of sustained and disruptive innovations were planned, agreed upon and actualized, bringing staff and the wider community into ongoing communities of practice.

Through this renewal process it became apparent that staff did not always know why they were perpetuating particular philosophies and practices. One teacher wrote:

> Clearly many of our practices were no longer effective and yet we were clinging to them because, I suppose, these practices were what we knew and they were also who we were. A few teachers started to read some current research on new pedagogies.
>
> (Latham et al., 2006, p. 54)

The Anna Jones Narrative

Over time, we focused less on the school as a whole or the children in one grade and more on the class teachers, and the ways in which they were moving their teaching to new times. For instance, one of these teachers' profile was built in lectures, tutorials, online through her professional journal and in her interactions with the pre-service teachers, other colleagues, parents and students. From her professional journal, Anna Jones explains some of the tensions she experiences daily:

> I realize that most of the questions are coming from me lately—I'm slipping back a little as I try and take the students on to where I want them to go, not where they are interested in going. I don't feel I can always relinquish that control. Tomorrow I'm going to consciously try a different starting point from their questions, and see where that goes.

We deliberately created a teacher who keeps facing her traditional past, slipping back to habitual modes of operating but still seeking needed change. Anna Jones is a highly reflective practitioner and a teacher/researcher. She became the kind of questioning, reflective teacher we encourage our pre-service teachers to become. Anna asks new kinds of questions about teaching and learning.

Recently we reduced the number of students in Anna Jones' virtual classroom to 20 in order to help our students hold on to and get to know these virtual people. We further developed their profiles as well as their learning folders on the online site. Along with this we built and strengthened the school and community around the school to give credence to the pedagogical and physical shifts in this school and in this classroom. For instance, the staff were far more responsive to what learners bring to the learning and the wealth of expertise brought by the community around the school. The Principal successfully applied for funds to renovate the playground in the school. The students in each grade are working on designs for the new playground, and the family committee has put in a vegetable garden with the children's support. As the viewer moves through the virtual school, the children's models and designs can be accessed in-progress (see the Virtual School website: www.dlsweb.rmit.edu.au/education/lathnervirtualschool/index.htm—password: Explore).

The authors purposefully made Lathner Primary a school on the edge. Thrown into this foreign territory, our pre-service teachers continue to discuss teaching and learning in this environment and how they might best meet the needs of their students. They form a teaching and learning community by talking face-to-face in and outside of university tutorial sessions, and writing online about the same school, the same classroom and the same students. "Experts" are invited into the virtual environment to add a rich layer of learning and further support pre-service understanding of the school community. Pre-service teachers' interactions with authors, for example, provide appreciation of authors' work and the research undertaken while writing a text. They also deepen comprehension about some of the complexities inherent in the text. These discoveries are discussed and interrogated in some detail, both online and in face-to-face tutorials. The following is taken from the *Creating Lathner Primary* blog.

> We decided to name this direction "Opening windows, Opening doors."
>
> In this spirit, students are often taught by teams rather than a single teacher, teams that include their peers and friends of the school. We are opposed to teaching behind closed doors. Teachers are being given increased opportunity to visit one another's classrooms in order to learn from one another. The principal, Brian Treadwell, takes many teachers' classes while they visit other rooms. This gives him a much stronger understanding of what children at the school need.
>
> Teachers are encouraged to move learning out to the wider community and to invite members of the community into the school to share their

stories, their knowledge and their skills. We recognize that some of these changes can be threatening to teachers as they may feel they are under constant scrutiny. We are working hard to help our teachers understand that they are being watched because they have a great deal to offer others. We want our teachers to know that we not only trust them, we also value what they bring and we want to learn from them.

These innovations in our school are opening up and stimulating new kinds of conversations in the staffroom (through the big coffee mug outdoors—see "Framing Questions within a Multimodal Environment") about teaching and learning.

Researching the Zone of Discomfort

> I was confused … I still haven't explored the school to its full potential but I realize I need to get lost and be open to new ideas and experiences.
>
> (Karl, a fourth-year pre-service teacher)

Boler (1999) argues that the first sign of the success of a pedagogy of discomfort is "quite simply, the ability to recognize what it is that one doesn't want to know, and how one has developed emotional investments to protect oneself from knowing" (p. 200) This discomfort asks students to leave the familiar waters of learned beliefs and explore the riskier critical depths of ethical and moral differences. Not unsurprisingly, learners are often reluctant to enter this zone, and we recognize the need to scaffold risk taking, using as many available modes as possible. Sequencing lecture material as a continuous narrative and complementary tutorial activities, accessing the research literature in timely ways, and sharing peer knowledge in structured online forums and tutorial group discussion all extend existing levels of understanding.

Guided ventures to connect what learners already know to less familiar territory we termed "sustained" innovation, while having pre-service teachers enter an unpredictable learning environment without a map was intended to be more *disruptive* in effect. Lathner Primary explores the potential of digital technology for both sustained and disruptive innovation, thus expanding spaces for rethinking routine pedagogical approaches.

Lathner Primary School is an environment in progress that has been "growing in," as past and present pre-service teachers with digital skills add content and animate the school. They augment the website with children in conversation audio-taped from actual primary classrooms. In this sense, the virtual school is far from a static concept. Over the past five years since its initiation, the narratives have evolved, and will continue to evolve according to our analysis of need through our future ideas in relation to the resources available. In the past year we have constructed two blogs at the virtual school. One blog was designed and belongs to the 4/5F students. It is a model of a student-generated and created resource that is authentic as its purpose is to inform family members of the day-to-day life in the classroom and to model classroom use of ICT.

The second blog, *Creating and Growing Lathner Primary*, was created to provide the visitor with background knowledge about the school. As well, we included resources teachers and pre-service teachers can access. On the site we wrote:

> We feel it is vitally important to disrupt habitual teaching narratives and get pre-service teachers interrogating the known. We want to allow them, in practice, to go beyond the known and experience teaching and learning where they take risks and experiment with more purposeful teaching and learning practices. We often ask the children we teach to take risks but we feel it is also important that we take risks. We believe that once pre-service teachers experience, learn from and start to trust a new set of practices they will hopefully transfer these practices as beginning teachers.
>
> By having all pre-service teachers participate in one school, we could begin to frame conversations around teaching and learning in the 21st century. We needed to ground our beliefs and see how they played out in the everydayness of classrooms. We needed to examine what these big ideas might look like, feel like and sound like.

As we continued to build Lathner Primary online, we depended largely on anecdotal responses from participants to evaluate the extent to which our aims were being achieved. We increasingly realize the need for more systematic, comprehensive feedback as part of an action research methodology. This involves planning, acting, reflecting, evaluating and initiating additions and improvements which have assisted in expanding and strengthening our virtual school over time. As a process-oriented collective approach, action research helps us to contexualize our research knowledge by monitoring our teaching and students' learning over time, making informed and systematic decisions about change.

Our research focus continually shifts as we modify the virtual school and the subjects that surround it. In the last iteration we gave far greater emphasis to disrupting habitual and unexamined practices as we encouraged risk taking. In this process of change we undertook five actions to support pre-service teachers:

- We presented a virtual school community that takes risks to enable their school to remain viable and flourish.
- We presented pre-service teachers with a mentor who values, supports and practices risk taking.
- As lecturers we identified and shared (with one another and with our students) ways in which we engage in risk taking.

For instance, Julie shares her risk taking in the online forum:

> My challenge as a lecturer is to allow for silences—moments of awkwardness even—when I could try and gauge what students were thinking, or not understanding. When I go to observe pre-service teachers in action now, I find that sitting at the back of the class watching students helps me pick up little things that pass among students I never saw at the front of the classroom: comments and questions the teacher doesn't hear, expressions of revelation or confusion, blank workbook pages. To stop explicitly teaching when I have covered the material and shift from my teaching to the students' learning (which some fear as giving up control) is the area of my teaching I need always to keep in focus, looking for the little signs of understanding/not understanding.

- We supported the benefits of disruption, taken from the literature, in lectures and tutorials.
- We asked students to dialogue about their risk taking in a shared supportive space in tutorials and online.

> The risks we are asking you to explore are things that take you and the children outside comfort zones yet you believe the risks to be worth taking because your teaching and your students learning will benefit. These risks often go beyond previously experienced practices. Although you haven't necessarily seen these practices implemented you would like to give them a go and you explain why and how these would be undertaken.
>
> (Gloria)

Even with a range of support structures in place, the analysis of pre-service teachers' ability to cope with disruption and risk taking is revealing. Many students describe risk taking apprehensively: "It scares me," one felt, as others articulated "letting go of the reins," "giving up control," "needing structure," "needing to know what works."

Allison expresses her fear of taking and not taking risks this way:

> I know I need to push myself and explore new knowledge and ways of doing things. However there is so much at risk; the children and their education, my professional reputation and employment. Too many times I have asked myself, "What if?" Maybe I should be asking "What if I don't?"

Ben, a peer, responds to Allison with the following:

> I think it's important to not fall in the trap of always wondering "what if" because that time could be better spent.... There are always going to be

> times when the risk we take doesn't work ... I am sure that the successful risks will heavily outweigh the failed ideas.... Personally, I want to try and eliminate the "if only" as much as possible. A great way to do that is to take risks, preferably educated ones at that.

Bronwyn's comments below are reflective of the schooling system she inhabited:

> Having just been spat out at the end of the kindergarten, primary school and high school/VCE assembly line, I asked myself as a learner, was I ever encouraged to take risks?

Sarah sums up her learning as a pre-service teacher at Lathner Primary to her mentor, Anna Jones:

> When I first met Eileen Trigony [the most conservative teacher in the school] last term, I realized ... that this is what I'm like. Not to say Eileen isn't a wonderful teacher, but her teaching style has nothing to do with the philosophy of the school and the culture you created in your classroom that I now love so much. This got me thinking that I need to change and try a different approach to teaching to be better able to engage students to learn.

Some of the changing viewpoints of the participants are being shaped by their active participation in the virtual school. They are developing shared understandings, with peers supporting them to take risks. These novice teachers are participating in a roleplay where interrogation of former beliefs is fostered and encouraged, and where the virtual and the "real" collide, allowing the creation of new possibilities.

Conclusion

A multiliterate approach offers potential to creatively rethink habitual practices, practices which are often deeply embedded in educational settings. Motivated by the desire to have students critically interrogate assumptions, we adopted Christensen's (1997) conceptualization of sustained and disrupted innovation. Our next task was to design a space where pre-service teachers could respond to the innovations, and take risks without penalty to gain practice and build confidence in "doing school" differently. The virtual school offers us opportunities to explore such ideas.

James Gee (2005), in discussing online environments as social semiotic spaces, notes the reflexive relationship between the design grammar of the interactive site and the individual practices and social interactions people bring to site content. It is the "external grammar" of the social semiotic space, or the ways in which people think about, value and act on the content and within the space which helps shape identities—in this case, teacher identities. By engaging in a roleplay, pre-service teachers become members of two different worlds simultaneously where they can be both themselves and someone other than themselves. Boal (1995) describes this state of being as "metaxis." In this state the participant can better understand "real life" through the virtual. The site of the virtual school and lack of a site map means that the viewer needs to play with the signs to see what happens and, therefore, how he or she might continue. The fact that random objects appear provides the site with a slightly surreal, or game-like quality. While exploring the virtual school might feel like a game, however, the participants need to read the signs as "real" teachers. Having had their sense of school "disrupted" by a mixture of elements included in the school site (giant vegetables, flying cupcakes, a white cat), they then need to access portals to locate themselves. Reading the class blog, accessing online forums, school policy, audio teacher profiles or committee notes all add layers of formal and informal understanding about the school. However, as in real life, such scaffolded information is not typically provided in an explicit or predictable way. Viewers need to play with the signs, repeat viewings and think in unconventional ways to fully explore the site. Collaborative approaches complement textbooks, lecture and tutorial information, enabling a more productive set of strategies to help pre-service teachers feel part of the Lathner Primary community. This further encourages individual, distributed and dispersed knowledge, characteristic of Gee's "affinity spaces" (2005, p. 225).

We understand that deep learning is more likely to occur when learners have time to tinker. Immersing pre-service teachers in Lathner Primary is deliberately dislodging embedded feelings about schooling; feelings often reinforced through concurrent professional practice experience. Borrowing elements from games and interactive sites, such as objects that open from indoors to outdoors, "draggable" classrooms and upstairs appearing as downstairs, we hope will encourage alternative ways of seeing and thinking about school. Using elements from computer games to illuminate aspects of teaching, we introduce teachers who enact different kinds of professional identities and model reflective practice.

Pre-service teachers have to learn to function in ways that comply with professional expectations and policy. However, modeling the virtual school on more lateral possibilities offers richer potential for rethinking schooling. Through invoking Christensen's (1997) concept of sustained and disruptive innovations, we aim to challenge norms and urge participants to think beyond predictable paths. Gee's (2005) social semiotic space model provides a concept to help the virtual school evolve more generatively in response to pre-service feedback. Moreover, a digital space provides a safe environment in which to take risks and make mistakes, as pre-service teachers design "curriculum innovation" and creative resources to extend their virtual students.

The school's growth in scope and complexity over the past few years has encouraged us to continue developing the concept, believing that it has the potential to offer rich learning and teaching understandings to other disciplines. While our concept is a populated classroom set in a primary school, the details of the space and texture of responses could transfer to myriad other environments where more reflective practices are sought by critical educators from all sectors. Nursing, for example, might adopt a similar approach to considering a variety of perspectives and educating beyond a skill set. Focusing on a shared environment which scaffolds and surprises participants enables enhanced ways of learning and reconstructing practice.

References

Bernstein, B. (1999). Vertical and horizontal discourse: An essay. *British Journal of Sociology of Education*, 20(2), 157–173.

Boal, A. (1995). *The rainbow of desire: The Boal method of theatre and therapy.* London: Routledge.

Boler, M. (1999). *Feeling power: Emotions and education.* London: Routledge.

Christensen, C. (1997). *The innovator's dilemma: When new technologies can cause great firms to fail.* Boston: Harvard Business School Press.

Cope, B., & Kalantzis, M. (2000). Multiliteracies: The beginnings of an idea. In B. Cope & M. Kalantzis (Eds.), *Multiliteracies: Literacy learning and the design of social futures* (pp. 3–9). London: Routledge.

Darling-Hammond, L. (1998). Teacher learning that supports student learning. *Educational Leadership*, 55(5), 6–11.

Duffy, F. M. (2003). I think, therefore I am resistant to change: What we know—or think we know—is our biggest roadblock to learning. *Journal of Staff Development*, 24(1), EJ. Retrieved December 11, 2007 from www.nsdc.org/library/publications/jsd/duffy241.cfm.

Economist.com. (2008). *From literacy to digiracy: Will reading and writing remain important?* Retrieved May 18, 2008 from www.economist.com/science/PrinterFriendly.cfm?story_id=11392128.

Fagerberg, J. (2004). Innovation: A guide to the literature. In J. Fagerberg, D. Mowery & R. Nelson (Eds.), *The Oxford handbook of innovations* (pp. 1–26). New York: Oxford University Press.

Ferry, B., Kervin, L., Cambourne, B., Turbill, J., Puglisi, S., Jonassen, D., & Hedberg, J. (2004). Online classroom simulation: The "next wave" for pre-service teacher education? In R. Atkinson, C. McBeath, D. Jonas-Dwyer & R. Phillips (Eds.), *Beyond the comfort zone: Proceedings of the 21st ASCILITE Conference* (pp. 294–302). Perth, December 5–8. Available from www.ascilite.org.au/conferences/perth04/procs/ferry.html.

Gee, J. (2003). *What video games have to teach us about learning and literacy.* New York: Palgrave Macmillan.

Gee, J. (2005). Semiotic social spaces and affinity spaces. In D. Barton & K. Tusting (Eds.), *Beyond communities of practice: Language, power and social context* (pp. 214–232). New York: Cambridge University Press.

Gibson, S. E. (2002). Using a problem based, multimedia enhanced approach in learning in the social studies classroom. *Australian Journal of Educational Technology*, 18(3), 394–409.

Green, M. (1973). *Teacher as stranger: Educational philosophy for the modern age.* Belmont, CA: Wadsworth.

Kress, G. (1995). Literacy or literacies: Thoughts on an agenda for the day after tomorrow. Unpublished paper.

Latham, G. (2007). *New Learning: Building surprise through the virtual.* Melbourne: RMIT University.

Latham, G., Blaise, M., Dole, S., Faulkner, J., Lang, J., & Malone, K. (Eds.). (2006). *Learning to teach: New times, new practices.* South Melbourne: Oxford University Press.

Laurel, B. (1991). *Computers as theatre.* Reading, MA: Addison-Wesley Publishing Company.

Lovat, T. (2003). *The role of "teacher" coming of age?* ACDE discussion paper. ACDE: RMIT University.

New London Group (1996). A pedagogy of multiliteracies: Designing social futures. *Harvard Educational Review,* 66(1), 60–92.

Oblinger, D. (2003). Boomers, gen-Xers and millenials: Understanding the new students. *EDUCAUSE Review,* 38 (4), 37–47.

Oblinger, D., Martin, R., & Baer, L. (2004). Unlocking the potential of gaming technology. *National Learning Infrastructure Initiative Annual Meeting,* January 26, 2004, San Diego, CA.

Papert, S., & Freire, P. (late 1980s). *The future of school.* Discussion. Brazil. Sponsored by the Catholic University of São Paulo and the Afternoon Journal TV Show. Broadcast in Brazil by TV PUC São Paulo and KTV Solucoes. Retrieved May 2, 2008 from www.papert.org/articles/freire/freirePart1.html.

Risco, V. (1995). Using videodisc based cases to promote pre-service teachers problem solving and mental model building. In W. M. Linch & E. G. Stutevant (Eds.), *Growing literacy* (pp. 173–187). Pittsburgh, PA: College Reading Association.

Schlechty, P. C. (2005). *Creating the capacity to support innovations.* Occasional Paper No. 2, Louisville, KY: Schlechty Center.

Senge, P., Scharmer, C. O., Jaworski, J., & Flowers, B. S. (2004). *Presence: Human purpose and the field of the future.* Cambridge, MA: The Society for Organizational Learning, Inc.

Afterword

Donna E. Alvermann, University of Georgia

I find it paradoxical, if not serendipitous, that less than an hour ago I responded in writing to a senior advisor to US Senator Edward (Ted) Kennedy regarding a bill for improving student literacy that will be introduced to Congress in 2009. Though not entirely relevant to the afterword that I am presently writing, my invited comments on the draft of that bill addressed what I perceive to be a general lack of attention to multiliteracies in the US education scene, outside of the academy. While perhaps not surprising in the context of the last two administrations, it is nonetheless disappointing to find that policy-makers still conceive of literacy as reading and writing printed texts for the purpose of demonstrating improved performance on high-stakes assessments.

In fairness to those who drafted the bill, I want to add that I could detect an emergent awareness of the social, economic, and technological changes afoot in literacy education in the world at large. Change takes time; be patient, I remind myself. Yet, in falling short of my expectations, the draft of the bill convinces me even more of the urgent need for a book such as *Multiliteracies in Motion: Current Theory and Practice.* Never one to dwell on what is lacking in a given situation, but rather on the possibilities that can come of it, I count myself fortunate to have had access to pre-publication copies of chapters in this timely and exceedingly well thought-out book.

The work represented in these chapters updates and expands on the New London Group's (1996) multiliteracies framework at a time of intense interest worldwide in bringing students' needs into the conversation of literacy educators on at least two fronts. First is the awareness on the part of teachers, curriculum developers, and teacher educators that students from diverse demographic backgrounds have their own notions of what counts as useful literate practices in relation to classroom learning and beyond. Second is the realization that in an era where page-to-screen shifts and multimodal texts are *de rigueur*, young people are choosing to construct and distribute remixed content that is eagerly read by others, often with requests for more of the same, or for better reasoned and illustrated content (Alvermann, 2008). In this respect, "far from being 'mindless consumers' and reproducers of existing media," young people today "actively engage with, rework, and appropriate the ideological messages and materials of the original text" (Black, 2008, p. xiii). This is multiliteracies at its best, and is also the message that several chapter authors convey in this book.

Another message—one that took me by surprise, but delightedly so—is the contention that multiliteracies should expand to account for elements of cyberpunk and techno-tribalism. What a treat to rethink concepts introduced by Bourdieu, Baudrillard, Lyotard, Maffesoli, and Deleuze and Guattari in the context of the multiliteracies framework! Skeptical at first, I found myself increasingly drawn to the argument, not for the novelty of it, but rather for the tensions that it revealed and for the opportunity to work through some of my own questions about the 1996 framework. I expect doctoral seminars will be equally enlivened by discussions focused on the need (or not) to enlarge upon that framework.

Other surprises awaited me as well. For example, I had for too long found excuses to avoid examining the research literature on *yuwen*, a concept that simultaneously incorporates reading, literacy, language, literature teaching, and learning in schools in the People's Republic of China. One reason for my reluctance to delve into this literature had been a lack of understanding on my part of the acculturation process that young Chinese children experience when they are introduced to reading. In *Multiliteracies in Motion: Current Theory and Practice*, I came to appreciate how Chinese school texts combine language and imagery in ways that mix modalities, genres, and voices quite unlike Westernized texts. Similarly, I came to appreciate the value of using a multiliteracies framework to reframe current curriculum debates involving science and literacy. It is an approach that the editors of a handbook on research methods, evaluation, and statistics after No Child Left Behind (Shelley II, Yore, & Hand, 2009) would likely have found compelling as well if they had been privy to its existence.

Finally, the chapter authors in *Multiliteracies in Motion: Current Theory and Practice* do not disappoint when it comes to offering insights into the pedagogy of multiliteracies for professional development and school renewal. Whether using the principles of multiliteracies to guide assessment practices, to facilitate culturally relevant experiences in digital environments, or to disrupt pre-service teacher education norms through a virtual school for rethinking learning, the authors boldly—and with evidence at hand—stake out a place for multiliteracies in framing current theory and practice in literacy education. What is left for readers of this book to do is a manageable, though no less challenging task: that of working with professional organizations and policy-makers at local, state, provincial, territorial, national, and international levels to keep the concept of multiliteracies in motion for this decade and beyond.

References

Alvermann, D. E. (2008). Why bother theorizing adolescents' online literacies for classroom practice and research? *Journal of Adolescent & Adult Literacy*, 52, 8–19.

Retrieved May 6, 2009 from www.reading.org/Library/Retrieve.cfm?D=10.1598/JAAL.52.1.2&F=JAAL-52–1-Alvermann.html.

Black, R. W. (2008). *Adolescents and online fan fiction.* New York: Peter Lang.

New London Group. (1996). A pedagogy of multiliteracies: Designing social futures. *Harvard Educational Review*, 66, 60–92.

Shelley II, M. C., Yore, L. D., & Hand, B. (Eds.). (2009). *Quality research in literacy and science education: International perspectives and gold standards.* Dordrecht: Springer.

Contributors

Donna E. Alvermann is Distinguished Research Professor of Language and Literacy Education at the University of Georgia.

Michèle Anstey and **Geoff Bull** run Anstey and Bull Consultants in Education (www.ansteybull.com.au). They provide professional development in literacy and children's literature, pedagogy and school throughout Australia and New Zealand. They also conduct tendered research, commissioned writing, speak at conferences, prepare professional development packages for trainers and advise on curriculum. Together they have published *Teaching and Learning Multiliteracies: Changing Times Changing Literacies*, 2006; *The Literacy Landscape*, 2005; *The Literacy Labyrinth* (2nd ed.), 2004; *The Literacy Lexicon* (2nd ed.), 2003; *Reading the Visual: Written and Illustrated Children's Literature*, 2000; *Crossing the Boundaries*, 2002; and various chapters in edited works and journal articles.

Ian Brown is Associate Professor with the University of Wollongong. He is the Associate Dean Teacher Education with the Faculty of Education. He lectures in visual arts education, visual design, information technology and pedagogy. Areas of teaching and research include visualization, visual literacy and assessment, cross-cultural design, graphic interface and interaction design. Ian's doctoral study explored implementation theory and policy processes.

Robyn Bush was an ESL teacher at a primary school in the south-western Sydney region at the time of contributing to this chapter. Robyn has taught in London as a classroom teacher and has worked as a project officer in the area of TESOL for the New South Wales Department of Education and Training before taking up a position as an Assistant Principal ESL in a primary school in south-western Sydney. Robyn's interests include visual literacy, supporting newly arrived ESL students and refugee students with interrupted or no formal education pre-migration.

Peter Caputi is Associate Professor in the School of Psychology at the University of Wollongong. His research interests are in applied psychology, psychometrics and quantitative psychology. He has published over 70 journal articles and book chapters. He has also co-authored or edited three books on methodology and Personal Construct Theory. Prof Caputi is currently a consulting editor for *The Journal of Psychology: Interdisciplinary and Applied* and the *Journal of Constructivist Psychology*. He is also currently Chair of the Assessment Committee in the Graduate School of Medicine at the University of Wollongong.

David R. Cole is Senior Lecturer in English and pedagogy at the University of Technology, Sydney. He has published widely in journals such as *Educational Philosophy & Theory*, *Prospect*, *Curriculum Perspectives* and *English in Australia*. In addition, he is currently editing books on literacy theory called *Multiliteracies and Technology Enhanced Education: Social Practice and the Global Classroom* (IGI) and *Multiple Literacies Theory: A Deleuzian Perspective* (Sense). He researches in the fields of affective literacy, multiple literacies theory and multiliteracies where he applies Deleuzian theory to open up questions in education. He published a novel in 2007 called a *Mushroom of Glass* with Sid Harta publishers, Melbourne.

Bill Cope is Research Professor in the Department of Educational Policy Studies at the University of Illinois, where he has been a faculty member since 2006. He is also Director of Common Ground Publishing, a company which develops mixed-medium print and Internet publishing software, now located in the research park at the University of Illinois. He is a former First Assistant Secretary in the Department of the Prime Minister and Cabinet and Director of the Office of Multicultural Affairs in the Australian Federal Government. His most recent books are edited collections, *The Future of the Book in the Digital Age* (Chandos, Oxford, 2006) and *The Future of the Academic Journal* (Chandos, Oxford, 2009).

Brenton Doecke is Associate Professor in the Faculty of Education (Monash). He has played an active role in debates about English literacy education for a number of years, and for five years was the editor of English in Australia, the national journal of the Australian Association for the Teaching of English (AATE). The chapter in this collection is one of many publications which he has co-authored with Douglas McClenaghan. He has been involved in many research projects in the field of English literacy education, including the development of Standards for Teachers of English Language and Literacy in Australia (STELLA), and the impact of standards-based reforms on the work of English literacy teachers in primary and secondary schools.

Beryl Exley is an experienced classroom teacher who is now lecturing and researching in language and literacy within the Faculty of Education at the Queensland University of Technology. Her award-winning doctoral thesis examined teachers' knowledge bases for language instruction in cross-cultural contexts. She has also authored research papers on multiliteracies pedagogies, grammar and critical literacy. In 2008 Beryl was selected as the

National Literacy and Numeracy Week National Literacy Ambassador in recognition of her publications and work in teacher education.

Julie Faulkner is Senior Lecturer in literacy in the School of Education at RMIT University. She has taught English at secondary level, as well as teacher education for many years. Her research and publications focus on questions of engagement and popular culture in relation to teenage learning, as well as the increasingly popular text forms associated with information and multimedia technologies.

Gustavo E. Fischman is Associate Professor in the Mary Lou Fulton College of Education at Arizona State University. His areas of specialization are comparative education, gender studies in education and the use of image-based methodologies in educational research. He actively teaches and collaborates on research projects in Argentina, Brazil, Mexico and the United States. Dr. Fischman has published four books, numerous articles and book chapters on critical pedagogy, teacher education, higher education and gender issues in education in journals such as *Educational Researcher*, *Comparative Education Review*, *Journal of Education Policy*, *Gender and Education*, *Revista de Educacion*, *Cuadernos de Pedagogia*, and *Educaçao & Realidade*, among others. He is the associate editor of *Education Review* and *Educational Policy Analysis Archives*.

Peter Freebody is Professorial Research Fellow in the Faculty of Education and Social Work at the University of Sydney, Australia. His research and teaching interests are literacy education, educational disadvantage, classroom interaction and research methods. He has published widely on these topics, including numerous invited contributions to international handbooks and encyclopedias. He has served on numerous state and national advisory groups in the area of literacy education and curriculum design. He has been senior consultant on the national online curriculum initiative conducted by the Curriculum Corporation and was lead author of the Framing Paper for the Australian National English Curriculum.

Mary Kalantzis has been Dean of the College of Education at the University of Illinois, Urbana-Champaign since 2006. Before then, she was Dean of the Faculty of Education, Language and Community Services at RMIT University in Melbourne, Australia, and President of the Australian Council of Deans of Education. She has been a Commissioner of the Australian Human Rights and Equal Opportunity Commission, Chair of the Queensland Ethnic Affairs Ministerial Advisory Committee and a member of the Australia Council's Community Cultural Development Board. With Bill Cope, she is co-author or editor of a number of books, including: *The Powers of Literacy* (Falmer Press, London, 1993), *Productive Diversity* (Pluto Press, Sydney, 1997), *A Place in the Sun: Re-Creating the Australian Way of Life* (HarperCollins, Sydney, 2000), *Multiliteracies: Literacy Learning and the Design of Social Futures* (Routledge, London, 2000), *New*

Learning: Elements of a Science of Education (Cambridge University Press, Cambridge, 2008) and *Ubiquitous Learning* (University of Illinois Press, 2009).

Gunther Kress is a distinguished Professor of teaching English at the Institute of Education, University of London.

Gloria Latham is Senior Lecturer in Literacy in the School of Education at RMIT University, Melbourne, Australia. Gloria is the co-author of *Learning to Teach: New Times: New Practices* and the creator of a virtual school called Lathner Primary.

Kimberly Lawless is Professor of Educational Psychology at the University of Illinois at Chicago. Currently she is the principal investigator on the Digital Literacy Assessment Project and the Global Ed II Project, which seek to understand middle-school students' use of content area literacy skills when engaged in online environments. In addition, Dr. Lawless has published more than 80 articles and book chapters in the areas of educational technology, instructional design and reading, and serves on the editorial boards of the *American Educational Research Journal*, *Contemporary Educational Psychology* and *Instructional Science.*

Theo van Leeuwen is the Dean of the Faculty of Arts and Social Science at the University of Technology, Sydney. He is a distinguished professorial author and researcher in the field of discourse analysis.

Lori Lockyer is Associate Professor in ICT in Education and Associate Dean (Research and Graduate) in the Faculty of Education at the University of Wollongong. Lori has been researching how technologies might support student learning for more than a decade—particularly in K-12, higher education and health education contexts. Her work in the multiliteracies area focuses on the integration of technologies in multiliteracies pedagogies and multiliteracies assessment.

Allan Luke teaches educational sociology and policy, language and literacy education at Queensland University of Technology, Brisbane, Australia. His current research projects include: a quantitative sociological study of the impacts of social class on Year 1 literacy teaching and learning; development of a digital assessment-for-learning model for at-risk adolescents re-entering formal education; and the evaluation of large-scale state interventions in Aboriginal education. His most recent books are: *Struggles over Difference: Texts and Curriculum in the Asia-Pacific* (State University of New York Press); *Pierre Bourdieu and Literacy Education* (Routledge) and *Curriculum, Syllabus Design and Equity* (Routledge).

Douglas McClenaghan is an English and Literature teacher at Viewbank College, a state secondary school in Melbourne, Australia. He has published articles and book chapters in the field of English curriculum and pedagogy, particularly in the field of student writing. His teaching and research interests lie in the exploration of reflective teaching practice and the development of alternative understandings of student literacy practices and their place in the English curriculum.

Annette Patterson is Professor and Head of the School of Cultural and Language Studies in Education at QUT (Queensland University of Technology) and Managing Editor of the *Australian Educational Researcher.* She has extensive teaching experience in high schools and universities and her research contributions are in the fields of secondary English education, curriculum history, reading and literacy practices. Annette's most significant work includes the analysis of classroom reading practices and subsequent development, with Bronwyn Mellor and Marnie O'Neill, of new ways of reading and working with literary texts in secondary English classrooms.

Darren L. Pullen is Lecturer in ICT, Professional Studies and Multiliteracies in the Faculty of Education at the University of Tasmania, Australia. He has worked with governments, industry sectors, enterprises (particularly health and training) and the education community to facilitate socio-technical change. His professional focus is on building viable humachine (human–machine) relationships and learning systems. Darren's previous employment includes being a Research Fellow in the health sector, ICT consultant and educator. His research interest is in the management of change processes with a particular interest in the micro-meso-macro level relationships between technology innovations and humachine relationships and interactions.

Jennifer Rennie is Senior Lecturer at Monash University where she teaches in undergraduate and postgraduate programs in teacher education. Her significant research contributions are in the fields of Reading Instruction, Primary English Education and Indigenous literacies. She has been an active member of a number of professional associations and is currently managing editor of the *Australian Journal of Language and Literacy.* Prior to working in higher education she worked extensively in both primary and high schools.

Louanne Ione Smolin is an independent education consultant and an adjunct faculty member at National Louis University. Prior to that she was Clinical Associate Professor of Curriculum and Instruction in the Department of Education at the University of Illinois at Chicago. She specializes in curriculum development and evaluation, particularly with respect to multimedia and technology integration in public school classrooms. She has developed professional development partnerships with numerous Chicago Public Schools, and has published journal articles and book chapters related to technology professional development. She has also presented her work at numerous national and international conferences.

Elizabeth Petroelje Stolle is Assistant Professor of Reading and Language Arts Education at Grand Valley State University. As a former classroom teacher in Illinois, she directly connects her research to student learning and teacher education, specifically focusing on teachers' use of new literacies and technology in the classroom and critical literacy. She was awarded the National Reading Conference student research award in 2007 for her dissertation, *Secondary content area teachers speak about literacy and technology: Tensions, complexities, conceptuatlizations, and practices.* Her writings have been published as chapters in several books and professional journals.

Len Unsworth is Professor in English and Literacies Education and Head of the School of Education at the University of New England. His publications include *Literacy Learning and Teaching* (Macmillan, 1993), *Researching Language in Schools and Communities* (Continuum, 2000), *Teaching Multiliteracies Across the Curriculum* (Open University Press, 2001), *Teaching Children's Literature with Information and Communication Technologies* [with Angela Thomas, Alyson Simpson and Jenny Asha] (McGraw-Hill/Open University Press, 2005), *E-literature for Children and Classroom Literacy Learning* (Routledge, 2006), *New Literacies and the English Curriculum* (Continuum, 2008) and *Multimodal Semiotics* (Continuum, 2008).

Bette Zhang Bin completed and received her PhD in literacy education from the University of Queensland, Australia. She has worked in the area of higher education as a Research Assistant, and has research interests in social interaction in everyday life, school and academic literacy, medical consultations involving children and intercultural communication. She is currently assisting a research project focused on students' diversity in local school communities at the School of Education, University of Queensland.

Index